RELIGIOUS IDENTITY AND RENEWAL IN THE TWENTY-FIRST CENTURY: JEWISH, CHRISTIAN AND MUSLIM EXPLORATIONS

DOCUMENTATION 60/2015

THE
LUTHERAN
WORLD
FEDERATION

Religious Identity and Renewal in the Twenty-first Century: Christian and Muslim Explorations

Edited by
Simone Sinn and Michael Reid Trice

LWF Documentation 60

EVANGELISCHE VERLAGSANSTALT
Leipzig

Bibliographic information published by the German National Library

The *Deutsche Nationalbibliothek* lists this publication in the *Deutsche Nationalbibliografie*; detailed bibliographic data are available on the internet at http://dnd.dnd.de

© 2015 The Lutheran World Federation

Printed in Germany · H 8006

This book was printed on FSC-certified paper

Cover: LWF

Editorial assistance: Department for Theology and Public Witness

Typesetting and inside layout: LWF Communications & Department for Theology and Public Witness

Design: LWF Communications/EVA

Printing and Binding: Druckhaus Köthen GmbH & Co. KG

Published by Evangelische Verlagsanstalt GmbH, Leipzig, Germany, under the auspices of

The Lutheran World Federation
150, rte de Ferney, PO Box 2100
CH-1211 Geneva 2, Switzerland

ISBN 978-3-374-04171-8

www.eva-leipzig.de

Parallel edition in German

CONTENTS

PREFACE

Martin Junge

Throughout history, religions have made significant contributions to transformation processes in society and provided a vision of life that has empowered people to work for change. Such a dynamic unfolds especially there where religious communities are open to renewal and transformation. As they are attentive to God's living presence, they see their own traditions in a new light. While some of these might need critical revision, others shine brighter than ever. It is crucial to learn how to relate one's own religious identity to the challenges and opportunities of one's time. This is a spiritual and a theological task that needs courage and commitment.

The sixteenth-century Reformation movement is a prominent case in point. Martin Luther and his contemporaries grappled with a tradition that had been handed down to them. Their struggle triggered the transformation of theological reflection, the reform of church structures and practices and the renewal of Christian life in general. The reformers firmly believed that listening to God's call "for today" was vital for discerning the way forward.

Such openness to God's living presence and the eagerness theologically to discern the signs of the times can be found in many religious communities. This publication provides insightful reflections and analyses by Jewish, Christian and Muslim scholars on religious renewal across the three monotheistic religious traditions. Renewal processes are subject to in-depth theological debates on how religions understand their own resources and criteria for renewal.

The Lutheran World Federation (LWF) has begun its journey toward the Reformation anniversary, which will culminate in the 500th anniversary of the dawn of the Protestant Reformation in October 2017. All LWF events and processes are carried out in accordance with three basic principles:

1. A strong emphasis on the polycentric character of the Reformation and the various contextual realities that gave rise to the Reformation

2. Close attention to the issues that move people and societies today, since the Reformation was not merely a moment in history, but is integral to the church's identity (*ecclesia semper reformanda*), and as such challenges the church to be open for renewal today

3. Commemoration and celebration of the Reformation anniversary in a way that affirms and strengthens ecumenical relations.

At a time when the world is becoming ever more religiously diverse, questions of reformation and renewal do not only occupy Christian circles alone. While other religious communities come from unique historical trajectories and theological premises, similar issues in relation to tradition and renewal have emerged. An interreligious conversation about the polycentric nature of religious communities and their negotiation processes regarding the boundaries of internal and external diversity helps us more profoundly to comprehend the complexity of the processes involved.

The essays in this collection were first presented at the August 2014 international interreligious conference, "Religious Identity and Renewal: Jewish, Christian and Muslim Explorations," co-organized with and co-sponsored by the LWF and the School of Theology and Ministry at Seattle University. I commend this collection of essays to all those who seek to deepen their understanding of resources for renewal in their own and in other religious communities in the twenty-first century.

INTRODUCTION

Michael Reid Trice and Simone Sinn

Religious identity is being profoundly challenged in our current age. Wherever religious life becomes a matter of debate today, the focus of attention quickly shifts to zones of conflict. Violence, hostility and hatred in the name of God or the sacred captures our attention. It is a mean trait of our age that hate is so closely aligned with religious identity. Examples differ by degree, even as a pattern is strikingly homogenous: religion is used to stigmatize and even obliterate the constitutive aspects of a shared humanity.

When one asks the question, What is the meaning and purpose of religion in human life? conversations around themes of nested identity (national, ethno-religious etc.) and cross-societal representation or manipulation of divine or sacred intention for humanity begin. Global dynamics and local aspirations seem to manufacture retribalized ethno-religious identities or create deep instability and socio-economic divisions. We witness a rise in the construction of physical or psycho-social borders that reclassify our humanity and transmogrify human beings into refugees of suspicious intent.

How can religious belonging make a difference and transcend the current protectionist trend for fear-based isolation? How is one expected to live a message of freedom amidst the restrictions of justice and deep moral trespass? Finally, how do we credibly account for the sacred that cares for humanity amidst the maelstrom of human ugliness?

In fact, religious people from every quarter of the globe, individually and collectively, counter militant religious expressions in creative ways across numerous platforms (social media, policy discussion, socio-religious affinity coalitions, etc.). These responses both resist the rhetorical or physical weaponization of religion, and represent the deep messages of human flourishing, societal health, global well-being and the need for soulful reflection on the spiritual virtues and messages toward the collective greater good of our unfolding future.

Even and especially amidst the maelstrom of human ugliness, human beings in the billions prove to be resilient in resisting untoward violence in their communities, standing against the radicalization of their faith, actively engaging their best spiritual selves in religious communities and hoping for a future society that refuses to accommodate itself to yesterday's animosities with its dead allegiances.

In the midst of these dynamics it has become evident that the question how faith communities deal with renewal in relation to their religious identity is vital—not only for their own self-understanding, but also for how they participate with others in society.

In anticipation of the 500th Reformation anniversary in 2017, Christians engage in lively debates on the meaning of Reformation, not just affirming its historical significance, but asking what kind of insights are relevant and helpful in constructively contributing to societal change today. Furthermore, it is pivotal for them to enter into conversation with experiences of renewal in other religious traditions. Sharing "memories of renewal" from different faith perspectives and analyzing the interrelationship between religious and social renewal helps to strengthen interreligious relations. In face of contemporary challenges and opportunities, it is necessary jointly to develop "visions of renewal" from the Holy Scriptures, faith traditions and theology. This includes identifying "places of renewal" in today's contexts, especially highlighting the role of local interfaith initiatives as well as interreligious cooperation in humanitarian, development and academic work.

In recognition of the challenges to religious identity and its renewal in the twenty-first century, a consultation of religious practitioners and scholars took place in August 2014 in Seattle, Washington (USA) under the auspices of the Lutheran World Federation (LWF) and the Seattle University School of Theology and Ministry. Over forty Jews, Christians and Muslims participated in a five-day consultation, convened to address the key, pervasive questions facing peoples around the world, and to provide multivalent religious responses to these questions. The responses to these central questions were agreed upon by attendees and planners as tantamount to sustaining a constructive religious impulse in society. The method used throughout the consultation was one of participatory engagement around themes that arose from the key questions. Presenters addressed the questions from their particular religious perspectives, and shared themes and concerns rather organically and naturally emerged. The essays in this volume were initially presented at the consultation in Seattle.

The reader is invited to walk through the five complete sections in the following pages. This introduction will further outline each section and identify some of the main supporting questions and themes respective of each section.

The first section, God, Generosity and Theodicy, responds to the key question, *What is the radical question for religions tomorrow?* Responses included the evolution of religions in the world, whether humanity is entering a post-religious epoch and how to make theological sense of massive suffering. Michael Reid Trice argues for a total reassessment of generosity as a theological and cross-religious focus that the world desperately requires today. Like an under-metabolized nutrient, generosity is something akin to deoxyribonucleic acid (DNA) as a self-replicating material present in all living organisms. The Muslim understanding of *Zakat*, as well as the Jewish interpretation of *Tzedakah*, attests to this nutrient, i.e., an ontological status of generosity rooted in the human being prior to human doing. Trice concludes that any future for the credibility of religion will require a comparative religious reclamation of scriptural generosity that confronts growing disregard and violence in the world. For his part, Anson Laytner responds to this section's key question by noting the deal breaker for many in the world, or what theologians call the challenge of theodicy, Why would a loving God let us suffer? In considering the Holocaust, Laytner states early on that either God is responsible for genocide or God is not responsible and has no power to do otherwise. Part of the crisis of our moment includes our distance from the divine. That is, when the Torah was written, the people knew where God dwelt; today, the post-modern crisis of meaning contributes to the human feeling of displacement altogether. We must not delude ourselves with theologies that rationalize human suffering in the world on the canvas of divine wisdom. Such responses do more harm than good, and discredit serious theological engagement. Laytner discovers a response to displacement in a model of enlightenment through the Xai Fung Jewish community in China, and asks the reader to consider another route to human well-being.

The second section, Religious Voice, Dialogue and Renewal, offers responses to the key question, *Who determines when the religious voice is truthful or diabolical?* An emerging theme of the conference was whether and how religions share a collective responsibility to identify when ideology is morally reprehensible. John Borelli's essay is aimed at the challenges of religious identity in the twenty-first century. First, religious dialogue is never meant to be the exclusive domain of experts; instead, dialogue belongs to our whole humanity, from local to global contexts. In a pluralistic world, dialogue requires a particular humility but never amelioration of the tradition or religious roots that shape one's worldview. Drawing on examples from Vatican II, and in particular *Nostra Aetate*, and with a view to religious pluralism, Borelli identifies three false starts for the practice of dialogue in communitarian contexts, one of these being the misconception that dialogue is a fully human undertaking. Whenever we dialogue, Jews, Muslims and Christians—and naturally additional religious streams beyond the confines of a consultation—are in the midst of the sacred or divine mystery, reminding us to listen to the stories of others and trust that our own story will speak first and best in a kind of holy attentiveness. Next, Shira Lander begins her essay by noting that renewal of religious identity in the future will not take place unless we have dealt with the substantial challenges of our past. These challenges include universalistic triumphalism, which is a cross-religious ideological methodology that advanced proselytization and forced conversion of other human beings. Contrariwise, religion in the public arena of the twenty-first century will necessarily need to include atheists, spiritual and secular humanists and others. If there exists a cross-religious "evangelistic" aim today, it is for religions to express their core values in unison and likewise to confront those who use the elements of faith in ways that cause and perpetuate substantial harm. And yet, the difficulty with dialogue is that it always transpires between the willing. What about the inclusion of extremist positions, which quickly demote dialogue into a debate on difference? Several challenges remain, one of which Lander signals for immediate concern: What are the limits of religious tolerance? There is a vast asymmetry between religious pluralists and extremist positions. And yet we will all inherit the present and gift the future, so the challenge we will be responding to in the decades to come is centered on how we will disrupt the cycles of hostility.

The third section, Memory, Tradition and Revelation, considered the question, *What makes a text sacred, and who has the authority to interpret it?* David Sandmel starts the discussion by exploring key concepts of Scripture and revelation understood in the classic rabbinic period. A text is never just a text; the Torah is never understood as narrow law, but by extension includes the *Tanach* and the entirety of rabbinic literature. This suggests that one is participating in Torah in the community's daily activity of transmission and interpretation of the text. After the fall of the Second Temple the rabbi can be understood as the avatar of Torah, or master teacher. In this way, Torah reflection includes the life of the community with its leadership, aiming to interpret anew where God is leading the people. In this way, Torah is the embodiment of God within the community; it is in one sense the incarnation of God's Word within the community. For Judaism, Christianity and Islam, the religious text is in both written and oral form, insofar as the former is meant to be spoken aloud and lived in community. Still, who determines when a text is just a text, or conversely when a text is an inspired act of divine revelation? Or, more to the point, what are the marks of a revealed text that make it sacred and not merely profane? The crisis of the authority of the text, and the authority to identify revelatory import within a text, creates problems for our age that will underscore ambiguity in sacred texts, begging the question regarding the rightful interpreter. The veracity of the lived text is evident in the life of the communities around the world who rely on these Scriptures. The communities who will identify the authentic use of Scripture when utilized for diabolical ends must correct aberrational interpretations.

Binsar Jonathan Pakpahan assesses the normative role of memory of the religious tradition, which is essential to the future of community identity. Following an analysis of two forms of memory—these being the event and the emotions attributed to the event—Pakpahan discusses the connection between ritual and memory, whereby the ruptured community re-members and re-actualizes its past in the present. How helpful is this practice of ritual to the future of religious well-being? What do we do with the memory of hostility or the so-called dangerous memory? The dangerous memory is in fact a form of forgetfulness, whereby a community develops a historical amnesia regarding the pain it caused other human beings and communities. Re-membering prohibits simply pardoning our humanity for the activity of former ills; rather, we remain in history and bear responsibility and accountability for the past. Finally, Nelly van Doorn-Harder assesses the tradition of the early Christian experience, which received the entire Bible as one continuous moment of incarnation, whereby Scriptures were aimed at initiation into the sacred practices of the believing community. Revelation is evident through the "insights of the heart," which opens Scripture to proper interpretation. In early Christian culture, the machinations of memory were central insofar as the transmission of faith (of hearing and recalling) was necessary for the formation of tomorrow's communitarian identity. What makes a text sacred? The answer depends on how that text is treated in community throughout history, to this very day. For Doorn-Harder, the text is reconfigured as sacred by the continuous efforts of those adhering to the Scripture, as a community that dedicates its vocational impulse to interpreting, transmitting and preserving these texts.

The fourth section, Twenty-First Century Formation of Community, asks, *What are the concrete realities that predominantly shape religious life today?* Catherine Punsalan-Manlimos responds to this question through the lens of a first-generation Filipina leader in the Pacific Northwest of the USA, where no dominant religious group persists; in the context of the US Pacific Northwest, religious identity is highly elastic. Thus, a predominantly non-monolithic interpretation of religious identity will necessarily include features of gender, ethnicity, culture and geography, among others. Punsalan-Manlimos identifies the cross-religious challenge of teaching children how to thrive in a pluralistic culture while remaining connected to the tradition and community that shaped them; the author draws on the narrative of second- and third-generation immigrant communities, where the diminishment of ethno-religious identity can become a crisis for families and larger communities alike. Indeed, how one forms roots amidst rootlessness is a key challenge in the formation and resiliency of any religious community. How less true is this of other geographical regions in the world today? Second, Paul Strasko, reflects on his experience as a rabbi in Germany. In a congregation of 2,700 members, including many Jewish immigrants from the former Soviet Union, he recalls the challenge of bringing even ten people together for worship. Three generations of Stalinism eradicated a community's self-evident sense of Shabbat-Shalom (of welcoming and greeting one another in the vitality of community life), as the soul of the community on which to build any future. In terms of formation, Strasko notes that the future of religious leadership in local to global contexts must relieve itself of particular delusions, ranging from a static understanding of any core, religious sense of community, to the delusion that religious institutions will self-evidently inform or shape the future. Indeed, the last century alone teaches us how it takes very little more than a stretch of religiously disconnected time to undo the moorings for the future on which that religious foundation is grounded.

Herbert Moyo's essay in this section covers the question of authentic religion, beginning first from his broader context as an African Christian. Moyo reflects on how religion must have authentic voice, leading to the love of God and neighbor. And yet, challenges include how religion responds to the political contexts embroiling contemporary life. For instance, even as religion must address governmental abuses, whenever there are differences of perspective—such as between mainline churches and African independent churches—society can become confused by the question of who authenticates the religious voice at these moments. At these times, what criteria do we use to determine if a particular ecclesial perspective represents religious authentic narrative? In the African-Christian context—where multiple forms of Christianity are thriving—there is a lack of agreement between traditional mainline and African initiated churches that bring a focus on healing ministry. In the case of healing ministry where adherents stop taking medications and get sick, new consensus must be quickly reached on the normative, scriptural interpretations that speak to human wellness. The formation of the religious community in the twenty-first century will require more levels of consensus in local contexts around the globe.

The fifth section, Intersection of Identities, is framed with this key, prevailing question in mind, *What is God's vision for the world, and how must humanity respond to this vision?* Celene Ibrahim-Lizzio begins with the mystery central to Muslim theology: that being created through the will of God suggests that humans are an outpouring of God's desire to be known. Scripture attests to God as both disappointed and genuinely interested in how we care for one another, for the world, for the integrity of our relationships, laws and systems of governance. The twenty-first-century *Umma* (community), like most communities around the world, is polycentric, with contextual theologies that are manifold and never reducible to one theological locus. The polycentric *Umma* in Muslim life requires an honest exploration of what it means to be one nation (people), and how people of faith operate with religious identity in a secular space, where even within families (in particular where both parents share different religious identities) there may be no single coherent religious narrative.

The final contribution of our text, and within this section, comes from Suneel Bhanu Busi. Busi also begins with a discussion on anthropology and explains how the Hindu creation story, and the enculturation of the caste system into Indian life, configures a repressive lens; through a complicated history, the moniker "Children of God" (*Harijan*) is today considered a derogatory reference for Dalits as illegitimate children in society. Busi discusses oppression in the form of ritual degradation and socio-economic political deprivation for Dalits, and then lands on the challenge of multiple belonging. Every individual carries multiple belonging.

The consultation was more than the component parts of these sections. It offered a template for thorough discussion by practitioners and scholars, with a view to our humanity prior to our expertise. The consultation participants consistently identified, from their own contexts, direct correlations between environmental degradation, global rates of poverty increase, the abuse of women and children, and phenomenal levels of displacement not experienced on our planet since the end of World War II. In a joint communiqué they affirmed:

> Communities are seeking renewal in many different ways. These include: reinterpreting difficult texts, the healing of memories and overcoming past divisions. Understanding more fully the historicity of the texts and of the divisions helps us to think anew about the constructive meaning of the texts in today's world. Each of our religious communities draws on rich interpretative expertise (midrash, tafsir, linguistic analysis, hermeneutics), and in reflecting on the interpretative challenges together we mutually benefit from this expertise.
>
> Theological education can be an important space where religious scholars discern the meaning of the Holy Scriptures and the traditions in ways that are true to the living relationship with the Creator. Jewish, Christian and Muslim identities are interrelated and their theologies have a rich history of responsiveness to one another. Today we see people of different generations in all of our faith communities asking radical questions about God in the face of tremendous human suffering. We realize that we cannot consider the future of our own faith community in isolation from others; our communities are closely related and the future of life in dignity is a shared concern.[1]

---

[1] www.lutheranworld.org/sites/default/files/Statement_ReligiousIdentity%2BRenewal_SeattleAug2014.pdf

Finally, the Japanese garden in the neighborhood of Seattle University is both a physical place and a metaphor, where integration of living ecosystems, in substance and aesthetics, are meant to stir both heart and mind. Religions attest to the human proximity to mystery, and the divine's desire for us to experience beauty, given first in the natural world, as a frame for our being on the planet. Part of a Japanese garden's beauty is located in the Japanese worldview (*wabi sabi*) that allows for both transience and imperfection, alongside order. Shy of choosing tomorrow's emerging systematic ideologies, religion reminds us that life is hemmed in by both limits and imperfection. Like a Japanese garden, how do we account for imperfection as a virtue, and not as a hindrance to our humanity? Should the moss sometimes win? The Japanese garden was purposely made to appear wild, to have unexplored and unplanned corners, to be spontaneous and not predetermined at every crevice and corner. It is arranged on purpose to be manicured in a way that never surrenders to the wilderness.

How will religions have a role in cultivating the human future on this planet? Renewal of religious identity in the twenty-first century will require new metaphors alongside authentic reclamations of our multiple identities, in order to interpret where mystery is spontaneously emerging tomorrow.

In the twenty-first century, diverse religious identities intersect every day. The classical borders for religious identity are both more porous and more vulnerable. In the face of this fluidity, the formation of religious identity requires a cross-religious aim, which we see today in the religious reclamation of early mysticism within the respective traditions. The aim is to go to the roots and to the depths of faith in community and the faith instinct generally, in whatever socio-and cultural-religious contexts we find ourselves. In a return to reshaping religious cosmologies that account for our full humanity, all human beings must ask how their respective religious identities enrich or skew a vision of our shared humanity on this planet, and explore the possible horizons of a shared witness to inhabiting the world today.

I. GOD, GENEROSITY AND THEODICY

THE FUTURE OF RELIGIOUS IDENTITY: A SPIRIT OF GENEROSITY

Michael Reid Trice

INTRODUCTION

What is the radical question for religions today and tomorrow? We start to locate this "radical question" by first assessing what the world needs from religion, assuming that religion is meant to participate in the healing of the world. So, we begin our inquiry with a quick sense of our socio-historical location in recent years. What is happening in the world? In a sampling of current world events we witness: religion or its aliases utilized to justify actions that include kidnappings of Church of the Brethren teenage girls in Nigeria; the murder of Israeli and Palestinian children in a blood revenge and the further escalation to inter-ethnic and inter-national conflict; the rapid rise of the Islamic State of Iraq and Syria (ISIS); a twenty-first-century refugee crisis for millions; the continued fight for rights by minority religious groups such as Ahmadiyah Muslims and Batak Protestant Christians in Indonesia; and the persistence of "Bible-based" white xenophobic Christianity in quarters of the USA. This brief socio-historical location Is part of our current global context where the principles of our faiths are used as cyphers for sowing or reinforcing conflict. That our hallowed virtues and values have become cyphers of this order is an abysmal fact of the coercion of religion. Of course, the news is not all bad: Mennonites and Lutherans participate in a ministry of reconciliation around the world as a means of overcoming the violence of their past; Muslims and Christians from Indonesia to Dearborn, Michigan, endeavor together alongside other co-religionists to combat anti-Islamic bias in the West and abroad; and practitioners and activists from all three Abrahamic faiths have more access to one another than at any time in modern history. Still, the serious challenge we face as co-religionists is that the bad news is so horrendously bad, even anathema, to the spirit of religion itself.

In a search for the "radical question" of religion today and tomorrow, we continue by asking specifically whether, in the tribulations of the world, there appears to be a deep need or hunger for a necessary yet under-metabolized nutrient that religion brings to the world. This would also have to be a nutrient that Judaism, Christianity and Islam have it within their power to provide to the world, both fully and unequivocally. Wherever we locate this hunger and lack of nutrient, we finally also locate the radical question for religion today and tomorrow, as this will be the greatest unmet need to which religion must respond. First, do we see a pattern of hunger and, if so, then what nutrient is missing? We see a pattern of hunger: alongside the examples described above, we see people on this planet plagued by a life with little or no hope due to consequences that range from the highest number of immigrants and internally displaced persons (IDPs) since the end of World War II, to ecologically-based droughts or flooding in some of the most vulnerable local communities in the world.[1] Swaths of our fellow human beings are embroiled in inter-ethnic and intra-religious conflict, which increases the ambiguity and confusion for all adherents of religion itself; and, finally, a growing set of armed conflicts, or potential hot-spots for armed conflicts, proliferate across the planet, ranging from the Ukraine to the Middle East and North Africa, and beyond.

We might too quickly rush for an antidote to the stories of humanity in conflict by believing that the missing nutrient in the world is peace. We simply need more peace, we might say. If so, then our radical question for our age is, How will religion and its adherents become relevant instruments of peace in the twenty-first century? This question of religious relevance for peace is certainly essential for us. And yet, in the paragraphs below I contend that there is a more immediate nutrient for us that we undervalue, and that we can nevertheless together locate in our faiths as a "spirit of generosity." Within each of the monotheistic religions—Jewish, Christian,

---

[1] At the end of 2013, the Office of the United Nations High Commissioner for Refugees (UNHCR) released its annual statistics showing that more than fifty-one million people were forcibly displaced at the end of that year, marking the largest number since the close of the Second World War. By 2015 this number had risen to 60 million; half of the world's refugees in 2013 are children. The report notes: "If displaced people had their own country it would be the 24th most populous in the world." At **www.refworld.org/publisher,UNHCR,ANNUALREPORT,,53a3 df694,0.html**

Muslim—there is an *a priori* spirit of generosity that is necessarily equally prior to, and instructive of, any religious commitment to peace, and that is absolutely essential for the world today. In fact, any viable commitment to peace withers when it does not originate in generosity. Generosity is that nutrient.

Here is the question I propose to ask as the radical question for religion today and tomorrow, What is the spirit of generosity that Jews, Muslims and Christians share from the heart of their communities, which is critical to humanity and the world in the twenty-first century? Given my assertions on behalf of generosity, this essay will proceed as follows: (1) it will briefly present a working definition of generosity; (2) it will assess how a spirit of generosity is meant to be an underlying disposition for human beings. This disposition will be assessed through the narrative of creation, within Scripture and in relation to classical thought; (3) in order to locate the source and font of cooperation between Jews, Muslims and Christians, the essay will explore the connection between generosity and holy envy; (4) it will then identify current historical statistics on the co-opting of religion by violence in the world, where both holiness and generosity fail; and, finally, (5) it will conclude with a practical application of generosity to the radical question of our day.

GENEROSITY—A WORKING DEFINITION

From a cultural point of view, generosity will elicit unique or distinctive features. In some cultures, any act of giving must be reciprocated, whereby accepting generosity is a commitment to relationship. In other cultures, the generous person or community is altruistic or empathetic, whereby the gift of giving is spoiled when accompanied by the expectation of a reciprocated gain to the giver. I suggest that we refer to generosity not first in terms of what human beings do, but rather in terms of who God is. In sacred Scripture, God's character is predominately generous and merciful, steadfast and loving. I mean generosity elicited in the Hebrew term, *hesed*, insofar as by *hesed* we mean generosity as an enduring loving kindness that originates first in God's character, as a God who desires to be in relationship with creation.[2] God is the most "merciful and compassionate," from which the world is derived, as is affirmed in the opening surah of the Qur'an. Christians too resonate with the theme of God's overflowing grace given as a gift to the world. Particular understandings on divine generos-

---

[2] God is "rich in *hesed* and fidelity" (Ex 34:6). In this context fidelity infers steadfastness, without which loving kindness would be frivolous in nature.

ity abound both within and between Judaism, Christianity and Islam. Any effort to provide an operative definition of generosity thus requires close scrutiny. For our purposes, generosity is a loving kindness that originates in, and models after, God's character first. Can we clarify this definition of generosity, so necessary within Judaism, Christianity and Islam today? We can, in an effort that takes us to the created order first.

A SPIRIT OF GENEROSITY

God acts (Hebrew Scriptures: Gen 1:1; Qur'an: Ibrahim, 14:32–34). That initial divine act of creation is first and foremost a supreme act of generosity toward human beings and the world, whereby creation itself—as the divine calling-to-order of things out of nothing—is the *primum movens*, or first act of the self-giving God to creation itself. The act of creation is a holy act; for Jews, Christians and Muslims, ours is the story of a God who enters into history and in so doing consecrates the world and all of the cosmos through creation. And, within the divine tapestry of the world, God also creates humanity. In the Genesis account, what do we make of this newest species, created as it was on the same day as the donkey and, yet, aspiring to the heavens? In short, what is this species to be and do in the world?

Between God's act of creating everything, and the human response to this creation, Christian theologians will respond to this question by speaking of the human being existing on a pendulum of sorts, simultaneously weighted between the presence of God (*coram Deo*) and the presence of the world (*coram mundi*). In God's presence, human beings are created as an act of generous love and, at best, they aim to reciprocate this generous love directly to God; in the presence of the world, human beings model divine generosity as coworkers, even co-creative partners, with the divine.[3] Living with the imprint of a generous, divine hand (literally in the *imago Dei* or image of God), means that humans reciprocate generosity toward God and toward one another, as to the whole world. This spirit of participation within divine generosity is present for Christians whenever we articulate the Oneness of God through all three articles of the Apostle's Creed—these

---

[3] Martin Buber, *I and Thou*, transl. Ronald Gregor Smith (New York: Charles Scribner's Sons, 1958), 112. Buber's popularized I-Thou relationship captures the intent of many of our great theologians, from Augustine onward, on the triadic relationship between God, the neighbor and the world. Buber writes that once generosity defines our relationships, "all else lives in its light." Emmanuel Levinas's *Entre Nous: Thinking-of-the-Other*, transl. Michael B. Smith and Barbara Harshav (New York: Columbia University Press, 1998), is also active in my thinking here. See, 201–207.

being creation by the Father, redemption through the Son and sanctification by the Spirit, whereby humanity participates in the creative, restorative and reconciliatory activities of a loving God in the world. Taken together, the whole story of creation is thus meant to be a cosmic narrative of generosity, with overlapping actions—one added atop another to the end of time.

The first great commission or scriptural obligation for human generosity, as a response to divine generosity, is found in Holy Scripture (Hebrew Scriptures: Gen 2:5; Qur'an: Al-Baqarah 2:177). Humanity is to tend and cultivate generosity toward others in creation itself. We are to "cultivate the soil," so to speak. This is our first shared responsibility, where no one works in the vineyard in isolation. In the daily application of this commission, Jews, Christians and Muslims basically follow three directions: a devotional life of individual and corporate worship as a cultivated response directed to God; a life of fidelity toward fellow human beings in the cultivation of kinship and community; and a life of stewardship directed to all creatures as to the planet. Standing as the human does between the weighted presence of God and the world, notice how the human response of generosity is not first and foremost an active verb. Instead, generosity is a definitive noun. That is, human agency as generous does not begin with the question, How shall I act in this given situation? Rather, in relation to the generosity of God's first act, humanity assumes generosity as a precondition of our identity that informs any action in the world: our question is not, What good thing must I do? but, rather, What does God intend me to be in my life? In this way, every individual act in our lives is prefigured for us by an underlying spirit or disposition of generosity, which is grounded in God's first act accounted for in Scripture.[4] Generosity is to be a disposition of our being.[5]

Perhaps too much is made of generosity. After all, human beings are a contradiction, often selfish, avaricious and unjust.[6] True indeed, and

---

[4] The essence of generosity prefigures action, analogous to Lamentations 3:22: "The steadfast love *(hesed)* of the Lord never ceases, his mercies *(racham)* never come to an end." Actions are evidence of a disposition of generosity.

[5] We have exemplars in our supplementary material to our primary religious texts. In terms of a true disposition of hospitality there is the story of Reb Aryeh Levin's Oath who, upon being robbed by a guest whom he had invited into his home, makes an oath to his wife against losing future generosity: "Let us promise one another and resolve in our hearts that this unfortunate and painful incident shall not serve as a precedent which might prevent us from welcoming needy guests again."

[6] Paul Tillich, *The Essential Tillich: An Anthology of the Writings of Paul Tillich*, ed. F. Forrester Church (Chicago: University of Chicago Press, 1987), 165–67. "The state of existence is the state of estrangement. Man is estranged from the ground of his being, from other beings, and from himself." See also, G. W. F. Hegel, "The

history is littered with the evidence of our malfeasance. But this fact does not dilute the truth that, within our most sacred Scriptures, Jews, Christians and Muslims have constructed a tent to house the irrefutable gift and obligation of a spirit of generosity to the world. We sometimes rush through these Scriptures as poetic flourish on neighbor-love, when in fact they are unique sets of formative prose on a shared disposition of generosity within our humanity, which all three religions profess. Consider these examples: In 1 Corinthians 13, Paul delivers his classic description of charity as a disposition of love (*agape*) that "bears, believes, hopes and endures all things" (13:7). For Paul, love is an expansive and broad staple of the Christian character in relation to God, and a character that is to inform charitable action. In like manner, the Islamic understanding of *Zakat* is grounded in a disposition of obligation. We miss the point of *Zakat* if we understand it to be simply an act of charity or alms giving; rather, *Zakat* is an underlying obligation from which the response of almsgiving generates. Thereafter, *Zakat* is a specific act of charity on behalf of the vulnerable in one's community. *Tzedakah* for Jewish self-understanding is likewise not first a magnanimous act of love, but is rather an underlying and even sacred duty to respond to the neighbor. In this way, the specific response of justice generates from a duty on behalf of those who are forsaken or find themselves in need. Taken together, generosity for Jews, Muslims and Christians is first an underlying disposition toward other human beings and the world that is framed as love, obligation, duty and justice, in solidarity with other human beings; these are all markers in a prevailing disposition of a spirit of generosity, of a defining loving kindness, within the partnership of the community and Individual to God, and within the story of God's first generosity to the world. Human beings can be selfish, avaricious and unjust, but this is not meant to be our disposition to the world, as is evident in Holy Scripture.

The connection between generosity and justice is also made in Western antiquity, which is informative to large quarters of religious, social and political life in the world today. Aristotle believed a disposition of generosity to be the necessary element for social life, a belief he shaped around the term, *koinonia*.[7] *Koinonia*, in classic Greek etymology, is the staple term for

---

Consummate Religion," in *Lectures on the Philosophy of Religion* (1827) (Berkeley: University of California Press, 1988), 447: "Human beings are inwardly conscious that in their innermost being they are a contradiction, and have therefore an infinite *anguish* concerning themselves."

[7] Aristotle, *Nicomachean Ethics*, ed. Paul Negri (New York: Dover Publications, Inc., 1998), I1097b-II, II59b27-30, and II6Ia1o-II; see also, R. G. Mulgan, *Aristotle's Political Theory* (Oxford: Clarendon Press, 1977), 14, 28. In Aristotle's work, the

healthy social and political life (i.e., in the polis).[8] There is no single English terminological equivalent to the Greek, *koinonia*.[9] Yet, if we describe it in English, *koinonia* is that experience of social life that includes three elemental and inseparable markers: generosity, community and justice. *Koinonia* takes place fully when all three markers are operative. In short, a disposition of generosity, a sense of shared belonging to one another, and a dedication to the prevailing virtue of justice, are all simultaneously active in social life, in friendship itself;[10] contrariwise, when one of these markers is diminished for too long, the whole house erodes and eventually fails. So central are these markers of *koinonia*, that philosopher Paul Ricoeur clarified the related intractability of generosity-community-justice to one another in social life. For Ricoeur, *koinonia* is best captured through the English term "solidarity."[11] To be in solidarity is to be generous, to seek to belong in community and to uphold justice within community. In this way, my neighbor's cultivated life is as central as my own.[12]

The above paragraphs teach us something of the nature of generosity through the auspices of creation, Scripture and classical thought. None of these avenues is meant to be exhaustive. They serve us momentarily insofar as they are panoramic. And if we take a step back and view our work, is it not true that our reflections on generosity to this point are somewhat self-evident, even plainly obvious in a cross-cultural way, once we seriously inspect the idea of generosity proper? Naturally, we must be disposed to generosity in order to seek solidarity with other human beings. If so, then

---

Greek *philia* is representative of *polis* life and implies "a general sociability, a desire to cooperate in shared activity of any sort, from the utilitarian business transaction to the close, personal relationships of true friends." This issue of generosity transcends Abrahamic sensitivities, and is identified herein as essential to socio-political well-being.

[8] Aristotle's use of this term is unique from Erasmian Greek, where early Christian Scripture understands *koinonia* in light of the body of Christ in the world. This later interpretation of the term allows for rich rhetorical play as well. Consider 2 Cor 6:14 – "What fellowship [Κοινωνία] has light with darkness?"

[9] One must be careful not to confuse Aristotle's understanding of *koinonia* with the Erasmian Greek adaptation that informed the Christian Scriptures, and which has been foundational to the modern ecumenical movement.

[10] Aristotle, *Nicomachean Ethics*, VIII, 149, 4.2.15. "Quarrels arise also in those friendships in which the parties are unequal because each party thinks himself entitled to the greater share, and of course when this happens, the friendship is broken up." Hospitality to the friend and fellow citizen is what Aristotle entitles "magnificence."

[11] Paul Ricoeur, "Eighth Study: The Self and the Moral Norm," in *Oneself as Another*, transl. Kathleen Blamey (Chicago: University of Chicago Press, 1990), 203–25.

[12] Aristotle, op. cit. (note 10), viii.

this suggests as a disposition that the world is flush in generosity. Perhaps so, but we might ask, If generosity is such an inexhaustible resource, then why is it also so scarce? In the USA we have lately experienced political gerrymandering in our highest legislative body that has moiled and now eroded a spirit of generosity through fierce protectionism, ideological division and calculating plotting of tomorrow's short-term gain at the expense of the country. Even Machiavelli believed that generosity was necessary for refining the art of compromise in public life, and yet today we are suffering from a scarcity of both. In socio-political erosion such as this, we are witness to how both the aspirations of justice, and an overall character of community well-being, suffer whenever generosity is absent. Aristotle appears correct about the symbiotic relationship between these three elements of socio-political life. Would this not hold true for us today as well? I believe so.

THE GIFT OF THE SACRED—SEEING THE HOLY

When a spirit of generosity is essential to our humanity as a gift from God, that gift is meant to be irrepressible. That is, a preeminent gift to the world by Judaism, Christianity and Islam is that these monotheistic religions see the integrity of our humanity as a shared virtue of creation, whereby all followers are obligated to exude a form of loving kindness, or a spirit of generosity, that frames the cosmos and us in it. This gift is evident in sacred Scripture whenever we are commanded to love, care for and stand in solidarity with our neighbors.[13] As we have already learned, the generous activity of loving one's neighbor is never merely a popularly conceived random act of kindness. Even so, each of these religions addresses neighbor-love in unique ways.

As a practitioner within Christianity I am obliged to love my neighbors because I see within them a reservoir of the holy, beginning from the unmistakable first act of a generous God. Creation and redemption are holy acts, and within my neighbor I witness the irreplaceable and irreducible mark of God's activity, created and redeemed as we are by a generous and loving God. In fact, through God's love I am freed up for my neighbor, whereby my neighbor and the mystery of God's creative act within my neighbor are mutually the aim of my love.[14] It is not enough to avoid killing my neighbor.

---

[13] See Lev 19:17–18; Mk 12:31; Sahih Al-Bukhari, Kitab Al-Iman, Hadith no. 13.
[14] Drawn from Leviticus 19:18: "You shall not take vengeance or bear a grudge against any of your people, but you shall love your neighbor as yourself: I am the Lord." Leviticus 19:34: "The alien who resides with you shall be to you as the citizen

Instead, in loving the neighbor I love both neighbor and God at the same moment.[15] I recognize within me a divine requirement for this disposition toward my neighbor. I am not merely meant to love and do unto them, as I would have them love and do unto me. Instead, I recognize that they are also my kindred, and thus the aim of my kindness, insofar as they too are the creation of a generous God.[16] The integrity of their humanity is never in question. Does God desire for them a fulfilled life? Yes. Am I to exhibit a spirit of generosity through loving acts toward them? Yes. Does my love for them mean that my neighbor must admit of a sense of the sacred in me in return? No. And this is the difficulty of such an explicit gift to the world; that gift might well go unrequited. The yoke of participation and belief is that the world to which you have an obligation for care will sometimes dismiss you, or even hate you, instead.

Given the sectarian divisions in the world—even between those who profess to practice Judaism, Islam and Christianity—we should further apply this gift of generosity to its logical end. As a person who practices the Christian faith, and within the encounter of people who are dedicated to Judaism and Islam, I become aware of the same hand that created and cultivated us all. Recall for a moment the note above on how human beings "cultivate the soil." There we said that religions and their adherents cultivate and tend in unique ways the commission of God's first (and indeed continuous) act in the world. Through the distinct aspects of worshipful devotion, of commitment to community and for the fullest expression of that community in its stewardship of the whole world, I recognize the distinct yet also familiar features of my own faith life in yours.

---

among you; you shall love the alien as yourself, for you were aliens in the land of Egypt: I am the Lord your God." My colleague Rabbi Anson Laytner reminds me that a fitting and even preferable translation to "love your neighbor as yourself" is in fact, "Love your neighbor. S/he is like you." See also, Matthew 19:19 – "Honor your father and mother; also, You shall love your neighbor as yourself." See also Mark 12:31, Luke 10:27 and Romans 13:9. See also Marvin Meyer (transl.), *The Gospel of Thomas* (The Gnostic Society Library, 2003), Codex II, saying 25, at **http://gnosis.org/naghamm/gosthom-meyer.html** "Love your brother as your soul."
[15] For further elucidation on Levinas, see Rudolf Bernet, "The Encounter with the Stranger: Two Interpretations of the Vulnerability of the Skin," in Jeffrey Bloechl (ed.), *The Face of the Other and the Trace of God: Essays on the Philosophy of Emmanuel Levinas* (New York: Fordham University Press, 2000), 43-62.
[16] There is a long and informative modern conversation on neighbor-love within Christianity. Two classic texts, which inform this conversation are, Paul Tillich, "Life and the Spirit, History and the Kingdom of God," in *Systematic Theology*, vol. 3 (Chicago: University of Chicago Press, 1963), 44; Matthew Lamb, *Solidarity With Victims: Toward a Theology of Social Transformation* (New York: Crossroad, 1982), 10.

For instance, I recognize the spiritual integrity, or marks of the holy, in your cache of scriptures, beliefs and liturgical forms and practices. I recognize in you the difficult and necessary moral discernments in the world that are different from my own but never altogether separate either. Over time, what I experience in you and in your religious fidelity are features that are genuinely unique from my own native cache of scriptures, beliefs etc. You cultivate in one way, I in another. In addition, what we cultivate in one another is a growing awareness of the integrity of expressions of the holy that abound in each of our individual labors. As I gaze across the vineyard what I witness in your cultivation has an aesthetic imprint on my life. This is what transpires in cultivating holiness; beauty is never far behind. I experience your expressions of the holy as "beautiful." I admire that beauty, am also somehow formed by it, and even yearn for those very expressions in my own faith life or community. I do not covet the beauty in you as though to control it; I am not required to convert from my own beauty as though to lose it. I experience this beauty as a gift, an invitation, and as a preamble to new cultivation and further invitation in the future.

This admiration of the holy-beautiful is what theologian and former bishop of Stockholm Krister Stendahl popularly phrased "holy envy." By "holy envy" Stendahl means that one is open to recognize "what is beautiful" in the other person's faith or community but not explicit in one's own. I admire and indeed wish in some way that your beauty would be reflected in my own religious tradition or faith.[17] Admiration or envy for the holy we see across religion is natural. And, I am suggesting that Stendahl's sense of "holy envy" between religions is only possible because the practitioners or, better, adherents of those religions, have some awareness of their activity within the cultivation of holiness first.

In terms of the holy we see in one another, we are mindful of a scriptural moral imperative that functions as a line-in-the-sand so to speak. That moral imperative is meant to protect both the neighbor (and ourselves), where obfuscation and deception mar our relationships, precisely where generosity is called for. For Jews and Christians, the Eighth Commandment of the Decalogue is clear—"You will not bear false witness against your neighbor." For Islam, Surah Al-An'am 6:151 is a composite prohibition against leading a life of deception toward the divine, family, friends and

---

[17] Stendahl noted that, with any approach to religious understanding, one should always "leave room for holy envy." The language for "holy envy" evolves in a lecture delivered on 27 February 1992 at the Center for the Study of World Religions, Harvard University. At his first mention of "holy envy" at a 1985 press conference in Stockholm, Sweden, Stendhal used the phrase "recognize elements." In 1992 he includes an aesthetic or "beauty," which I am including above.

what is expected of you in relation to those in your care. Asserted positively during the Second Vatican Council, we read the unprecedented declaration, *Dignitatis Humanae* (*The Declaration on Religious Freedom*, 1965), as a crucial document for human rights and the protection of religious freedom.[18] *Dignitatis Humanae* asserts that the dignity of the person, as to the community of faith, is not to be trespassed. Likewise, neither an object of scorn nor the aim of conversion, human beings are free and immune from coercion or any harm by oppression through the auspices of religion.[19] Taken together, the Abrahamic faiths reveal a prohibition from deception, misrepresentation and even coercion of the truth within one another. In addition to prohibition, we recognize the invitation to experience people and religions as pathways of dignity and beauty. We are invited to experience the holy. In this manner, Jews, Muslims and Christians are to co-exist between prohibition and invitation, in the world.

Sometimes we glimpse the holy, living between both prohibition and invitation. Consider the October 2007 declaration from leading imams and scholars within Islam, which was addressed and sent to Christian leaders around the world. The declaration, aptly titled "A Common Word Between Us and You," called for Muslims and Christians to endeavor in peaceable communities of well-being, remonstrated to "love the Lord our God" and to "love our neighbor as ourselves." Christian leadership around the world responded, including the then president of the Lutheran World Federation, Rev. Mark S. Hanson. Hanson recalled a visit to the Hashemite Kingdom of Jordan, in a delegation that met with Prince Ghazi bin Muhammad, who later became one of the principle authors of the "Common Word" declaration. During the visit and in discussion about the origins of the Abrahamic faiths in that region of the world, Jordanian advisor Aakel Biltajj noted the specific honor of having so many Abrahamic holy sites in the care of Jordanian sovereignty. Recalling this story, Hanson wrote:

> I acknowledge this letter in gratitude [...] and I accept it in the belief that Jews, Muslims, and Christians are called to one another as to a holy site, where God's

---

[18] *Dignitatis Humanae*: Declaration on Religious Freedom, On the Right of the Person and of Communities to Social and Civil Freedom in Matters Religious, Promulgated by His Holiness Pope Paul VI, 7 December 1965, at **www.vatican.va/ archive/hist_councils/ii_vatican_council/documents/vat-ii_decl_dignitatis -humanae_en.html**

[19] It is no small demonstration of such a prohibition in favor of human integrity that today the National Palatine Museum in Rome exhibits the colorful opening salvo of Vatican II just an inch from the papal bull that ordered the excommunication of Martin Luther, the latter of which rendered the rupture between Catholics and Protestants irretrievable in the sixteenth century.

living revelation in the world is received in reverence among the faithful and not in fear of our neighbors.[20]

At other times, we do not glimpse the holy and instead transect the prohibition against false witness. When that happens, healing early wounds can take generations. Consider Christian Reformer Martin Luther's sixteenth-century anti-Judaic writings, which drew on and contributed to a generalized Christian anti-Semitism. In 1982, the Lutheran World Federation called all Lutherans everywhere to "purge" hatred and contempt for the Jews. Many Lutheran local responses of repudiation of Luther's anti-Judaic writings took place in the 1990s. There is no question that these historical anti-Judaic writings were used as seeds of modern anti-Jewish sentiment to dangerous effect. Their repudiation offered a necessary theological and historical corrective that is leading to trusting relationships with Jewish neighbors, and that allows Lutherans to mature alongside other communities of faith around the world.

Prohibition against trespass, and invitation for authentic encounter, are the lessons here, for the future of religions laboring together in the world. These examples of prohibition and invitation serve as a historical prelude to the serious challenges for human and religious dignity that we face in the world today. We have entered a time where together we must name the unholy and exorcise what Pope Francis calls the "demonic" from our societies, if we hope for a future that we desire our grandchildren to inherit.[21] Our challenges today are at the axis of religion and violence.

THE UNHOLY

Quantitative statistics on the collusion of religion and violence in the world assist in locating the serious challenges we face today. First, in my own country, the USA, we experience problems with pockets of radicalized

---

[20] See Response of Mark S. Hanson, at **www.acommonword.com/response-from-bishop-rev-mark-s-hanson**. Luther puts the matter plainly in his *Commentary on Galatians*, (Chapter 5, and Verse 14): "You do not need any book of instructions to teach you how to love your neighbor. All you have to do is to look into your own heart, and it will tell you how you ought to love your neighbor as yourself." From Martin Luther, *Commentary on the Epistle to the Galatians*, transl. Theodore Graebner (1998), Chapter 5, Verse 14, at **www.gutenberg.org/files/1549/1549-h/1549-h.htm**

[21] In talking about the unholy, terms like "demonic" or "diabolical" are ontologically freighted via the Enlightenment framework and anthropology. In our effort not to personify it or give "evil" agential status, we can end up either trivializing it or rendering it the symmetrical opposite.

religious groups. The reputable Southern Poverty Law Center reported in 2008 that it was monitoring 844 active hate groups within the country. In February 2011, those numbers rose to well over a thousand. The Center reports that, "Since the year 2000 the number of hate groups (in the USA), has increased by 54 percent."[22] These numbers coincide with a general sense in the citizenry of an erosion of public trust, shrinking capacity to maintain financial solvency or advancement and ideologically balkanized and protectionist groups that reinforce community identity.

In January 2014, the Pew Forum on Religion and Public Life, released statistics on their 2012 and 2007 study on religion and violence in the world.[23] The number of countries in the world affected by religion-related violence has doubled over the past six years. Women face harassment due to religious dress in nearly a third of countries in the world (32%), up from a quarter (25%) in 2011 and less than one-in-ten (7%) in 2007. Roughly three-quarters of the global population lives there where overall levels of sectarian hostilities were rated high or very high in 2012. Half of all countries in the region of the Middle East and North Africa currently experience sectarian violence. Globally, sectarian violence took place in nearly one-in-five of the world's countries in 2012 (18%), up from 8 percent in 2007. We also know how sectarian violence does not respect national boundaries, where networks appear like neural fibers across regions of the globe.[24]

These statistics bely a form of trespass by our own co-religionists, who hail from the same root stock of our cherished values, if we believe them when they say they practice Judaism, Islam and Christianity. What is taking place in today's world, and indeed the hunger that informs the necessary radical response of religion today, is like oxygen deprivation. There are coastal waters in the world where nothing grows. Lacking oxygen, life collapses. Take a submersible and travel to the bottom of those bodies of water; you enter a graveyard of organic matter. Where our children are murdered, whole communities are threatened with biological agents or invasion, the widow and orphan in the forms of today's immigrants and

---

[22] See Southern Poverty Law Center "Hate Group Numbers Up By 54% Since 2000." February 26, 2009. Accessed November 17, 2015. **https://www.splcenter.org/ news/2009/02/26/hate-group-numbers-54-2000**.

[23] See PewResearch Religion and Public Life Project—Religious Hostilities Reach Six-Year High, at **www.pewforum.org/2014/01/14/religious-hostilities-reach- six-year-high/**

[24] Philip Jenkins, *The Next Christendom: The Coming of Global Christianity,* 3rd ed. (Oxford: University Press, 2007), 234. Jenkins notes the neural reality that is no respecter of national boundaries in his accounting of the Rwandan massacre in the 1990s, which spilled over into Angola, Zimbabwe, Namibia and Uganda.

refugees are left exposed to religious zealots, and on and on we enter into an equivalent kind of death zone at the bottom of our humanity.[25]

A death zone is that peculiar place where a spirit of generosity, and accompanying community, justice and solidarity are hobbled if not altogether absent in any way that glimpses peace.[26] Philosopher Etienne Balibar describes the plight of what some Latin American sociologists provocatively call "[...] *población chatarra*, [or] garbage humans, [who are] thrown away, out of the global city," from this-side-of-the border to across-the-border.[27] These are the ones who are neglected, abandoned and forgotten. They are refugees who wake up "in the face of a cumulative effect of different forms of extreme violence [or] death zones of humanity [...]."[28] Where religion is co-opted by violent intent, rationality also fails. Well-reasoned yet insane arguments from charismatic leaders can commit us to an inexplicable and contradictory trespass of whole communities, stirring great injustices even in the name of justice itself.

In our day, and in examples from our holy texts, we could say that what is unholy is so because at the heart it is a disconnection of our place in relation to God and neighbor in the world. Erecting an image of sacrilege in an arbitrary appeal to Scripture, even in the name of God, can weaponize religion and skew this core relationship. Such appeals are in fact meant to be outside the respect of God or religion. The Christian Scriptures (Mt 2:40, Mk 12:29), the *Shema* (Deut 6:4) in the Torah, and the Qur'anic reflections on the nature of God (Al-Ikhlas, 112:12) all begin at the Oneness of God who creates and cares for God's whole creation. Our Scriptures attest to the unholy in the form of hostility, a co-optation of our very values and violence that can reach a horrific scale. We hear from the stories of those

---

[25] Gustavo Gutiérrez, *A Theology of Liberation: History, Politics, and Salvation*, transl. and eds, Sister Caridad Inda and John Eagleson (New York: Orbis Books, 1973), 69–72. There is a cry of injustice that some quarters of the world have little access to find voice. I recommend more on this topic by reading Gutiérrez's classic account.

[26] Geneviève Jacques, *Beyond Impunity: An Ecumenical Approach to Truth, Justice and Reconciliation* (Geneva: WCC Publications, 2000), 36. "The more difficult question in the aftermath of conflict or massive violations of human rights is how to respond to the *victim's need* for justice by bringing the accused to the bar of justice" [author's own italics].

[27] Etienne Balibar, "Outlines of a Topography of Cruelty: Citizenship and Civility in the Era of Global Violence," in *Constellations* Volume 8, No 1 (Oxford: Blackwell Publishers Ltd, 2001), 15–29.

[28] Ibid., 24. Reflecting on the global context of a death zone, Balibar refers to it as topographical, and thereby all-encompassing in social life. "This [geopolitics], among other reasons, is what leads me to discuss these issues in terms of a 'topography', by which I understand at the same time a concrete, spatial, geographical, or geopolitical perspective."

who have walked through those shadows of death so that they experience a form of theft, and then a denial of the theft, somehow stealing from the past, the present and opening a wound in an uncertain future as well.[29] Judaism, Christianity and Islam—millions upon millions draw on their core texts to respond to God's first act of relationship, to raise their families, to lead upstanding and righteous lives, to exhibit every small and significant show of solidarity in community and, at the core, to be generous in life.

THE RADICAL QUESTION

So, What is the spirit of generosity that Jews, Muslims and Christians share from the heart of their faiths, which is critical to humanity and the world in the twenty-first century? Our response is no less true even when it sounds redundant: That spirit of generosity is a disposition in us to live holy lives, aligned to relationship with God, for the sake of love and solidarity with one another in the world. A life of generosity means that we share specific obligations in the world. I would like to suggest four specific obligations for living into this radical question.

First, generosity is a radical response to conflict. Even so, generosity appears to evaporate when people feel under threat due to conflict. It becomes an abstraction that fails to give us sustenance. This is always most evident when co-religionists attack each other, having reverted to (say) ethnicity as their primary identity. At these times generosity must be made more concrete through ritual, or shared ritual, in order to remind communities of the principles and values so that they do not settle for lesser more balkanizing identity. In 2014, in Sarcelles, France, rabbis, imams and pastors joined together with other dignitaries to stand against anti-religious bias. Co-religionists from Washington D.C. to South Korea, endeavor in their communities and alongside one another to confront hate speech. Ritual calls on the long, holy memory or anamnesis that requires a response from communities in conflict, and this century will require greater strategy for integrating ritual in communities engaged in conflict.

---

[29] The US Presidential Task force on the Holocaust underscores the principle reflections of those serving on the commission in their introductory letter to President Jimmy Carter: "We cannot grant the killers a posthumous victory. Not only did they humiliate and assassinate their victims, they wanted also to destroy their memory. They killed them twice, reducing them to ashes and then denying their deed. Not to remember the dead now would mean to become accomplices in their murders." Report to the President: President's Commission on the Holocaust, Elie Wiesel, Chairman, 27 September 1979. US Govt. Printing Office, Washington, D.C.

Second, we have a responsibility to amplify the story of God's generosity to the world as an unremitting "yes" to people and communities desirous of a whole and flourishing life. In work and life we have networks of people for whom we care, and to whom we reach out, especially across sectarian divisions, for purposes of peace and well-being.[30] They hope for this generosity of spirit from us, as we do from them. Creating structures in our communities to tell the true-to-life experiences and stories of hope from those suffering under persecution is a form of resistance. The power of a local example of resiliency and resistance can oxygenate a whole community.[31] Dietrich Bonhoeffer, Martin Luther King, Anne Frank and Abd El-Kader, were not aware how their impact in the present would be a witness to millions upon millions in the future.[32]

Third, from local to international contexts, we must truly learn together equally and resoundingly to identify the unholy or diabolical with an unequivocal "no!" to the violence and its allegiances that erode human life, community and justice. When three-quarters of the global population live amidst sectarian hostilities, we require leadership that opposes the radicalization of belief and instead heightens core values. If we believe there is no justification for trespassing human rights, then we challenge such movements as they threaten human rights, and we seek to put pressure for the purposes of quelling hostilities at their source.

And fourth, as Philip Jenkins notes, we live in a post-colonial world where the religious voice will be shaped beyond affiliation to countries or their allegiances, so that our mutual appeal to God transcends a world framed by the Enlightenment.[33] In this new world, we are also transcending our expectations for communication and the nature of community. We live amidst unprecedented technological advances in organized communication.

---

[30] Consider the comments on this matter by Said, Abdul Aziz. "Islam and Peace-making in the Middle East: Keynote Address for USAID Ramadan Iftar." Lecture delivered at American University, Washington, DC, 16 September 2008, at **www.american.edu/sis/islamicpeacechair/upload/Islam-and-Peacemaking-in-the-Middle-East.pdf**

[31] Karima Bennoune, *Your Fatwa Does not Apply Here. Untold Stories from the Fight Against Muslim Fundamentalism* (New York: W.W. Norton, 2014). "I am seeking a new way of talking about this all together, that is grounded in the real life experiences and hope and people on the front lines."

[32] Abdelkater El Djezairi (Abd El-Kader: 1808–1883) was an Algerian religious and military leader who struggled against the French colonial forces. His constant regard for human rights, even for the religious rights (mostly Christian) of his own prisoners of war, and for saving the Christian community of Damascus from a massacre in 1860, won him admiration by friends and enemy combatants alike.

[33] Jenkins, op. cit. (note 24), 231–36.

Popularly compared to the advent of the printing press, our technological gain is categorically disruptive by a much greater factor than that of set type. And that gain is growing exponentially. In Seattle students from around the world with an interest in religion, also make their living in the tech industry. They ask, What hinders us from coordinating a visible global summit of religious leadership through emerging technology?

A coordinated and sustainable virtual summit dedicated to a future intended from the heart of our sacred Scripture, is not a bad idea. In fact, I would say it is just a matter of time. Too much social and political dislocation and religious entrepreneurialism is stirring at the heart of our young, who have more access to one another through increasingly less expensive technology. It is only a matter of time before this generation will elevate this form of advanced coordination as a necessary mark of religious relevance in the world. Will they tire of violence in a global context where proper networking of the religious voice for peace is possible? So far, those advances are taking place largely external to religious self-understanding. That could rapidly change.

Consider, from within the Christian community, how Pope Francis is a disruptive example of a religious leader committed to placing simply-stated generosity at the heart of his ministry. An appeal to more coordinated communication will seem naïve to the socio- and geo-political complexities of the world today, not to mention the internal complexities within our religious communities. But that critique would mistake informed aspiration for ignorance. Religion is aspirational. Religion aspires to assist humanity in living a holy life. Every worthwhile religious aspiration is dangerous to ideologues who would rather justify oppression under the ruse of a righteous god. Today, where images of violence and death saturate media, what inhibits us from aspiring to a mode of telling the manifold stories of generosity to a world hungry for an under-metabolized nutrient of human life?

In terms of leadership, we live in a time where our brightest minds from across disciplines and fields could assist in the cultivation of ideas and strategies for how religion will express itself today and tomorrow. This is a bad time in history to be a violent ideologue. That may seem counter to the horrendous violence we see in the world. But there are increasingly fewer places to conceal atrocity in a world reaching hyper-alert status of observation. And their peddled wares purchase less and less for an increasingly conversant world. For the first time in history on a global scale, people have the technological capacity to pay as much attention to the UN's condemnation of violence as to the social networks that rise up overnight on behalf of the beleaguered. Now would be the time to amplify a message of generosity that brings to life true peace in a world, and yet only when religions unequivocally refuse any message of apostate violence. Name it as unholy and repudiate it. And reclaim a core message of loving kindness and life that draws on a generosity after which the world is sorely hungry.

Religion today and tomorrow must take up the challenge and obligation to speak and act together in a spirit of generosity. If we join together in refuting the unholy, what then? Perhaps the conflicts we seek to quell, and stories we need to tell, will be respectively extinguished or mocked. Either way, to deny this generosity is to promote our irrelevance in the future. Thus, what is at stake in our decision to live together in a spirit of generosity today is nothing less than the credibility of our aspiration to God and the world, both for this generation and for the generations to come.

JEWS, GOD AND THEODICY

Anson Laytner

THE PROBLEM

The Jewish people faces many challenges today: intermarriage and assimilation threaten our small numbers through attrition; the physical threat of ongoing conflict between Israel and the Palestinian people, and beyond to include the larger Arab and even the Muslim world; and the spiritual threat of secularism.

The Pew Research Center Religion and Public Life's Report on American Jews reported that twenty-two percent of the American Jewish participants claim "no religion" and that the majority of respondents do not see religion as the primary component of Jewish identity. A full sixty-two percent ground their Jewish identity in ancestry and culture, while only fifteen percent base it on religion. And among Jews who gave Judaism as their religion, fifty-five percent nonetheless base Jewish identity on ancestry and culture and sixty-six percent did not view belief in God as an essential constituent part of Jewish identity.[1]

While many Jewish experts claimed to have been surprised, even shocked, by these results, I confess to being relieved. The results of the Pew Research Center appear to indicate that the majority of American Jews have embraced an ethnically-based sense of Jewish identity, which

---

[1] A Portrait of Jewish Americans, at **www.pewforum.org/2013/10/01/jewish-american-beliefs-attitudes-culture-survey**. Compare these statistics with the national norms: In the 2012 survey by the Pew Religion and Public Life Project (**www.pewforum.org/2012/10/09/nones-on-the-rise**), nearly a fifth of those polled said that they were not religiously affiliated—and nearly thirty-seven percent of that group said they were "spiritual" but not "religious."

is more in line with their Israeli Jewish counterparts and also with Jewish tradition. And all this, I think, is a good thing because the radical question facing Jews today still has to do with God's apparent absence during the Holocaust, which we Jews call the *Shoah*. Therefore, if Jewish identity were primarily based on our religion, and so many Jews have problems with God, we would be *auf tzuris*, in really big trouble.

Jews can be agnostic or even atheistic and still consider themselves Jews, and if this is surprising, then the following short digression on the changing nature of Jewish identity over the centuries might prove helpful. Thereafter, I will connect Jewish identity with the issue of theodicy and review a number of the traditional theodicies; then I shall suggest an old/new God concept as a way of dealing with the issue of theodicy; and finally, I will conclude by linking the issue of God's presence to that of our changing religious identity in the twenty-first century.

On Jewish identity

For Christians and Muslims, Jewish identity is straightforward enough: "Judaism" is a religion. It is almost logical. You, Christianity and Islam, are both religions and you are related to us, therefore Jews must constitute a religion too. Would that it were that simple; it would make things a lot easier for us.

A brief review of Jewish mythic origins (or history) is in order: In the beginning, God created Avraham, who begat (with a little help) Yishmael and Yitzhak; and the latter begat (also with a little help) Esav and Ya'acov; and the latter begat (with lots of help) twelve sons and one daughter (who did not matter except where her family's "honor" was concerned). Muslims see Avraham and Yishmael as the founders of their faith, the first Muslims. Jews see Avraham, Yitzhak and Ya'acov both as founders of our nation and our religion. Belief, practice and tribe are uniquely blended in the Jewish covenant with God.

Ya'acov, according to this transformational myth, wrestled with a divine being and was bestowed the name "Yisra-el" and his sons' descendants were called "B'nai" or "children" of Yisrael. According to the Torah, these tribes, together with a mixed multitude, returned to Cana'an from Egyptian slavery and settled there, first in loose association, then in a kingdom—make that two kingdoms—Yehudah (Judah), comprising the tribes of Yehudah and Benyamin, and Yisrael (Israel), for the rest.

The kingdom of Yisrael was destroyed by Assyria and its citizenry dispersed, some to Yehudah and some to points unknown. Yehudah was destroyed later and its élite exiled to Babylon, where Judaism as we know it began to be formed.

The word "Yehudi" or "Jew" in English comes from "Yehudah" or "Yudaea" (Judaea) as it was called by the Greeks and Romans. The linguistic connection between our name and our geographic origin is clearer in languages other than English. "Judaism" was the religion of the people of Yehudah, the Yehudim, regardless of where they lived. Ironically, it was precisely during its near fatal struggle with the Roman Empire that the faith of the Jewish nation almost went international as its message found a receptive place in the pagan Roman Empire. (Remember how Jesus supposedly criticized the Pharisees for their zealous proselytizing.[2])

Christianity came into existence during this same period, first as a Jewish sect and eventually becoming an independent and truly international faith. Among the first things Emperor Constantine did after bestowing imperial status on Christianity was to make conversion to Judaism a capital crime. Islam, the other international faith in the Abrahamic line, usually viewed Judaism in more complementary terms than did Christianity. But Islam also encouraged, sometimes violently, Jewish conversion to Islam, and like Christianity forbade the reverse. Thus Judaism remained primarily the faith of the Jewish nation-in-exile, awaiting the messiah's arrival and the return to our ancestral land, as traditional Jews do to this very day.

Fast forward to the age of the so-called European Enlightenment. The emerging nation-states of Western and Central Europe gradually began to emancipate and integrate their Jewish resident alien populations, with the proviso that said Jews abandon their national identity and instead identify themselves solely as members of a religious group. One might say that when this separation in identity occurred, "Judaism" the religion, was born. Ironically, in reaction to this offer of citizenship, modern anti-Semitism was born as well. Anti-Semitism focused on the idea that Jews constitute a different nation, or race, than the French or the Germans, for example, and that this alien nation, regardless of how many centuries it had been in residence, was inimically hostile to its host nation-state. Anti-Semitism is a hatred that goes far beyond religious prejudice; it is something that even conversion to Christianity cannot overcome. The Nazis represent the apogee of European anti-Semitism.

Jews in Europe responded to the offer of emancipation and the reactive rise of anti-Semitism in a variety of ways: some by modernizing their observance in the hope of obtaining equal rights (the contemporary Reform, Conservative and Orthodox movements of Judaism), some by becoming revolutionaries and challenging the oppressive status quo (Bundists, socialists, Communists, anarchists, etc.) and some by choosing to retain the traditional self-definition as a nation-in-exile with a faith and land of its own (paradoxically both the Zionists and the ultra-Orthodox).

In America, Jews were viewed both as belonging to a faith-group, Judaism, but also as being racially outside the white European Caucasian fold.

---

[2] Matthew 23:15.

Jews from Germany, the first major group to arrive in America, preferred the religious self-definition but the mass immigration of Jews from Eastern Europe in the early twentieth century, American anti-Semitism, the Holocaust and the birth of the state of Israel, all reinforced the traditional self-definition once again.

So here we stand: we are both a religion and an ethnicity. But I would say that we Jews primarily think of ourselves as a people. A people is different from a religion. A people is different from an ethnicity. A people is different from a nation. Peoplehood is an ancient designation with few cognates in the modern world and therefore it is difficult for many today, including many Jews, to understand and accept. (One thing however is clear: If there remains a shared ethnicity among us Jews worldwide, it exists only in our DNA, otherwise it is largely mythic—but real to us nonetheless.)

As the Yiddish saying goes: "It's hard to be a Jew!"

THE PROBLEM OF THEODICY

What does this question of identity have to do with the questions about God posed by the *Shoah*? If being a Jew were simply a matter of ethnicity, how we relate to God would not matter, except on the individual spiritual plane. But since we are a people, a nation with a unique religion and a self-perceived singular relationship with God, the issue of God's presence or absence during the Holocaust is most significant because it threatens the entire structure of Jewish identity. I want to suggest that the challenges Judaism faces regarding this issue are shared by Christianity and also Islam. While the question of theodicy is hardly new, I believe that it remains the radical question facing our three faiths today because of its implications for our god-concepts, and the concept of divine providence in particular.

The *Shoah* and other modern genocides strongly undermine the traditional concept of divine providence. Mass murder is very hard to reconcile with divine goodness, particularly because our three faiths all traditionally hold that God can and does intervene in history—but the same challenge holds true for the suffering of the individual as well. Baldly stated, either the Holocaust (and every other genocide) is part of God's plan—which makes God ultimately responsible for genocide; or God is not fully in charge—an idea that threatens the entire construct of traditional Jewish faith, and perhaps other faiths as well.

What makes the issue of theodicy more of a radical question in our day than before is the fact that modern scientific thought offers further challenges to our traditional god-concepts.

For many people today, science has wreaked havoc on our understanding of the universe and on our ancient views of God. The world literally is not the same place it was when the Torah and Talmud, the New Testament and the Qur'an, were written. At one time, people literally knew where God dwelled; today, in an apparently infinite and expanding universe, where is God's abode? Our sense of place in the scheme of things—and indeed the whole scheme of things—is radically different from those of ancient times, yet our god-concepts have largely remained the same.

Science in turn bred "the scientific perspective" which in turn gave birth to "secularism," both of which cast a skeptical eye on any knowledge or theory that is not objectively (i.e., scientifically) verifiable. This has resulted in a sustained critique and sometimes an outright attack by philosophers from the European Enlightenment to our own day; by way of example, witness the recent spate of books by the "new atheists."[3] All this has threatened our religious worldviews, as perspectives that have existed for several millennia, if not more.

Central to the worldviews of our three faiths is the concept of divine providence. Beginning with the Torah, our religions teach that God is actively involved in history; selecting individuals through whom to reveal the divine will; intervening in human affairs; testing, punishing and rewarding individuals and whole nations based on their adherence to divinely revealed moral laws and as part of some divine plan. To that end, even the so-called natural evils, like earthquakes or tsunamis, have been believed to be used by God for divine ends.

According to our religions, because we believe the Creator operates with a plan, we must accept whatever happens as God's will, even perceived evils. "Submission" is the term used in Islam, and it applies equally to the Jewish and Christian traditions as well. However, it seems human nature to expect only the good from God. For example, although some survivors of a plane crash might attribute their survival to God's will, most people would probably shun the corollary that it must therefore also have been God's will that everyone else perished—although that never stops some fool clergy from saying so.

Over the centuries, much effort has been spent to explain an apparent conundrum: God is omnipotent, but evil and suffering happen. Humanity's free will does not let God off the hook because, being omniscient, God would know the outcome of our bad choices in advance and still choose not to act. In any case, since God cannot or will not intervene to prevent suffering, God could be accused of standing by idly while the blood of humanity

---

[3] Two wonderful condemnations of religion, specifically the Abrahamic ones, are, Sam Harris, *The End of Faith* (New York: Norton, 2004), and Christopher Hitchens, *God Is Not Great: How Religion Poisons Everything* (New York: Twelve Books, 2007).

is being spilt.[4] Without explanation, this conundrum leads to one of two consequences: either God is neither good nor just or God is not omnipotent.

Today, as a result of centuries of effort, a sufferer has a veritable smorgasbord of theodicies from which to choose to ease their spiritual suffering. Here is a taste of some major ones from the Abrahamic faiths[5]—and please forgive me for generalizing:

- Suffering allows us to distinguish and appreciate the good life. If we did not have suffering, how would we know what good feels like?

- Suffering is punishment for sins committed and therefore is seen as discipline lovingly administered by God—like a parent providing corporal punishment—meant to redirect one to follow God's ways. One should accept such suffering with gratitude, analyze one's behavior for sin, and modify one's deeds. This view has been applied both to the suffering of the nation and to the suffering of the individual.

- Suffering is a test or trial of individual faith, such as Avraham or Iyov was subjected to. It is an honor to be chosen—and God never gives one

---

[4] This is acknowledged in a *midrash* on Cain's murder of Abel, in which God admits responsibility both for creating human beings with a flaw and for being an apathetic bystander. Responding to God's question, "Where is your brother Abel?" Cain retorts:

> You are He who is the guardian of all creatures and You ask of him from me?...I have killed him. But You created the evil inclination (yetzer ha'ra) in me. You are the guardian of everything, yet You allowed me to kill him. You are the one who killed him...for if You had accepted my sacrifice as You did his, I would not have grown jealous...This resembles the case of two who quarreled and one is killed. But a third fellow was there who did nothing to intervene between them. Upon whom does the blame rest if not the third fellow?

In this *midrash*, Tanhuma to Beresheet (Genesis) 9, God acknowledges that Cain is right because the proof-text is read not just as a plea: "His blood cries out to Me (*ely*)" but also as an accusation: "His blood cries out against Me (*aly*)," because God had clearly violated one of His own commandments: "Do not stand upon the blood of your fellow" [Vayikrah (Leviticus) 19:16]. According to this *midrash*, with regards to human evil, God is at least partially at fault, just as surely as is the perpetrator of the wrong.
[5] Space prohibits a more complete listing. For example, Hindus and Buddhists consider life's experiences—suffering and pleasure, joy and sadness—to be illusory. Their spiritual task is to attempt to comprehend the reality behind the illusion. Suffering and joy are one and the same, like dreams, while the object of life is enlightenment, the transcendence of all passions and attachments.

more than one can handle. Traditional imagery likens the sufferer to smelted metal, a pruned tree, a clay pot, which gets knocked to test its mettle, or a poked fire. Since God only tests the righteous, one should embrace these trials, like Rabbi Akiva did when he was tortured to death by the Romans. In the Jewish tradition, this sort of suffering is called "sufferings of love."

- Suffering is an inexplicable mystery and should be accepted with an attitude of submission. Individuals are encouraged to place their trust in God's goodness and in God's plan for each person, even if it includes suffering. There is a divine integrity to events, even if one fails to perceive it.

- Suffering in this world does not matter since this life is only the vestibule to eternal life in the world-to-come. Some good people suffer in this world—their sins are wiped clean—so they do not have to be punished in the hereafter.

- Suffering happens for no apparent reason or without justification, or so asserts the Jewish "arguing with God" approach. When suffering happens, one can and should protest to God, against God, for allowing these perceived injustices to occur, just as Avraham, Moshe and other Jews have done in the past.

- A Jewish mystical approach would suggest that as an unintended result of God's "self-contracting" to allow space for creation to exist, God created a good but imperfect world. Our job is to act as God's partners by repairing the world.

- Suffering happens because, although God is omnipotent, God chooses not to use that power in a broken, unredeemed world but instead is present with us in the ordeals we suffer, even to the point of suffering with us, but will act to vindicate the sufferers in the future.

- Similarly, a distinctly Christian approach holds that when we suffer, we share something with Jesus, because in human form he suffered as we do, and there is comfort in knowing this.

- The deist solution is to assert that God is like a watchmaker who, after making the world, withdrew from the field of action and let "the machine" run on its own. In traditional terms, this means affirming God's general providence is operational, but denying that personal providence exists. With a little fine-tuning—like removing the watchmaker—this could be an atheist understanding of suffering too.

- A contemporary view posits that God is not omnipotent but rather has limited powers to the degree that humanity also has some power. Consequently, God is neither responsible for what happens nor capable of intervening.

- Some Christians and Muslims embrace the existence of "Satan" or "Shaitan" as an opposing power to God. Human life and commensurate suffering are the battleground between these cosmic forces. Therefore, one prays to God for support and strength against the Evil One/Deceiver.[6]

I could go on—and I have not even got to Hindu and Buddhist rationalizations! For me as a Jew, the *Shoah* represents the zenith of human cruelty to other human beings and the nadir of divine activity in the face of immense suffering. For me, the Holocaust has created an irreversible rift between the religious past—and its views on suffering and its God-concepts—and the present day.

It is my belief that it is time for radical change. It simply makes no sense for our thinking to have evolved in so many ways yet to remain static in the field of faith. One needs to ask if our god-concepts ought to remain tethered to ancient perceptions or be allowed to grow and change. In fact, our god-concepts have always been changing, it is just that our faiths did not acknowledge this as being the case. In truth, we Jews have many god-concepts all linked by the theological conceit that "God is One."

I believe that the concept of divine providence and other traditional concepts are in dire need of transformation. I believe that these rabbinic tenets are as outmoded in our day and age as the sacrificial cult of the Temple in Jerusalem eventually became. Our prophets questioned the primacy of sacrifice over ethical behavior, but animal sacrifice was a near universal form of worship in the ancient world. Then prayer without sacrifice became more common and, in our case, once the Temple in Jerusalem was destroyed, prayer completely replaced sacrifice. Today, the idea of animal sacrifice as a form of worship is appalling to most people. Similarly, we need a revolution in Jewish theological thought, something as radical in our day as envisioning a form of Judaism without the Temple and priests and sacrifices was at the beginning of the Common Era.

---

[6] This perspective is shared by dualistic religions such as Zoroastrianism and polytheistic religions such as Wicca.

Kaifeng Jewish theology

I shall draw on another field of interest of mine in order to suggest the direction our faiths, or at least my faith, might take in addressing these challenges. For years, I have been a student of the Jewish community in Kaifeng, China, a group that survived without persecution for over a thousand years and persists to this day. Although tiny in numbers, the Kaifeng Jews blazed a trail that was unique for its cultural adaptation.

We often have no idea of the extent to which Judaism has borrowed from other theologies and philosophies down through the ages. The foundations of biblical Judaism may be found in ancient Egyptian, Mesopotamian and Canaanite cultures. Post-exilic, proto-rabbinic Judaism borrowed from the Zoroastrian faith and Hellenistic thought. Medieval rabbinic Judaism nourished itself on Aristotelian thought via Islamic thinkers and from Islam itself. In Europe, Jewish thinkers adopted and adapted ideas from Christian theologians and from philosophers from the eighteenth through the twentieth centuries. This is what Jews everywhere have always done in order to survive and grow.

In the case of the Kaifeng Jews, because they lived in China, they borrowed from Daoist and Confucian thought as they settled into their new cultural home.[7] The only difference between what happened in Europe and the Middle East on the one hand and China on the other is that, in no small part due to population size and isolation, the Chinese Jews assimilated almost to the point of disappearance while, further to the West, foreign ideas were assimilated but the Jewish people flourished.

Nonetheless, the incorporation of Chinese ideas into Kaifeng Jewish religious thought represents a unique synthesis. While admittedly this Sino-Judaism has not had any influence in the history of Jewish thought as did, for example, the incorporation of Hellenistic thought into proto-rabbinic Judaism, which evolved into the Judaism that is practiced today, and which also laid some of the foundations for Christianity and Islam, it is nonetheless significant in its own right.[8]

---

[7] Jordan Paper, *The Theology of the Chinese Jews, 1000–1850* (Waterloo, ON: Wilfrid Laurier UP, 2012), has drawn attention to the cultural bias of the dominant Ashkenazi Jewish community when it comes to examining the so-called "exotic" Jewish communities and their attitude towards the Kaifeng community is part and parcel of this bias. Thus, while it may indeed be said that the Chinese Jews absorbed foreign ideas into their faith, the same may be said, and indeed ought to be said, about the Jewish communities of Europe and the Middle East as well. What is fit for the Beijing duck ought to be fit for the goose and gander as well!

[8] Andrew Plaks argues for a culturally-neutral, but appreciative, perspective in his essay, "The Confucianization of the Kaifeng Jews: Interpretations of the Kaifeng Stelae Inscriptions," in Jonathan Goldstein, *The Jews of China* (Armonk NY: Sharpe, 1999), vol. I, 38–39.

The Kaifeng Jews wanted to have their faith and practices be understood in light of the dominant culture, much as Jews everywhere always have. In the Chinese situation, they were fortunate to live in a society that fostered syncretism and which was indifferent to doctrinal differences in a way unimaginable in the monotheistic Middle East or Europe. Consequently, the Kaifeng community was able to embrace basic Confucian and Daoist concepts and relatively easily blend them with their own Jewish ones. The focus of both faiths on human relationships rather than theology made this synthesis particularly rich and it was able to sustain the community for many centuries.[9]

What lessons might this unique synthesis potentially hold for contemporary Jewish thought and life? Given the problems rabbinic Judaism has today, particularly with the Holocaust but also with secularism, and coupled with the interest many people have in Eastern faiths, perhaps the Kaifeng Jewish materials have something of value to offer the spiritually restless souls of our post-Holocaust, contemporary world. Consequently, I thought it might be spiritually worthwhile—and intellectually "fun"—to explore the Kaifeng Jewish materials—recorded for posterity by Jesuits and other missionaries—for what they might offer to our own Western-style Judaism. Also, since our three faiths tend to eschew innovation and revere the traditional, the Kaifeng Jewish concepts also provide me with a precedent—spiritual/intellectual cover, if you will—on which to base my own thinking, which follows afterwards. I will focus my reflections on the themes of God, God's role and the human role.

First, about God: When talking about God, the Kaifeng texts use the term *Tian*, which is not a proper name or even a word meaning "God," like the Hebrew *El* or *Elohim*. It is impersonal, even abstract. At best, like its Hebrew counterpart *Shamayyim*, *Tian* is a word with a dual meaning, referring both to the actual sky and to a figurative or symbolic "Heaven." Rather than using the anthropomorphisms of the Torah, Talmud and prayer book—terms like father, king and so on—the Chinese Jewish texts assert that the divine, i.e., Heaven, is a mystery, as something truly beyond our comprehension. This is hardly an alien idea for it is precisely what both the Jewish philosopher Maimonides and the Jewish mystics taught.

Second, God's role: The biggest difference between the Chinese Jewish "theology" and mainstream Jewish theology has to do with the concepts of revelation and God's intervention in history. In the Chinese Jewish texts, Heaven's only intervention—if it is that at all—is the giving of Scriptures.

---

[9] That the Kaifeng community almost ceased to exist is due to its small numbers and long isolation, to the integration of its members into the larger society, and to China's own long eclipse during the late Qing dynasty and the subsequent turmoil of the early Republic.

According to the traditional Jewish perspective, revelation is something God gives to Moshe and, through him, to Yisrael and the world. Here, however, revelation is the attunement of the human being to something that is omnipresent and immanent. In the Chinese Jewish view, it is through human endeavor and self-improvement—not unlike Maimonides's views on the levels of the intellect and the prophetic mind—that an outstanding person like Avraham or Moshe can gain enlightenment and perceive the *Dao* of Heaven. In Avraham's case, his enlightened state made him the first to "know" Heaven and therefore he is honored as the founder of the faith. In Moshe's case, his highly developed personal character led to his perceiving the mystery of Heaven and then to his composing the Scriptures and the commandments therein. But the revelation was theirs to achieve, not God's to bestow. Absent from the texts is any substantive reference to Yisrael's miraculous exodus from Egypt or its biblical years, or to God's use of history and nature as either reward or punishment.

And third, humanity's role: What emerges as most striking about the Kaifeng Jewish materials is their humanistic focus. As in traditional Jewish thought, *Tian*, though ultimately unknowable, could be known both through the creative power of nature and through the Torah. In the Kaifeng texts, *Tian* orders both the natural world and the human world. It is the role of the exceptional human being to perceive it, experience it and try to communicate it to other people. The ordinary person has only to practice the *Dao* as expressed in the Torah, i.e., the *mitzvot*, or commandments—honoring Heaven with appropriate prayers and rituals, respecting one's ancestors and living ethically—in order to put oneself in harmony simultaneously with the *Dao* of the natural world and the *Dao* of Heaven.

For the Chinese Jews, as for Jews everywhere, the *mitzvot*, the commandments, provide for Jewish continuity. They constitute "Jewish civilization" and, wherever Jews wandered, there too went the *mitzvot*. The Kaifeng Jews were traditionalists in their observance. They prayed three times a day, observed Shabbat and the holidays and kept kosher and tried to live ethically. The Kaifeng Jewish adoption and adaptation of *ziran* (self-awareness), remind us of the importance of personal spiritual development and the need for self-evaluation/self-cultivation as an integral part of observing the *mitzvot*. One is engaged in *ziran* not just for one's own sake, but because one's personal ethical behavior both shows respect for one's ancestors and provides a model for future generations to emulate.

This sense of connection with the past and future was probably heightened for the Kaifeng Jews by their adoption of Chinese cultural norms of *xiao* (filial piety) and "ancestor reverence." Ancestor reverence gave them a unique sense of being contemporary links in the chain of a proud and ancient civilization. It was a way of honoring and connecting with the past and emphasizing the responsibility of the present generation to prepare the way for the future.

To summarize these three points noted above: *Tian*–Heaven, or God, exists, with no description possible, although it is perceivable. *Dao* or *Torah* is *Tian's* ordering of both the natural world and the human world. It too exists in some immanent way and is communicated to us by exceptional human beings. Accepting this, the ordinary person has only to practice the *Dao* as expressed in the Torah and thereby live their life in harmony with the *Dao* of Heaven. It is a faith that is firmly planted on earth and rooted in the proper doing of daily deeds, yet its practice allows one to feel a sense of unity with the totality of existence, with past and future generations, and to aspire to a perception of the Whole.

I believe that there is much we can learn from the Jews of Kaifeng that can be of value for our own search for meaning in this secular world of ours. Today, when so many Western Jews are falling away from both traditional Jewish practice and their identity as Jews, perhaps we can turn to the novel interpretation of Judaism by the Kaifeng Jews for a reinvigorated form of faith.

Their emphasis on human behavior and on the ability to perceive an immanent Presence is more in keeping with the humanistic tenor of our own age than a system based on a transcendent God's intervening in history to give the Torah, on our observing God's commandments (out of fear, or love, or both) and waiting for God to intervene in history once again.

Toward a new God-concept

Let me now return to the topic of God and build upon what I discussed briefly when I talked about *Tian* to propose an old/new God-concept.

In Hebrew, the word God is *Elohim* or *El* or *Elo-ah*, all cognately related to the Arabic "Allah." But what does God–*Elohim*–mean? Strictly speaking, *Elohim* is not a name; it's a job title, and one that many ancient Near Eastern deities were given by their peoples.[10] But for us Jews, God also has a personal name, several of them.

In Shemot (Exodus) 3, in what ought to have been a humorous skit, after encountering God in a talking Burning Bush, Moshe asks for God's name. Imagine Moshe's consternation when God replies "*Ehyeh-Asher-Ehyeh*," meaning "I will be who/what I will be." God tells Moshe to use that name when he speaks in God's name to Pharaoh and the Israelites. God also says

---

[10] Thus Ya'acov vows after his vision of the ladder that if YHVH will do "x" and "y" for him, then YHVH will be his god–(and if YHVH fails to help him, then Yaakov is free to choose another, higher performing deity)–see Beresheet (Genesis) 28:20–22.

to Moshe, "you may also call me '*Ehyeh*' ('I will be') for short." What a sense of humor! Imagine going up against the king of the greatest empire of its day and demanding: "Thus says 'I will be,' let my people go." No wonder Moshe had trouble to convince Pharaoh!

God has another, related name, comprised of the Hebrew letters "yud hay vav hay," which may be rendered in English as "YHVH," and it is used throughout the Bible and in Jewish prayers to this day. This name is called the Tetragrammaton and in Jewish tradition is unutterable, both because it is believed to be God's holy, ineffable name and also because its pronunciation, which only the High Priest knew, was lost when the Temple was destroyed. Biblical scholars often pronounce it as Yahweh—but who knows? (Personally, I believe YHVH to be the sound of breath entering and leaving our bodies and should be pronounced accordingly.)

When we Jews see the letters "YHVH," we say "*Adonai*" meaning "Lord" and most Bible translations and Jewish prayer books follow this convention. Christians later took the Hebrew vowels of "*Adonai*" placed them under the Tetragrammaton and got Jehovah. Thus God acquired another name.

In Jewish tradition, it is entirely proper to use a diminutive for God's personal name, like using Rob in place of Robert, or Sue rather than Susan. Instead of *Ehyeh* or YHVH, we can say "*Yah*" as in *Hallelu–Yah*! Traditional Jews simply call Yah "HaShem" which simply means "The Name." The Name, YHVH, also has meaning of its own: The letters YHVH represent a combination of the present and future tenses of the verb "to be." So God's name is literally (and grammatically) pure potential: Is-ness. Will Be-ing.

What does this mean? I think it may mean that God is always in a state of becoming. God is not yet whatever God will be.[11] In other words, God is not perfect but is in a state of perpetual perfectibility.

Reading the Torah, we see no indication that God is perfect. Instead, God changes His mind, regrets what He did, gets angry and does things that are downright disturbing, even scary. That is far from being perfect. But God is improving—just look at how much better behaved God appears to be by the rabbinic era—but do not take my word for it, look at how God also is depicted in the Christian Bible or in the Qur'an too. The God we share, conceived in the early centuries of the Common Era as being perfect and omni-everything, is a far cry from the God depicted in the more ancient Jewish Scriptures. The point is not that God changes, but that our conceptions of the divine do.

The Name YHVH suggests that God's essence is forward-looking and future-oriented, as in fact the Torah has God say by way of self-description.

---

[11] For more on this interpretation, see Arthur Green, *Radical Judaism: Rethinking God and Tradition and Ehyeh: A Kabbalah for Tomorrow* (Woodstock, VT: Jewish Lights, 2003).

After the Golden Calf episode, Moshe again asks to know God. But God says: "You cannot see My face, only My back,"[12] meaning "You can only see where I've been, but that is not Me." So Moshe is only allowed to view God's passing by, much as we might see the wake of a ship without seeing the ship itself pass in front of us.

Traditionally, Judaism has accepted the premise that God is essentially unknowable. Thinking of "God" as "YHVH" is the essence of the second of the Ten Commandments: not to make any images of the divine. If any single perception of God is given the mantle of absolute truth, whether by virtue of antiquity or by canonization, it becomes a humanly sanctified image—an idol, so to speak—for subsequent generations.

Because "God" is ultimately unknowable, all our theologies are flawed in that they are all limited by our human capabilities. Nonetheless, they also all point to a shared truth: that humanity perceives a Something or some Being somehow greater than all of us. In this regard, I like to compare "God" to a multifaceted gem that offers many different facets for observation. Each individual, each generation, every faith, is capable of describing only a few divine facets—and then, sadly, historically, we argue with other individuals and other faiths about what we have observed—but no one can ever know the whole "gem."

Each religion has a unique perspective of this "gem" and has built distinctive systems of belief and practice on its perspective. Our theologies are our metaphysical constructs based on our perceptions of the divine and there is unique validity to each perception and to all the religious systems built on those perceptions. But, at the same time, it is important to remember that our efforts at theology are like the parable of the blind men and the elephant, with each of us having the capacity to describe but one part yet think it the whole.

Today, the world appears smaller than it once was; we know more about each other than ever before thanks to advances in travel and communication. Consequently, "God" today is perceived by some to be more universal than any faith tradition ever imagined "God" to be. But, even in the best expressions of traditional religion, the universal God of the Jews is still peculiarly attached to the Jews; the universal God of Christianity is wedded to the church; and the universal God of Islam reveals His word only in Arabic—even the "no-God" of Zen Buddhism prefers ceremonies and meditation to be performed Japanese style! However, "God" belongs to us all, however and whatever we perceive "God" to be; no matter how we choose to dress and address the divine.

We may think we know God in some way through the past deeds attributed to God by our ancestors in their stories, or through our own experiences, but

---

[12] Shemot (Exodus) 33:18–23.

that does not constrain God, because God ultimately will be whatever God will be. And we will understand God to be however we understand God to be and however we experience God to be. Consequently, I think that many of us need to let go of past conceptions of God in order to build our own relationships with the divine. We need the freedom to perceive God in our own ways, to reinvent God, as it were, for our own day and our own needs. It is not "God" we are changing; only our human God-concepts because YHVH–"God"–is beyond all our words, past, present and future; beyond all our imaginings. Dare we permit ourselves to let go of "God" and embrace the mystery of YHVH?

A NEW THEODICY AND VISION FOR THE FUTURE

For Jews, the desire to know God is often linked to the issue of understanding why bad things happen to basically good people. Regarding the story cited above, about Moshe wanting to see God's face, one rabbinic interpretation was that Moshe wanted to understand God's way in the world, i.e., the question of God's justice and unwarranted suffering. Rabbinic opinion was split on what, if anything, was revealed of him.[13] The question however has haunted us down to the present day.

Therefore, How to make sense of unwarranted human suffering with a God like YHVH? I start by leaving God out of the equation and building from the ground up. To begin with, we can make sense of suffering simply by observing how we ourselves deal with suffering, i.e., how we live it. Life–whatever happens to us–is what it is; but we make it what it will mean for us. The meaning of suffering is not found by asking "why?" but by asking "to what end?" Every experience is either a stepping stone, or a mill stone, for our future, depending on how we perceive it and how we use it. But we alone are the ones to imbue our experiences with meaning.

Second, experience, both my own personal experience of suffering and that of the Jewish people in particular, and humanity in general, has taught me not to see God's hand in individual human lives or in human history. Nor do I expect any kind of miraculous divine intervention. I have let go of that god-concept. Cancer strikes whomsoever it will strike, regardless of their moral character; tsunamis and earthquakes kill without regard to those in their paths; armies and mobs annihilate and maim their enemies, armed or not, real or imagined. Based on what I know, divine providence does not seem to play a role in any of this; a lot of what happens to us, individually and collectively, is simply a matter of luck.

---

[13] Talmud Bavli, Menahot 29b.

I struggle to embrace the traditional Jewish teaching, which tells us to accept whatever happens in life, both the apparent good and the perceived evil, as divinely given[14]—except that I do not ascribe them to God's doing. Instead, I try to accept whatever happens as a follower of Daoism might embrace the *yin/yang* operation of the Dao. Both can happen; both are part and parcel of the divine whole we call life.

In terms of traditional Jewish theology, I suppose I accept the idea of general providence but reject the concept of personal providence. The evidence just is not there. But: I know from my own experience that YHVH Is and is true to my tradition; I also hope that YHVH is somehow and in some way present in our lives for the better. While I never will definitely know if YHVH actually "cares"—if I may be permitted this anthropomorphism—I nonetheless draw inspiration—and hope—from ancient speculations about an empathic God, One who somehow suffers when we suffer, who somehow rejoices when we rejoice and somehow is upset by human suffering and injustice.[15]

Since I choose to let God be YHVH and remain inexplicable, this means that we, and we alone, must choose to be responsible for human behavior here on earth. Fortunately, all of our faiths have good solid values to help us find the path to right living. For the ancient rabbis, the key operative element in our world was the concept of *hesed*, usually translated as loving-kindness, but also meaning mercy, favor, faithfulness, piety, benevolence, righteousness and graciousness. From *hesed* come *gemilut hasadim*, or acts of loving-kindness. So important were these that one sage, Shimon the Just, taught that they were one of the three pillars upon which the continued existence of the world depended (the other two are Torah and worship), while a later sage, Rav Huna, taught that one who only studied Torah but did no deeds of loving-kindness was like one who has no God.[16] Deeds of loving-kindness are the quintessential, demonstrable acts of Jewish piety and the desire to be holy (like God is holy).[17]

---

[14] See, for example, Talmud Bavli, Berahot 19a, 33b, 54a, 60b; Megillah 25a; Pesahim 50a; and the *Tziduk HaDin* prayer of the Jewish funeral service.

[15] The rabbis of the classical period greatly developed the concept of an anthropo-pathetic and empathetic god, conjecturing that God, or His Shekhinah, suffered when Israel suffered, was enslaved when Israel was enslaved and will be redeemed when Israel is redeemed. God is said to feel pain when Israel feels pain and God weeps and mourns for the destroyed Jerusalem and its Temple just like a king of flesh and blood. See Anson Laytner, *Arguing with God: A Jewish Tradition* (Northvale, NJ: Jason Aronson, 1990 & 1998), 83 and texts referenced in notes 41–49, 268.

[16] Pirkei Avot 1.2 and Talmud Bavli, Avodah Zarah 17b.

[17] See Vayikrah (Leviticus) 19:2. The rabbis taught (playfully) that God personally performed deeds of loving-kindness for us to emulate: God clothed the naked (Ahdam and Hava), visited the infirm (Avraham, after his circumcision) and buried the dead (Moshe), among other things. See Talmud Bavli, Sotah 14a.

I believe that the concept of *hesed*, or loving-kindness, is global; it is only articulated differently. I think it is analogous to the concepts of *agape* and *caritas* in Christianity, to *rakhma* in Islam, to *karuna* in Buddhism, to *ren* and *de* in the Chinese Confucian and Daoist traditions and to *daya* in Hinduism. It may be, along with our various versions of the Golden Rule, the closest thing we have to a universal (global) religious truth.[18] Loving-kindness is the best we are able to offer our fellow creatures, both human and beast. It builds bonds of connection; of unity, love and trust; and enables us to heal, or to repair, our world.

Life's crises are never easy, but by treating one another with loving-kindness we can help support one another through almost everything. God will not necessarily be invoked to assist from above—and even if invoked, it is highly unlikely God will intervene—but YHVH may be said to be present in the love shown, in the joys shared, in the solidarity demonstrated and, if we have the skill, in the peacefulness created.

The late Rabbi Zalman Schachter-Shalomi, or Reb Zalman as he preferred to be called, said that worldview shattering events such Auschwitz—Hiroshima and the moonwalk were two of his other favored examples—necessitate a paradigm shift because they rendered many aspects of traditional Jewish theology irrelevant.[19] At the same time, he felt they had the transformative power to launch a new era of human civilization, one in which all human beings would reach out toward one another rather than to continue to live in fear and mistrust. He believed that no faith had a monopoly on religious truth and instead spoke in favor of an "organismic" model that saw Judaism as one of many tributaries of the divine river.

Let me add to his splendid vision by noting that, if the critical question of our time concerns the meaning of suffering and related problem with traditional God concepts, then the ultimate answer lies in our (a) accepting our limited human ability to know the divine; (b) setting aside the resultant centuries of religious and ethnic intolerance; (c) truly practicing the ideals of our respective faiths; and (d) finally learning to live and work together to save ourselves and heal our planet. The Torah has Moshe say the following in God's name:

> Surely this commandment [...] is not too baffling for you, nor is it beyond reach. It is not in the heavens...neither is it beyond the sea [...]. No, the word is very close to you, in your mouth and in your heart, that you may do it. See, I have set

---

[18] For more on this see Karen Armstrong, *Twelve Steps to a Compassionate Life* (New York: Anchor Books, 2010).

[19] See Ellen Singer (ed.), *Paradigm Shift: From the Jewish Renewal Teachings of Reb Zalman Schachter-Shalomi* (Northvale, NJ: Jason Aronson, 1993).

before you this day life and good, death and evil [...]. Choose life, that you and your offspring may live.[20]

God knows this was good advice—and it is applicable for us even to this day!

A STORY ON THE TASK AT HAND

Let me conclude with a parable of my own making.[21] One day the owner of a garden assembled the gardening staff and said to them: "Tomorrow I am going on a journey. My journey may be of long duration; it may be short. I do not know when or even if I shall return. But here are some instructions to follow in my absence. Take care of my garden. In the meantime its fruits are yours to enjoy." The next day, after giving instructions to the various teams of workers, the owner left.

Weeks passed into months, and the months turned into years. Eventually the gardeners began to disagree on the interpretation of the owner's instructions. One group maintained, "This is what the owner meant," while another group insisted, "No, this is what the owner intended." As time went on, the two groups of workers found it harder and harder to agree on what needed to be done. Their argument raged persistently, neither side convincing the other, neither gaining the advantage over the other. They no longer understood that they were all tilling the soil of the same garden. Eventually the disagreement over whose interpretation was right became so heated that it consumed everyone's attention and work in the garden ground almost to a complete halt. People despaired that the owner would never return.

Finally, a third group arose and spoke to the contending sides:

"Brothers, sisters! While you argue this way and that, the garden is going to ruin. Have we not been given this wonderful garden to care for and its produce to enjoy? Don't all our interpretations help the garden grow? Does it even matter whether or not the owner returns? If the owner returns and sees that we have worked well, we shall be rewarded as promised. In this case we should continue our work. And if the owner never returns, then we shall have this garden and all its fruits as a reward in itself. In this case too it is to our advantage to continue working. Who knows what the future will hold? But let us cease this arguing to and fro. Let us return to our work at once. From either standpoint, our reward is in our continuing to work the garden."

---

[20] Dvarim (Deuteronomy) 30:11–20.
[21] Adapted from a story originally published in Laytner, op. cit. (note 15).

II. Religious Voice, Dialogue and Renewal

Challenges to Religious Identity in the Twenty-First Century

John Borelli

Remembering and the Future

Inevitably for many not so young Catholics like myself when we focus our minds to what might be ahead of us in this twenty-first century regarding religious identity and renewal, we begin by recalling how we got to this point. Is not Confucius credited with giving encouragement to reinvigorate the past in order to know what is new?[1] Thus, to consider the challenges to religious identity in an interreligious context, or specifically in an Abrahamic context, we begin by gaining inspiration from the past in order to recognize what may be ahead. I think this tendency is true for older Lutherans and older ecumenists from other churches as well.

Let me briefly explain why I am particularly cognizant of what was unfolding fifty years ago in my church that made a significant impact on my identity as a Catholic and my relationship today with fellow Christians and Jews and Muslims. Fifty years ago, Catholics were halfway through the Second Vatican Council or Vatican II. On 18 September 1964, a draft was brought to the floor of Vatican II for its "great debate." The next few months were critical for the survival of that draft, which eventually would make a huge difference in the lives of Catholics and, I truly believe, in the lives of fellow Christians, Jews and Muslims. Originally, this little text had the title "On the Jews," but that was changed to "On the Relation of Catholics to Non-Christians, above all, to the Jews" for its first presentation to the

---

[1] Analects 2, 11.

council fathers in November 1963 as a chapter within a larger draft on ecumenism. Pope John XXIII wanted this council to be ecumenical from the start, that is, to take into consideration the promotion of relations among Christians for the restoration of unity. That was revolutionary in itself for Catholic identity, fifty years ago.

CONTEXTUALIZING THE DISCUSSION

The Lutheran World Federation (LWF) came into being in 1947. It is currently engaged in a project on "Lutheran hermeneutics," which its leadership hopes to bring to fruition in 2017. It seeks to strengthen the capacities of member churches to understand the Word of God that comes through Scripture as well as the Lutheran theological heritage and to renew both church and society. The LWF engages in ecumenical and interreligious work, and among its five major bilateral ecumenical dialogues is one with Catholics that will be fifty years old in 2017. The LWF also engages in a number of interfaith projects.

The Evangelical Lutheran Church in America (ELCA) is a member of the LWF. Not the only Lutheran church in the USA, the ELCA is one of the most successful churches in the ecumenical movement, a true bridge church. Created out of three Lutheran churches in 1988, the ELCA entered relationships of full communion with six churches from 1997 until 2009. According to the ELCA, "Full communion is when two denominations develop a relationship based on a common confessing of the Christian faith and a mutual recognition of Baptism and sharing of the Lord's Supper."[2] Lutherans in America have cosponsored an ecumenical dialogue with the United States Conference of Catholic Bishops since 1965 through several rounds that has produced several excellent resources. As the 1990s unfolded, the ELCA was successful in developing a number of bilateral initiatives with Jews and Muslims.

Seattle University is one of twenty-eight Jesuit colleges and universities in the USA. In the US today, Jesuit universities bring together people of many faiths, secular as well as diversely religious, both ecumenical and multi-religious in representation. The usual way we negotiate this diversity is to push the question of faith to the background and promote a consensus on justice. This has been our history in the US, namely, to cooperate in social justice and to downplay discussions of faith and morals. In the last half century, we have got better at doing the latter. In 1974,

---

[2] See **www.elca.org/en/Faith/Ecumenical-and-Inter-Religious-Relations/Full-Communion**.

at a General Congregation of all Jesuits, the Society of Jesus, committed itself deeply to social justice as essential to its identity. In 1995, at another General Congregation, Jesuits committed themselves to interreligious dialogue as essential to their identity. The first commitment has been more visibly successful. For us, Jews, Christians and Muslims, the dialogue of social justice is far easier than interreligious relations as such. However, a genuine dialogue about justice cannot occur by setting aside one's faith. We still need more dialogue about faith.

TAKING OWNERSHIP

If we leave any of this work of Christian unity or interfaith relations to the experts, then it never belongs to our communities and has little impact on how we speak of our identity as Christians, Jews or Muslims. This is the first challenge that I wish to put on the table. Reaching back into the past, I realize that I have been struggling with this for thirty-five years of public work in ecumenical and interreligious dialogue. Some complain, "When do we in the pews benefit from all this formal dialogue?" On the other hand, the leadership and many members of our communities too easily want to leave dialogue to the experts as something that is happening somewhere else and usually on the fringe of the life of their communities. The ELCA could not have effected its agreements on full communion without church-wide effort. We need to emphasize that dialogue is already happening all around us and to encourage discernment and reflection on these everyday efforts with regard to our faith.

We often forget about the dialogue of life or dialogue in community, where Christians, Jews, Muslims and others, through friendship and sharing what is really important in their lives, have the most extensive encounters. I agree that the social and political context for dialogue is critical. I also agree that among immigrant communities in the USA, ethnic bonds create friendship and interreligious exchanges that are less frequent, if not impossible, for various groups in their home countries.

Still, whatever the context, we need to encourage more reflection on how the dialogue of life profoundly affects us. Too often, members of our communities believe that dialogue is for those who take leadership in interfaith associations to promote justice and charity in their communities, or for those who engage in formal exchanges on particular topics, or for those professionals who explore the nature of religious experience. Yet, our friendships, our associations and the quest for spiritual enrichment in our increasingly diversely religious societies will have much to do with our identities as Jews, Muslims and Christians in the future.

Just before the new millennium, while I was working at the US Conference of Catholic Bishops, with my counterpart at the National Council of Churches of Christ and the director of the Institute for Ecumenical and Cultural Research at St John's University, Collegeville, Minnesota, we planned a two-part interfaith consultation on the theme, "Living Faithfully in the United States Today." This transpired over two five-day summer conferences, and the result was a profound reflection on the dialogue of life. Asking for no advance papers and giving everyone an initial question, we discovered how the dialogue of life unfolds, first through storytelling, then with some trust to frame important issues and key questions, then allows fear, prejudices and feelings of isolation to come out, and finally then to celebrate each other's joys and form mutually supporting communities in a pluralistic society. That was 1999 and 2000, and I still feel close to those participants.[3]

The 1963 draft on ecumenism that laid the groundwork for Catholics to enter into dialogue with Lutherans and others, was the first official Catholic text of this high status to use the term "dialogue." That first draft on ecumenism in 1963 was a timid one. Positive relations with other Christians, was something very new for most Catholic officials fifty years ago. The drafting commission, the Secretariat for Promoting Christian Unity, used the term "dialogue" only three times. The response was so positive from the twenty-five hundred bishops gathered at the council that the next draft used "dialogue" a dozen times. In addition, the new 1964 draft would use another important expression, "on equal footing," to describe Christians meeting one another.[4] Its earlier chapter four, "On the Relation of Catholics to Non-Christians, above all, to the Jews," did not use the new Latin term *dialogus*" but an older one *colloquia* for dialogue with Jews:

> Since the common heritage of the Church with the synagogue is so great, this Holy Synod intends in every way to foster and commend mutual understanding and esteem, which is the fruit of theological studies and fraternal conversations [*colloquia*].[5]

---

[3] The text is available, at **http://collegevilleinstitute.org/wp-content/uploads/2013/02/Living-Faithfully-in-the-United-States-Today.pdf**.

[4] For an explanation of the importance of "on equal footing," see George Tavard, "Sisters and Strangers," in Marsha L. Dutton and Patrick Terrell Gray (eds), *One Lord, One Faith, One Baptism: Studies in Christian Ecclesiality and Ecumenism in Honor of J. Robert Wright* (Grand Rapids: Eerdmans, 2006), 328; George H. Tavard, *Vatican II and the Ecumenical Way* (Milwaukee: Marquette University Press, 2006), 42.

[5] For all Vatican II texts, the Latin text is the official text and translations are interpretations. I am using English translations of drafts by Thomas F. Stransky, C.S.P., an American priest who was invited to be one of the founding staff mem-

The text was still only a preliminary one. The next public draft, the one up for its great debate in September 1964, was actually a freestanding declaration, separated from the eventual *Decree on Ecumenism,* entitled "On the Jews and on the Non-Christians," and mentioning Muslims for the first time:

> In obedience to the love for our brother and sister, we ought to pay great attention to the opinions and teachings which although they differ from our own in many ways, contain nevertheless many rays of that Truth which enlightens everyone in this world. This applies above all to Muslims who adore the one God, personal and judge, and they stand close to us in a religious sense and they draw near to us with many expressions of human culture set before us.

Note that neither conversations nor dialogue are mentioned specifically for relations with Muslims as would later be encouraged in the final draft. But, we can already observe how this draft, though it would pass through further transformations into a final, richer form, was a real beginning for Catholics in relations with Jews and Muslims. Other Christians have also commented most positively on the final document, which goes by its first two Latin words, *Nostra aetate.*

Actually, the 1964 records reveal that there were as many as eight drafts of this text on interreligious dialogue, depending on how you count them, the first and eighth differing significantly. It was the shortest of the sixteen documents of Vatican II and in many ways the most controversial. While the draft decree on ecumenical relations was received so well that its outcome was seldom in doubt, the draft of a separate declaration on interreligious relations faced significant challenges. In early September 1964, two weeks before the public debate, it was leaked to the press. A rather poor English translation appeared first in the *New York Herald Tribune* and the next day in *The New York Times,* and these two paragraphs from the section on relations with Jews caused considerable reaction:

> Furthermore, it is worthy of remembrance that the union of the Jewish people with the Church is a part of Christian hope. With unshaken faith and deep longing, the Church awaits, in accordance with the Apostle's teaching (cf Rom. 11:25), the entry of this people into the fullness of the people of God, which is that fullness Christ has founded.

---

bers of the Secretariat for Promoting Christian Unity in 1960. Still alive today, he experienced Vatican II and the changes in these drafts first hand. He and I have been working on a volume that traces the genesis and development of this draft on interreligious relations that was eventually named from the first two Latin words in the promulgated text, *Nostra aetate.*

> May all, then, take care that whether in catechetical instruction and preaching on the Word of God or in daily conversation, the Jewish people is not represented as a rejected race, and that nothing is said or done that could alienate souls from the Jews. They should also guard against attributing what was done during Christ's passion to the Jews of our own time.

The second paragraph makes it look like Jews are to be tolerated only because Christians live by the hope that one day they will be one with the church. Rabbi Abraham Heschel identified the Christian hope as nothing less than the annihilation of Jews and spiritual fratricide. "I am ready to go to Auschwitz any time, if faced with the alternative of conversation or death," he wrote.[6]

Although the final version of *Nostra aetate* would meet with the approval of Jewish leaders, the question of mission and dialogue still affects our communities and interreligious relations.

Vatican II occurred within a much larger context, in what is now called a century of ecumenism. In the mid-twentieth century, like the LWF, the World Council of Churches (WCC) came into being and incorporated two important aspects of cooperation among the churches: Life and Works, Christians working together to promote justice; and Faith and Order, Christians working together to end the scandal of their disunity. These initiatives as well as a series of missionary conferences that gave rise to the idea of a WCC reached back even into the last two decades of the nineteenth century. The WCC today has projects related to Christian self-understanding within an interreligious context. Discussion of dialogue and relations among the pluralism of Christians gave rise to discussion of dialogue and relations among the pluralism of followers of various religions.[7] Although the Catholic Church has not become a member of the WCC, a Joint Working Group (JWG) was formed soon after Vatican II in 1965, and continues to this day as a productive forum for dialogue.[8] By 1967, the JWG issued a working paper on "ecumenical dialogue" aimed at joint profession of faith.[9]

Young Christian adults today may know little of this general history, but they reap enormous benefits because of the good will and cooperation, including full communion in many instances, that exist among many of

---

[6] Edward Kaplan, *Spiritual Radical: Abraham Joshua Heschel in America, 1940-1972* (New Haven: Yale University Press, 2007), 260.

[7] This was the argument of my article, "The Origins and Early Development of Interreligious Relations during the Century of the Church (1910-2010), " in *U. S. Catholic Historian* 28, 2 (Spring 2000), 55-80.

[8] **www.oikoumene.org/en/what-we-do/jwg-with-roman-catholic-church**

[9] The Secretariat for Christian Unity, *Information Service* 1967/3, 33-36.

their churches and congregations. This, in turn. has impinged on Christian identity. The success of the ecumenical movement has created new challenges to Christian identity.

Vatican II helped Catholics recover something that had been lost in a long nineteenth century of reaction to the modern world. Catholic scholasticism, especially in its pre-nineteenth-century forms, shared something with Renaissance humanism, what John O'Malley calls a "reconciling dynamic." They both, he says, "looked upon 'the other' with curious, sometimes admiring eyes, and they sought to learn from an encounter with that other."[10]

THREE ENDURING FALSE STARTS

In my experience, there are three mistakes that we can make from the start when we take on questions of identity in a pluralistic context. First, we can emphasize the ideal rather than the lived. Ideals are good, giving us something to strive for, guiding our decision making and helping us to begin to understand someone else who belongs to another religious tradition than our own. None of our religious identities exists in the ideal realm but the lived realm. As Pope Francis responded initially to the question about his own identity, "I am first of all a sinner."[11] We too often compare ourselves ideally with the lived realities of someone else's religious tradition. The last form of this mistake has caused immeasurable harm, and still does today, in the relations among Jews, Christians and Muslims.

A second false start is being too autobiographical in our quest for identity. Nowadays, there is great emphasis on personal narrative, which is good in that it provides a basic way of initiating the dialogue of life. Every man and woman has something of their own to give us; every man and woman has their own story, and their own situation, and we should listen to it. The first problem comes when we forget that for us as believers—Muslims, Christians and Jews—there is someone else in conversation to us, speaking to us, calling us and challenging us, namely the divine person. God

---

[10] John W. O'Malley, S.J., "Dialogue and the Identity of Vatican II," in *Origins*, Catholic News Service Documentary Service, 42, 25 (November 22, 2012), 400. One can view O'Malley giving this address and other lectures and download some on the topic of Vatican II and identity, at **www.georgetown.edu/vatican-II-dialogue. html**. O'Malley has published the best single volume history of Vatican II that more than adequately explains the ecumenical and interreligious initiatives of Vatican II. John W. O'Malley, S.J., *What Happened at Vatican II* (Cambridge, MA: Harvard University Press, 2008).

[11] "The Exclusive with Pope Francis: A Big Heart Open To God," in *America* (30 September 2013), 18.

is the significant participant in each of our narratives. Prudence, which we Christians say is a gift of God's Holy Spirit, guides us in how much we should listen to others. Prudence should also guide us in how much we should listen to ourselves. Prudence should guide us to listen to others more than we speak ourselves.

Related to giving too much attention to ourselves is another mistake—privileging our own religious identity and tradition. Indeed we speak out of our faith perspectives. We need to be careful about imposing our narrative on others and the way in which we frame questions on others. Joint preparation and preliminary discussions help remedy this often committed mistake. There are those who have studied another religious tradition extensively such that they feel that they can perceive from within the tradition. It is a desirable goal for one engaged in the study of the history of religions. But, wisely, some know that this is very tricky and not a state of mind that they ever totally possess. We should always be open to learning, and in this exercise, it is important to emphasize learning the perspectives of others rather than getting our story out.

CHALLENGES

Earlier I gave the first challenge, namely, convincing our co-religionists, our fellow Jews, Muslims and Christians, to join us in this enterprise because challenges to our self-identity arise in a healthy multireligious context and that in such a context we construct our religious identity in dialogue with others. In the future, our religious identity will increasingly take our relationships with one another into account. Dialogue is not something for the experts. Dialogue is a feature of our identity.

A second challenge is to realize that models and modes for interreligious activity change just as forms of communal religious life do not stand still. We run a risk if we allow our identity to depend too much on comfortable structures. True, structures serve their purposes, sometimes accomplishing what they set out to do, but then preserving them too rigidly becomes full-time work and creativity is lost. Besides, new generations may require adjustments to structure. We have observed this about ecumenical structures. In the USA, the Federal Council of Churches gave way to the National Council of Churches, which may or may not give way to Christian Churches Together in the USA. A better example in the USA is the National Conference of Christians and Jews that ran from 1928 until just a couple of decades ago. It was the flagship of interfaith organizations in the modern world. It served its purpose, promoting good citizens and ending religious bigotry while allowing participants to walk the thin line between civic dialogue and public discussions of faith and morals before many of our communities were ready for such engagement. The changes of mid-century called for newer forms of engagement. Were the early participants accused of promoting "indifferentism" (one faith is as good as the next)? Yes, they were. Were they accused of compromising their faith? Yes, they were. We honor those pioneers who served not by preserving their old structures but by building on their achievements and meeting present needs. Too many of our co-religionists are so loyal to present institutional structures that they are prevented from experiencing God's grace. I am not suggesting that structures be thrown away completely but adjusted so as to be both faithful to what we believe and helpful to those who participate.

A third challenge is to address an increasing agnosticism in our societies. Hostile polemics from atheists and angry agnostics are not new, and in the past few decades we have known a new round of debates from scientists who are styled "New Atheists." Such individuals are not ready for dialogue but their arguments require of us careful attention to both a vision of science and the style of their arguments. Dialogue is not polemics, and the latter is what many non-believing challengers prefer. At the same time, there are those religiously sensitive intellectuals who say they do not believe in God but are open to conversation on matters of common concern. The Vatican's "Courtyard of the Gentiles" is a model for this kind of encounter though it privileges the church.[12] Recognizing that the Spirit of God works in the world as well as in the church, the time has arrived for both sides to enter the field on more equal terms. We need what some have called a "New Aereopagus" as a common space for the exchange of ideas and experience. The dynamics for this among Jews is certainly different, as recent discussion of Jewish identity has shown.[13] And, yet another dynamic exists among Muslims when addressing unbelief.

Thus far, these discussions with agnostics have shown how the arts provide a field in which Christians and nonbelievers have gifts to share with one another that may provide for fruitful encounter. For us believers, how we appreciate the arts for expressing our deepest insights about human nature and God's work in our lives also give us insight into another's spiritual cultures. Non-believers are not lacking deep insights and feelings. The same fourfold process for the dialogue of life works here too: narrative, framing, clearing away misunderstandings and prejudices, then mutual celebration and support. Where secular thinkers are sensitive to faith, there

---

[12] Georgetown University hosted a courtyard 19-21 April 2014, at **www.georgetown. edu/news/faith-culture-common-good-event-announcement.html**.

[13] Jon D. Levenson, "What Are They? Modernity and Jewish Understanding," in *Commonweal* (February 24, 2012).

is every reason to clear away as much misunderstanding as possible and for Christian thinkers to share with them their explorations of the same phenomena, even as they hear unbelievers unravel their doubts. Also, a dialogue between our ways of life would be attractive to today's spiritual seekers—those who identify as spiritual but not religiously affiliated. Finally, religious freedom is an area in need of attention. Religious freedom applies to both public and personal life. The liberal tradition, with which many agnostics identify, developed the idea of religious freedom in public life and equality of all persons before the law as well as all religious institutions. How much religious freedom exists within our own communities?[14]

A fourth challenge for us is what Pope Francis calls a twofold transcendence: toward God and toward our neighbor. Any type of personal discernment concerning our religious identity is more than an adventure. It is a journey, but it is not simply a journey. It is the path that God provides for us. The journey symbol is dominant in our traditions. Our traditions begin with the story of an act of faith expressed by a journey when God said to Abraham, "Go from your country." The journey out of ourselves allows us to meet God and to meet others. Closeness with God brings us closer to others. Put simply, this is love of God and love of neighbor. This is something that Muslims reiterated in their 2007 consensus statement, *A Common Word between Us and You*.[15] Closeness is a key word: be near. We need to explore this common understanding from our traditions in light of our special relationships with one another founded on faith of Abraham.

To borrow again from Pope Francis in a question and answer session that he gave in summer 2014 with the priests of the Diocese of Caserta, to dialogue two things are necessary: one's identity as a starting point and empathy toward others. If I am not sure of my identity and I go to dialogue, I may end up relativizing my faith. Such a dialogue is not authentically interreligious.[16] Let me add a caution: we have often erred by thinking that we needed too much certainty of our identity. We spend so much time talking about our identity that we never get around to dialogue. Empathy is important too because it keeps us from thinking that dialogue involves only ourselves speaking. That is monologue. Empathy also prevents us from condemning another's point of view without taking the time to try and understand.

---

[14] These suggestions are developed by Drew Christiansen, S.J., in a forthcoming essay review of representative works of "religious atheism," in *America: The National Catholic Weekly*

[15] **www.acommonword.com/** .

[16] See **http://en.radiovaticana.va/news/2014/07/28/pope_has_casual_qa_with_priests_of_caserta/1103586#** .

One of the signs both of uncertainty about one's religious identity and a lack of empathy is proselytizing. This still falls under love of neighbor as a form of human transcendence. The relationship between mission and dialogue is one of the neuralgic issues of dialogue. I believe that we have not found the words to express it adequately, and it will continue to haunt, if not taunt, us in years to come.

The journey is not only when God draws us to a place but also when God sends us out. As a result of Christians talking about this in the past fifty years, I think we have at least convinced most Christians who hold fast to the conception of mission as being sent that proselytism is wrong. The term has come to refer to using unfair means and pressuring techniques to draw them into the church, that is, any effort to influence people in ways that de-personalizes or deprives them of their inherent value as persons or the use of any coercive techniques or manipulative appeals that bypass a person's critical faculties or play on psychological weakness. There are numerous agreements among Christians to this effect. However, Christian language for understanding dialogue means that this problem of using words such as "mission," "evangelization" and "evangelism" with the word "dialogue" will not go away. It continues to create problems for relations with Jews and recalls difficult times in the past with Muslims and others.

In 1991, the Pontifical Council for Interreligious Dialogue, which has been responsible for promoting relations with Muslims, put out a statement, "Dialogue and Proclamation."[17] It incorporated the wisdom of an earlier reflection, issued by the same office in 1984, that drew on the experience of those engaged in interreligious dialogue worldwide since the end of Vatican II and the lessons learned. There was an objection to the earlier statement from the Congregation for the Evangelization of Peoples and the struggle between those who focused on mission and those who focused on dialogue continued. The same experience was being felt in the WCC, brought on by those who remained uncomfortable with interreligious dialogue. In early 1990, the dialogue sub-unit of the WCC undertook a four-year study culminating in a consultation that also included delegates from the Catholic Church and produced a study document, "The Baar (Switzerland) Statement: Perspectives on Plurality."[18] The Vatican was finishing its own study, "Dialogue and Proclamation," at the same time.

---

[17] The text is on the Vatican website, at **www.vatican.va/roman_curia/pontifi-cal_councils/interelg/documents/rc_pc_interelg_doc_19051991_dialogue-and-proclamatio_en.html**

[18] **www.oikoumene.org/en/resources/documents/wcc-programmes/interre-ligious-dialogue-and-cooperation/christian-identity-in-pluralistic-societies/baar-statement-theological-perspectives-on-plurality**.

Here is how the 1991 "Dialogue and Proclamation" defined dialogue drawing on the earlier 1984 statement of the Pontifical Council for Inter-religious Dialogue, "Reflections on Mission and Dialogue":

> In the context of religious plurality, dialogue means "all positive and constructive interreligious relations with individuals and communities of other faiths which are directed at mutual understanding and enrichment," in obedience to truth and respect for freedom.[19]

Here is the Baar Statement: "We see the plurality of religious traditions as both the result of the manifold ways in which God has related to peoples and nationals as well a manifestation of the richness and diversity of humankind."[20] Let me cite another passage from "Dialogue and Proclamation" that reveals what I think is the real tension at work in both texts:

> Interreligious dialogue does not merely aim at mutual understanding and friendly relations. It reaches a much deeper level, that of the spirit, where exchange and sharing consist in a mutual witness to one's beliefs and a common exploration of one's respective religious convictions. In dialogue, Christians and others are invited to deepen their religious commitment, to respond with increasing sincerity to God's personal call and gracious self-gift, as our faith tells us, always passes through the mediation of Jesus Christ and the work of his Spirit.[21]

These two texts, coming as they do about the same time, reveal on the one hand a reluctance of many Christians at the time to use the more common expression "religious pluralism" and opt instead to employ the somewhat awkward "religious plurality." This latter term is hardly used today. Twenty-five years ago, theologians and church leaders shied away from "religious pluralism" because they felt it gave too much support to a particular position that all religions are but expressions of a single form of religion and we need only find the common denominator to understand the nature of religion. Such a simplistic view might still be rampant among those who have never studied religion. Those who take the time to reflect on their interreligious encounters come to realize that differences matter. It is also probably true that there were those Protestants who were holding fast to Karl Barth's distinction between faith and religion. They were influencing the outcome of the Baar text. On the Catholic side, there were those Catholics holding fast to something imposed on the text of the *Declaration on Religious Liberty*

---

[19] Op. cit. (17).
[20] Op. cit. (note 18).
[21] Op. cit. (note 17).

(*Dignitatis humanae*) of Vatican II and against the will of those drafting it, that the one true religion subsists, can be found, in the Catholic Church.[22] Without these distinctions between Christianity and the rest of the religious world as existing in a different realm, some Catholics and Protestants alike felt that there would be no motivation for mission. But, terms such as religion, faith and mission leave much room for interpretation.

Nowadays, most use the term religious pluralism to mean "engaged religious diversity." First, it is not just that various religious groups live side by side and participate in the same political and social structures; rather, religious groups end up influencing one another. Religious communities change through this engagement. Secondly, many engaged in dialogue find closeness and companionship across religious borders, at times, an intimacy and friendship that is greater than they have with their co-religionists. In the academic study of religion, the field on comparative theology is growing. Empathy and dialogue, with a healthy sense of self-identity, are finally catching on more widely. We know that we have certain expressions in each of our traditions, terms scripturally based and with considerable history of use, like "mission," "evangelization," "chosen people," "righteous Gentile," "good Samaritan," "jihad," "people of the book" and so forth, which sound positive to speakers and less so to listeners. We need to continue to pay attention to these as we explore questions of self-identity and dialogue.

A fifth challenge for all of us, Muslims, Jews and Christians, is to face squarely how we each claim an Abrahamic character. We understand ourselves as a people who hear God and act.

In the prayer of the church, morning and evening prayer, hymns from the Gospel of Luke are recited each day, the Song of Zechariah (the Benedictus, Lk 1:68-79) in the morning and the Canticle of Mary (the Magnificat, Luke 1:46-55) in the evening. Both mention Abraham: "Our father Abraham" and "the promise he made to our fathers, to Abraham and his descendants." And the liturgy each day refers to "the sacrifice of Abraham, our father in faith." Jews mention Abraham in the central series of prayers of every worship service, the *Amida*/standing prayer. Muslims mention Abraham and his family at the end of the five daily prayers.[23]

---

[22] The text actually says: "We believe that this one true religion subsists in the Catholic and Apostolic Church, to which the Lord Jesus committed the duty of spreading it abroad among all men."

[23] The references to Jews and Muslims are taken from the responses of Rabbi Daniel Polish and Professor Amir Hussain to the address of Patrick J. Ryan, "The Faith of Abraham: Bond or Barrier? Jewish, Christian and Muslim Perspectives, 13 and 14 April 2011. A digital version is available, at **http://digital.library.fordham.edu/ cdm/singleitem/collection/mcginley/id/4**

There are those, for example, no less a scholar as Jon Levenson, who hold that Abraham is so different for each of us, for Jews, for Christians and for Muslims that he disclaims using Abrahamic as an umbrella term.[24] Jesuit scholar Patrick Ryan suggests otherwise: "We Muslims and Christians and Jews may live together more fruitfully and more peacefully if we recognize the polyvalence of Abraham, the polyvalence of great concepts like faith and revelation, community and the path of righteousness."[25] In addition, perhaps we might see our Scriptures as commentaries on a story that has had much appeal to those who have sought God beyond the visual images that we fashion and to those who have waited in silence for the Word of God.

A sixth challenge is how fragile progress can be among Christians, Jews and Muslims. A whole range of issues from international politics, to social challenges, to religious matters impact relations among our three groups. When one of our religious leaders misspeaks, we know so immediately. Developments in the Middle East seem to undo years of careful progress. It is the special feature of these relations that makes them fragile and easily bruised. None of us should consider the other two foreign or exotic religions. The remedy is a mixture of time and therapy. We need to come to know one another as we are now and as we have lived these past many centuries together as well as to study more carefully or relations based on scriptural language. We have defined ourselves over and against one another for so long it seems unavoidable for us to understand our present identity without making reference to one another. If Christians form stronger ecumenical bonds so that the world may believe, Jews and Muslims pay attention and wonder about missionary efforts directed at them. We are also condemned to live the consequences of our collective history; yet, we should work at developing a stronger desire to define ourselves in relationship one another than by what separates us in the politics and developments in the Middle East.

A seventh challenge is how much the texture of the theological dialogue has changed with the inclusion of a growing number of Jewish scholars

---

[24] Jon Levenson, "The Idea of Abrahamic Religions: A Qualified Dissent," in *Jewish Review of Books* (Spring 2010), see **http://jewishreviewofbooks.com/articles/244/ the-idea-of-abrahamic-religions-a-qualified-dissent/**; Jon D. Levenson, *Inheriting Abraham: The Legacy of the Patriarch in Judaism, Christianity, and Islam* (Princeton: Princeton University Press, 2012).

[25] Patrick J. Ryan S.J., "The Faith of Abraham: Bond or Barrier?," in *Origins: CNS Documentary Service* 41, 5 (9 June 2011), 73, note 20, also at **http://www.google. ch/url?sa=t&rct=j&q=&esrc=s&source=web&cd=2&ved=0ahUKEwj4xduM5 ajJAhUBKywKHVZ7Dh4QFggiMAE&url=http%3A%2F%2Fwww.fordham.ed u%2Fdownload%2Fdownloads%2Fid%2F3475%2Fspring_2011_lecture.pdf& usg=AFQjCNHLoQuS4dbpTkzbgBHGSeR6tcbY_A&bvm=bv.108194040,d.bGg**

of the New Testament and Patristic period. The *Jewish Study Bible* and the *Jewish Annotated New Testament* belong among the resources that every Christian seriously involved in pastoral work and in Christian-Jewish relations should have.[26] I look forward to the day when we have as many Muslim scholars of the New Testament and early centuries of Christianity. All three of our traditions need to encourage good, solid scholarship of the other two traditions. Jews and Christians share a Scripture and a common set of experiences during the early Roman Empire. The fact that the apostolic church was a movement among Jews should not create a distance between Jews and Christians on the one hand and Muslims on the other. The experience of the one God who had spoken through the prophets was what Muhammad was seeking when he retired from the polytheism of Makkah to the quietness of the cave. He articulated his experience in the language that he had understood, taken from a shared oral tradition. We have much to explore together.

I am struck by how often Pope Francis used the word "path" in his 2013 Apostolic Exhortation, *Evangelii Gaudium*. It appears twenty-two times, and "new paths" at least three times. Clearly he is encouraging Christians and others to look on their lives as spiritual journeys and to see how we are all companions on the journey. This is an eighth challenge for us. There are increasing numbers of people identifying less and less with religious institutions and defining themselves as spiritual seekers. This is coupled with a renewed interest in spiritual practices within Christianity. For example, many religious orders have come to understand that their future depends on teaching lay people how to live their charism. This is certainly true of the Jesuits. The Spiritual Exercises of St Ignatius, once something that incorporated young men into the Jesuits, are readily available to laypersons. Ignatian forms of prayer are promoted through retreats and other means. So, it is no wonder that Pope Francis, a Jesuit, used "path" so many times to convey how he would like Christians to live the joy of the gospel. Dialogue is less about a faith in institutions than about how we live and understand our faith in relation to one another as we each traverse our paths. Dialogue is less about common ground than about how we traverse the way that God has given us.

Fewer young people identify with religious communities, and there is an increasing number of "nones" or non-affiliated. Whether these are trends or not remains to be seen. Yoga and other borrowed forms of spiritual practice

---

[26] Amy-Jill Levine and Marc Zvi Brettle (eds), *The Jewish Annotated New Testament, New Revised Standard Version* (New York: Oxford University Press, 2011), and Adele Berlin and Marc Zvi Brettler (eds), *The Jewish Study Bible* (New York: Oxford University Press, 1985; 1999).

are more popular than ever. A debate rages in some circles on whether or not one needs to know something about Hinduism to practice yoga as a spiritual way of life. This means to me that spiritual hunger remains stronger than ever. We can certainly understand ourselves by what we believe, but more significant is what we do as people of faith. Our faith should give us joy, and joy should define our companionship with one another and with all.

One final and ninth challenge that I wish to mention comes from another phenomenon on the rise—double-belonging or even multiple religious belonging. Related to this is an increase in marriages among our communities, a continuing sensitive issue among our communities. There is more than one phenomenon here. For example, particular Christian identities are challenged by ecumenical success. If churches reach full communion, will their distinct characters be lost in this new and desired relationship? Even as churches lay aside the obstacles to full communion are they laying aside their identities? An achievement like the *Joint Declaration on the Doctrine of Justification* requires Catholics and Lutherans no longer to define themselves over and against one another regarding this key doctrine on which, according to Martin Luther, all stands or falls. Lutherans and Catholics, and indeed all Protestants who celebrate the Reformation of 500 years ago, face a special positive challenge to look at the 500th anniversary of Martin Luther's Wittenberg Reformation of 1517 in a way that commemorates what Catholics and Protestants now share in positive ways from this five-hundred-year history.[27] More to the point of everyday life, couples from two church traditions forge a way of life that reflects their beliefs and their desire to nurture their love as a couple. Many choose to practice in two churches.

Jewish–Christian couples face more difficult but not insurmountable challenges. Some find ways to balance their religious backgrounds in a harmonious family life. The children from these homes may feel a double-belonging. We have yet to see the long-term effects of this. Even when one Christian joins another Christian community, they do not abandon the past completely. The variety of phenomena surrounding double-belonging will influence Jewish, Christian and Muslim identity in the future.

CONCLUSION

I began this reflection by reference to the past, fifty years ago and the events at Vatican II that had an enormous impact on Catholic identity.

---

[27] See the suggestions made by the Lutheran-Roman Catholic Commission on Unity, *From Conflict to Communion* (2013), at **www.lutheranworld.org/sites/default/ files/From%20Conflict%20to%20Communion.pdf**.

Similar developments were occurring among other churches as well. As a result of those changes, dialogue became a defining factor of Christian identity. Those developments also explain why we are here today asking the questions that we are.

In 2012, when we celebrated the fiftieth anniversary of the opening of Vatican II on 11 October 1962 at Georgetown University, we invited Archbishop Michael L. Fitzgerald, M.Afr., to participate. He was at the opening of the council as a young priest and later, in 1987, just after the first World Day of Prayer in Assisi in October 1986, began serving as secretary for the office soon to be named the Pontifical Council for Interreligious Dialogue. He delivered the homily at the liturgy we celebrated at the beginning of the conference. In his homily, the archbishop turned to Pope John's example and his opening address at Vatican II, *Gaudet Mater Ecclesia*:

> The task before the Church is an arduous one, no easier today than it was fifty years ago. Yet it was one which John XXIII faced with equanimity. He wished to distance himself from "the prophets of doom", discerning the work of Divine Providence in the events of the time. He proposed that the Spouse of Christ, the Church, should have recourse to the "medicine of mercy" rather than "the weapon of severity". He had a childlike trust in God, a trust that had allowed him to announce the Council with the assurance that the Holy Spirit would guide it to results beneficial for the whole Church.[28]

Perhaps, the archbishop was just setting the stage for Pope Francis who would emphasize mercy over severity in witnessing the joy of the gospel. Here is how Pope John put it this way fifty years ago:

> But for this teaching [the deposit of the faith] to reach the many fields of human activity which affect individuals, families, and social life, it is first of all necessary that the Church never turn her eyes from the sacred heritage of truth which she has received from those who went before; and at the same time she must also look at the present times which have introduced new conditions and new forms of life, and have opened new avenues for the Catholic apostolate.[29]

---

[28] Archbishop Fitzgerald's homily and the presentations at the October 2012 Georgetown University conference on Vatican II can be found, at **www.georgetown.edu/vatican-II-dialogue.html**.

[29] Archbishop Fitzgerald gave his own translation of the pope's opening exhortation, *Gaudet Mater Ecclesia*, which can be found in its Latin form, at **www.vatican.va/holy_father/john_xxiii/speeches/1962/documents/hf_j-xxiii_spe_19621011_opening-council_lt.html**. Archbishop Fitzgerald's homily was published as "Dialogue for Life," in *The Tablet* (8 December 2012), 13–15. Another English version of

We faced new challenges fifty years ago and, as a result, we accomplished a great deal. Now, we face new challenges as we face into a new century. I identified nine such challenges:

- Convincing our fellow Jews, Christians and Muslims to join us in dialogue and in promoting it as a way of being Jewish, Christian and Muslims, not leaving this to experts

- Emphasizing living our faith and not our structures for our identity

- Addressing the new agnosticism around us

- Applying Pope Francis' two-fold transcendence to which we are all called: love of God and love of neighbor

- Discerning our Abraham character in relationship with one another

- Overcoming the fragility of our relationships due to political and social developments and the prejudice that remains from our shared histories

- Encouraging scholarship of one another's Scriptures and traditions, learning the languages and other tools of understanding so as to change the texture of our dialogue for the better

- Emphasizing our spiritual companionship over our institutional identities

- Addressing the growing phenomenon of double-belonging in our midst.

Perhaps there is yet a tenth challenge which will serve as my concluding point. The generation of pioneers is mostly gone who were there at Vatican II and at the critical mid-century assemblies and meetings that affected the WCC and the LWF. The generation whom those pioneers instructed is nearing retirement. The "new generation" has indeed had a different set of ecumenical and interreligious experiences. A change of generation can be significant for the churches. I have already observed how allegiance to a particular church is a casualty of the success of the ecumenical movement. Many younger Christians more easily change churches or perhaps even are reluctant to identify with a single church. They feel comfortable in more than one church. Relationships, especially marriage, worship

---

this passage can be found in Xavier Rynne, *Letters from Vatican City* (New York: Farrar, Strauss & Co., 1963), 267.

experiences and social engagement in the mission of the church, become more important factors for church affiliation than doctrine. These developments expand to interreligious experiences.

As he was nearing retirement as President of the Pontifical Council for the Promotion of Christian Unity (PCPCU), Cardinal Walter Kasper undertook a project that concluded in a volume, *Harvesting the Fruits: Basic Aspects of Christian Faith in Ecumenical Dialogue*.[30] In it he refers to a new generation moving up: "A new generation of ecumenically minded and motivated Christians, especially among the laity, is taking up the torch of the ecumenical movement, but with a different emphasis with respect to its predecessors."[31] When he presented the book he spoke in more detail why this project for the new generation:

> Second, after 40 years a new generation stands ready to take up the torch to continue the ecumenical journey. It is normal, indeed it is necessary, that this generation have new and fresh ideas, but it should not start again from zero; rather, it can count upon a solid foundation. The harvesting text seeks to inspire the new generation and to show it that dialogue is worthwhile and that something can be achieved with unceasing effort, with patience and courage.[32]

This applies not only to ecumenical relations about which Cardinal Kasper was speaking, but to our interfaith relations as well. We need to find ways to engage our congregations, parishes, synagogues and mosques more in ecumenical and interreligious work. Local relations in our towns and neighborhood more and more have a global dimension. Our young people are more pluralistic, more comfortable with the benefits of a secular society and more global than ever before. We need to pay considerable attention to our spiritual companionship as Christians, Muslims and Jews because this will increasingly play a greater role in how our heirs will self-identify in the future. In other words, there are libraries of information and achievements to be studied, and we need to promote that kind of indispensable work. But, while we mine the riches of the past and interpret them for the present, we need to pay attention to the paths to the future.

One of the great minds of Vatican II was the Dominican theologian, Fr Yves Congar. Almost immediately after the close of the Vatican II, he reflected on the major consequence of missing the point of Vatican II and looking at the words, the texts, of the council and losing sight of its tra-

---

[30] Cardinal Walter Kasper, *Harvesting the Fruits* (New York: Continuum, 2009).
[31] Ibid., 2.
[32] "Harvesting the Fruits' and the Future of Ecumenism," in *Origins* 39, 37 (25 February 2010), 599.

jectories. This is how he put it on 13 December 1965, just five days after the council ended:

> The danger is that one will not seek any more, but will simply exploit the inexhaustible warehouse of Vatican II. Then a post-Vatican era would open up in the way a post-Tridentine era existed. It would be a betrayal of the aggiornamento (the updating of the church to modern times) if we thought it could be fixed once for all in the texts of Vatican II.[33]

---

[33] Jean-Pierre Jossua, O.P., *Yves Congar: Theology in the Service of God's People* (Chicago: The Priory Press, 1968), 182.

THE ROLE OF THE RELIGIOUS VOICE IN THE TWENTY-FIRST CENTURY— A JEWISH PERSPECTIVE

Shira Lander

HOW WE GOT TO THIS POINT—NO FUTURE WITHOUT CONFRONTING THE PAST

For the better part of our religious histories, monotheistic religions have made universalistic claims. And they have made these sweeping declarations using particularistic language. I will speak on behalf of my own faith, Judaism. For our part, Jews have made claims like: "*all* the land that you see I will give to you and to your offspring forever" (Gen 13:15); "Abraham shall become a great and mighty nation, and *all* the nations of the earth shall be blessed in him" (Gen 18.18); "For you [that is "we"] are a people holy to the Lord your God; it is you the Lord has chosen out of *all* the peoples on earth to be his people, his treasured possession" (Deut 14:2); and "There is no other god besides me, a righteous God and a Savior; there is *no one* besides me" (Isa 45:21). These are only a brief selection of such biblical affirmations.

The previous, that is twentieth, century, brought large-scale conflicts that religious institutions not only failed to prevent, but were complicit in fomenting, either through tacit support or through indifference. Theologians soon realized that if they were to speak with credibility on these divisive issues of the day, they would also have to put their own house in order. Religion had found itself on the ethically indefensible side of too many battles not to undertake a serious process of self-examination (*heshbon hanefesh*), *teshuvah*, *tawba* and *metanoia*. Particularly the failure of religious institutions in the Holocaust raised profound questions about the role of religion in responding to racial, ethnic and political violence. Initially, many religious leaders responded with action. This approach was well-articulated by the Lutheran theologian Dietrich Bonhoeffer in reflections written while he was incarcerated by the Nazis at Tegel military prison: "Let us honor these priceless possessions [of freedom and brotherhood] for a while by silence, let us learn to do the right things for a while without speaking about them."[1] This call to action over words was an appropriate reaction to the horrors of Nazi Germany. Heroes, like Magda and Reformed Church pastor André Trocmé of Le Chambon, France, took action that saved countless lives. Yet, over time, under the moral weight of this catastrophic devastation, North American and European religious leaders and many of the faithful realized they could no longer forge ahead, business as usual. Universal, triumphalist claims—wherever their authority was rooted—had wreaked havoc and would demand reconsideration.

This reconsideration of dangerous strains within religious traditions produced institutional responses as well as individual theological reflections. Many religious councils were formed to examine the legacy of prejudice and hatred that could be found in their respective traditions. Institutional responses often came in the form of denominational statements, such as the famous Roman Catholic Ecumenical Council declaration *Nostra aetate* of 1965. Additionally, numerous theologians undertook the enormous and vital task of confronting this legacy and reforming their traditions so that they, in the words of the German Roman Catholic theologian Hans Hermann Hendrix, "will always be aware that theology at all times runs the danger of initiating, by way of polemics, a chain reaction of religious disqualification, which via social ostracism will lead toward physical threats of the worst kind."[2] Several leading Christian theologians of other denominations have heeded the instruction of Roman Catholic Johann Baptist Metz "not to indulge any longer in theological thought which is directed towards possibly forgetting about, or in fact remaining untouched by, the occurrence of Auschwitz,"[3] like Lutheran Norman Beck, Methodists Alice and Roy Eckardt, American Baptist

---

[1] Dietrich Bonhoeffer, *Gesammelte Schriften*, vol. 3: "Theologie-Gemeinde: Vorlesungen, Briefe, Gesprache, 1927-1944" (München: Chr. Kaiser Verlag, 1958), 479-80, ed. Eberhard Bethge, as translated and quoted, in Eberhard Bethge, "Turning Points in Bonhoeffer's Life and Thought," in *Union Seminary Quarterly Review* 23.1 (Fall 1967), 3-21, here 18.

[2] Hans Hermann Hendrix, "In the Shadow of the Shoah," in Michael A. Signer (ed.), *Humanity at the Limit: The Impact of the Holocaust Experience on Jews and Christians* (Indiana University Press, 2000), 66-78, here 69.

[3] Johann Baptist Metz, "Ökumene nach Auschwitz," in Eugen Kogon and Johann Baptist Metz, *Gott nach Auschwitz* (Freiburg: Herder, 1979), 121-44, here 138, quoted in Hendrix, ibid., 69.

Walter Harrelson, and Disciples of Christ Clark Williamson. As the Canadian Roman Catholic theologian Gregory Baum has written, Auschwitz "summons us to face up to the negative side of our religious and cultural heritage."[4]

For the better part of the last century, the majority of my Jewish colleagues and I wasted little energy and ink distancing ourselves or disavowing horrific statements and acts made in the name of Judaism by ultra-Orthodox or extremist or radical Jewish groups. Viewing them as marginal, or fringe, elements with hardly any following, we chose to look the other way in the hope that they would just disappear. They did not consider us Jews, and we essentially returned the favor by not dignifying them with a response. After Baruch Goldstein opened fire on the mosque in the tomb of the patriarchs in 1994 and Yigal Amir assassinated Prime Minister Yitzchak Rabin in 1995, many of us realized that we could no longer remain silent. As long as Jews, of whatever stripe, were acting in the name of the people called Israel, we, I, had a responsibility to speak out against them. Most recently the Price Tag gangs in Israel reflect the actions of extremist Jews. The Torah that I had learned condemned these acts of violence, and I was compelled to denounce them.

As was the case with Christianity, Jewish attempts to confront dangerous strains within our tradition have also come from both institutional and individual sources. One example of institutional effort with which both David Sandmel and I were closely involved is *Dabru Emet*. This historic document, issued in 2000, affirms the "inalienable sanctity and dignity of every human being" regardless of religious faith, and singles out "improving the lives of our fellow human beings and for standing against the immoralities and idolatries that harm and degrade us"[5] as the primary task of religion for the twenty-first century. Other individual attempts have been made by Jewish scholars Michael Kogan, David Novak, Tvi Marx, Michael Signer and Israel Yuval, to name just a few.

This call for reform of religious approaches to the "Other" has coincided with another trajectory in world history: the advent of religious diversity, which accompanied the inexorable growth of globalization, telecommunication and physical mobility. The religious faithful found themselves living alongside of and/or increasingly aware of people whose religious traditions were different from their own. This demographic phenomenon precipitated divergent responses within religious traditions: on one end of the spectrum, some religious communities welcomed this religious diversity. Through the

---

[4] Gregory Baum, "Introduction," in Rosemary Radford Ruether (ed.), *Faith and Fratricide: The Theological Roots of Anti-Semitism* (Eugene: Wipf and Stock, 1997), 7.
[5] **www.jcrelations.net/Dabru_Emet_-_A_Jewish_Statement_on_Christians_and_Christianity.2395.0.html**

interfaith dialogue movement, they explored one another's commonalities and differences, advocating tolerance and mutual respect as the appropriate theological response to this intimate encounter with the religiously Other. This response has come to be known as "religious pluralism."[6] Religious pluralism, not to be confused with religious diversity, "is the engagement that creates a common society" out of the sea of diversity. Pluralism requires that people of diverse religious backgrounds get to know and respect one another, that they honor their differences yet seek to find common religious ground on which to build a civil society. These religious groups joined together in dialogue, interfaith worship, community service partnerships and political coalitions. On the other end there were those who reacted to the phenomenon of religious diversity by circling the wagons, clinging to their traditional exclusivism even more tenaciously, and rejecting any reconciliation or even dialogue with religious outsiders. How religious communities situated themselves vis-à-vis the religiously diverse world in which they found and will continue to find themselves was the defining question of the previous century.

CHALLENGES FOR THE TWENTY-FIRST CENTURY—THE LIMITS OF TOLERANCE

Humanity now stands well beyond the dawn of this next century, with these two camps well-defined and firmly entrenched, and the question facing us now as we move forward is, How will we, the pluralists—those who advocate the values of tolerance and mutual respect—relate to those with whom we share religious texts and traditions yet who seek to destroy us, who repeatedly resort to violence to promote or impose their universal, exclusivist triumphalism? Does my encounter with those for whom intolerance is corollary to their religious beliefs stretch the limits of my tolerance and mutual respect? Central to that existential question are the questions about how we will negotiate that relationship, what means will we use to communicate with the most extreme Other: How do we deal with the asymmetry that exists between these two camps? Will the only remaining voices passionately devoted to religion and religious ideals as we move deeper into the twenty-first century be those that want to turn the clock back on social issues and use violent means to terrorize and silence their opposition? Before we can begin to address these questions, it behooves us to try to understand what motivates those who preach hatred and pursue violence.

---

[6] Diana L. Eck, *The Manyness of God* (St. Lawrence University, 1987). See more recently Eck's "From Diversity to Pluralism," in *On Common Ground: World Religions in America* (2013), at **www.pluralism.org/encounter/challenges**.

Saira Yamin, professor of Conflict Analysis and Resolution at the Asia Pacific Center for Security Studies in Hawaii, has written extensively about religious violence. When religious identity is a primary component of group identity and firmly rooted in society, that identity relies on religious rituals, rites and storytelling for its creation, reinforcement and perpetuation.[7] When the group perceives itself threatened, either physically, economically or spiritually, it will marshal those mechanisms of rituals, rites and storytelling to "defend itself" and strengthen group ties. A common feature of this defense is to define one's group in contrast to others, demonizing and dehumanizing those who are portrayed as unlike or even hostile to the group.[8] Yamin calls this phenomenon of shoring up religious group identity in opposition to non-members "religious pseudo-speciation." After delineating the typology of religious violence in its various manifestations around the globe over the last quarter century, she proposes the following complex network of factors to explain the phenomenon:[9]

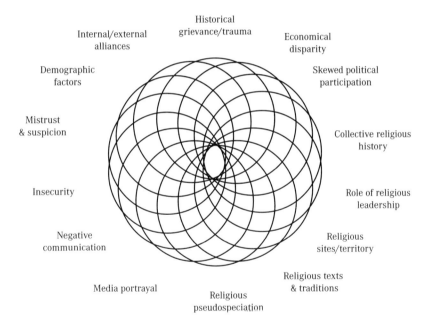

Historical grievance/trauma

Internal/external alliances

Economical disparity

Demographic factors

Skewed political participation

Mistrust & suspicion

Collective religious history

Insecurity

Role of religious leadership

Negative communication

Religious sites/territory

Religious texts & traditions

Media portrayal

Religious pseudospeciation

---

[7] Saira Yamin, "Understanding Religious Identity and the Causes of Religious Violence," in *Peace Prints: South Asian Journal of Peacebuilding,* vol. 1, no. 1 (Spring 2008), 13.

[8] Ibid., 12.

[9] Ibid., 3.

As we can see, the phenomenon of collective religious hostility and violence is exceedingly complex and multi-sourced. Fortunately, Yamin groups these into five components and organizes them into a hierarchy of causes: [10]

Alliances: resources of support and funding: providing fuel and vigor

Demographic factors: relative strength of groups, ability to consolidate and mobilize

Socio-economic and political factors: rank disequilibrium, political participation, econonomic factors

Psychological factors: communication, media, perception, collective history, historical grievance, pseudospeciation, insecurity, mistrust and suspicion

Religio-psychological contextualization of dispute: role of religious leadership, cultural religiosity, dispute over religious sites and territory; manipulation or selective use of religious text

I will attempt to address how religious leaders and thinkers might intervene at each level of this typology to disrupt or divert religious groups' formation of hostility and instigation of violence.

I. ALLIANCES: SOURCES OF SUPPORT AND FUNDING: PROVIDING FUEL AND VIGOR

It is unlikely that religious leaders positioned outside these groups will be accepted into the inner circle of allies as dialogue partners. Religious leaders can, however, attempt to forge alliances with these groups' allies farther out in the circle. Sitting down with people of unlike minds may break ties that support and fuel religious hostility and violence. Allying with those moderate religious leaders who are working within these circles

---

[10] Ibid., 4, adapted.

can provide an alternative to violence by offering support, whether with financial or human resources. Too often peace missions become embroiled in political conflicts in ways that are not helpful. I urge caution in this area and warn against taking sides in religio-political conflicts. Religious leaders can easily become pawns in conflicts that are barely understood because of their visibility and influence. It is too facile to side with the perceived victims and condemn the oppressors; doing so succumbs to the oppositional paradigm that locks parties into cycles of hostility and violence, inadvertently fueling the violence and encouraging the us/them mentality that sustains the conflict. The task of religious leaders in the twenty-first century is to disrupt the kinds of oppositional thinking and alignments that undergird religious conflict. This can be done by sponsoring dialogues between parties to the conflict, as was the case in Northern Ireland, and by partnering with political strategists who also reject this oppositional paradigm in favor of a dialogical, relational model.

II. Demographic factors: relative strength of groups, ability to consolidate and mobilize

The best efforts to preempt the demographic factors of religious violence are programs that reach out to disaffected and unemployed youth and make early interventions. Many of these programs are supported by religious institutions and staffed by people with deep religious commitments. Religious leaders can urge their communities to partner with the growing number of peace-building organizations and programs throughout the world. Programs such as MEET (Middle East Education Through Technology), in collaboration with MIT, which bring Israeli and Palestinian youth together to acquire advanced technological and leadership tools while empowering them to create positive social change within their own communities, can help break the cycle of distrust and disaffection that violent religious leaders prey on to implement their destructive approach to religio-political agendas.

III. Socio-economic and political factors: rank disequilibrium, political participation and economic factors

The third factor is more commonly the domain of religious leaders. Those who serve congregations address issues of socio-economic inequality and political participation from the pulpit. Religious leaders and institutions often provide the safety net that government agencies either cannot or will not. This is religion's age-old response to socio-economic inequality. Yet, religious leaders have seriously to consider the ways that structural inequalities embedded in global commerce fail to ameliorate persistent suffering in too many regions of the world. Although religious institutions often play a key role in getting out the vote, ensuring equitable voter access and political lobbying in democratic countries, these institutions have not done enough to articulate how the political process can best express their religious anthropology in non-democratic countries. Those of us living in democratic countries too often assume that democracy is the fulfillment of our religious principles, yet we surely recognize that all forms of government are imperfect and particularly in this historical moment that democracy may not be right for everyone. If we have learned nothing else from the fallout of our intervention in Iraq, it is that nation-building does not translate from one socio-historical context to another.

IV. & V. PSYCHOLOGICAL FACTORS: COMMUNICATION, MEDIA, PERCEPTIONS, COLLECTIVE HISTORY, HISTORICAL GRIEVANCE, PSEUDOSPECIATION, INSECURITY, MISTRUST AND SUSPICION; RELIGIO-PSYCHOLOGICAL CONTEXTUALIZATION OF DISPUTE: ROLE OF RELIGIOUS LEADERSHIP, CULTURAL RELIGIOSITY, DISPUTE OVER RELIGIOUS SITES AND TERRITORY; MANIPULATION OR SELECTIVE USE OF RELIGIOUS TEXTS

Religious leaders can also influence the fourth and fifth factors. Just as religious leaders work closely with local law enforcement agencies in cities and towns around the USA and Europe to track extremist group activities, they should work similarly with international law enforcement agencies to help them interpret religious groups' communication, media and perceptions that are being monitored to look for early warning signs of pseudospeciation, insecurity, mistrust and suspicion. Religious leaders can become familiar with the collective history and historical grievances narrated by the extremist wings of their co-religionists and not only relate an alternative narrative but acknowledge the truths within the Other's collective history and trauma. For me this has been most difficult in my conversations with Palestinians. So much of our own identities are defined by oppositional relationship to the Other that leaders in both of our communities equate acknowledgement and validation of the Other's narrative with betrayal and sedition. Breaking this internal dynamic of fear and intimidation can only happen with dialogue that takes place outside the political sphere. Too many religious leaders have been seduced by the power of politics and have forgotten their role as teachers and pastors. Religious leaders are in a unique position to mediate between the halls of government and the sanctuaries of their congregations. Teaching those who desire to practice their own religion freely—especially religious traditionalists—that this freedom comes at the cost of protecting the religious freedom of others is a primary responsibility of religion in the twenty-first century.

Navigating conflicting religious voices

Unlike many of my colleagues in the southwest, a deeply religious part of the USA, I do not lie awake at nights worrying about atheists (or anti-theists) and their wholesale attack on religion. The rejection of god is less worrisome to me than the rejection of the moral values and ethical ideals that I believe lie at the core of all religions. This raises yet another pressing question for our century: How do we arbitrate among competing claims to religious authority? What criteria do we use to judge whether one interpretation of religion is more or less valid than another? Or, Who determines when the religious voice is truthful or diabolical? Do religions share a responsibility to identify when ideology is also morally reprehensible? It seems to me shortsighted and unproductive to sit in judgment of this or that religious voice which we find morally objectionable. As I have articulated above, such an approach merely perpetuates the oppositional structures that undergird the conflicts that produce such voices to begin with. Any approach to this conundrum must seek first to understand these voices and second must find a way to break the structures that sustain them.

Although there are resources in Jewish tradition for confronting these challenges, the predominant approach has failed to offer such a solution. In Jewish tradition, a false prophet is determined in hindsight, by the efficacy of his prophecy: "he who speaks in the name of the Lord and the word does not come true (Deut 18:22)." Yet prophecy has been considered dead by the majority of Jews since the dawn of the Second Temple period, close to two and a half millennia ago. The source of authority in the post-prophetic era shifts to biblical interpretation. So the question that confronts Jews in this era is whose interpretation is true, and whose is false? How do we adjudicate among these varying interpretations? Rabbinic discourse, as reflected in the Talmud and contemporary literature, is inherently pluralistic, sometimes agonistic, but always multi-vocal. A famous Talmudic debate between Rabbi Eliezer and Rabbi Joshua over a minute point of Jewish law is finally left unresolved with the declaration: "These and these are the words of the living God."[11] How does this message of dialectic apply to the current conflict between the diametrically opposed approaches to religion and the violence that too often results from such opposition?

Robert Erlewine explores these questions in his book, *Monotheism and Tolerance. Recovering a Religion of Reason.* The kind of symmetrical relations articulated in the notion of pluralism, as advocated by Diana Eck, John Hick and Jürgen Habermas, has run its course and proven to be only applicable in certain contexts. Erlewine argues that monotheistic religions

---

[11] b. Rosh Hashana 27a.

cannot fully embrace this even-handed arrangement because they make core claims that are inherently asymmetrical and agonistic, or adversarial, toward the Other.[12] He identifies a kind of triumphalism in these pluralistic philosophies of Eck, Hick and Habermas that privileges the universal over the particular. In these systems, particular faiths must give way to commonly held principles; their traditional principles must conform to a universal and common understanding of humanity. Because these approaches do not take into consideration the inner conflicts between the particular and the universal that can be found within religious traditions, Erlewine argues, they have failed to chart a course to bridge the chasm between so-called fundamentalist and liberal strains of religions.

A close examination of Jewish tradition reveals a dialectic between the particular and the universal that cannot be dissolved into universalistic pluralism if the essential character of monotheism is to be maintained/preserved. Following the thought of the German-Jewish philosopher Hermann Cohen, Erlewine appeals to a discourse of reason, which ultimately holds in tension particularistic assertions about the nature of the universe, like revelation, salvation or chosenness, together with a universal ethics that fully take the Other into consideration. This common, neutral discourse enables adherents to account for particular truths in ways that do not appeal to insider, or particularist, language and worldview. He concludes that reconstructing and reconfiguring one's religion in rational terms both strips it of violence and "shows why the agonism at the heart of the monotheistic worldview can be embraced by a rationalist position, with rigor and integrity, while ethics and concern for the Other remain paramount."[13] This is the path religious leaders must follow if they are to break the death-grip that currently locks parties of religious communities against each other.

Let me illustrate what this might look like with examples from Jewish tradition. On the one hand, Judaism teaches that salvation is available only to Jews. In the language of the third-century codification of Jewish tradition, the mishnah, "all Israel has a share in the world to come."[14] In commentaries compiled over the first six centuries of the Common Era, a debate over this concept is recorded:

> Rabbi Eliezer stated: All non-Jews are denied a portion in the age to come, as it is written (Ps. 9:18), "The wicked will return to Sheol, all nations who have forgot-

---

[12] Robert Erlewine, *Monotheism and Tolerance. Recovering a Religion of Reason*, Indiana Series in the Philosophy of Religion (Bloomington: Indiana University Press, 2010), 177.
[13] Ibid., 181.
[14] m. *Sanhedrin* 10:1.

ten God." As to the phrase, "The wicked will return to Sheol"—this refers to the wicked Israelites.

Rabbi Joshua argued: Had the text read, "The wicked will return to Sheol, all nations" and ended there, I would have agreed with your opinion. Now that the text adds the phrase, "all nations who have forgotten God," I infer that there are righteous people (*tzaddikim*) among gentile nations who indeed merit a portion in the age to come.[15]

Despite the Jewish tendency to speak of salvation in particularistic, exclusivist ways in liturgy, which admittedly was conceived as private conversation between Jews and God, the point of view articulated by Rabbi Joshua, which embraces a universal ethic, is clearly in tension with the particularistic point of view articulated by Rabbi Eliezer. But this is an insider conversation. How is this internal dialogue translated into universally comprehensible language that bridges the gap between opposing camps of the religious divide?

Religion and reason in the public realm

The rational approach to religious conflict requires that religious leaders get involved in the public realm in ways that some of us trained in western democracies, who legislate separation of religion and state, might make us uncomfortable. This leads to my final challenge for the religious voice in the twenty-first century: What should the role of religion be in the public realm, in the political life of nation-states?

The so-called "secular" public sphere requires participants, whether religiously motivated or not, to employ rational, moral and political arguments for their positions on legislative, judicial and penal issues that can be understood by all of their fellow citizens. The creation of a general moral discourse subjects religious values to a kind of universal scrutiny that has eluded it in previous centuries.[16] This examination has produced numerous critiques of religion in general and of Christianity, Islam and

---

[15] Tosefta Sanhedrin (ed.), Moses Zuckermandel, chap. 13, p. 434, para. 2; Sanhedrin 105a and Rashi, at *ha shear nokhrim*, transl. Gilbert S. Rosenthal, "Hasidei Umoth Ha-Olam: A Remarkable Concept," in *Journal of Ecumenical Studies* 48.4 (Fall, 2013), 468.

[16] Although public religious debates forced participants to bridge the particularities of each other's religious discourse, the discourse was still Judaeo-Christian or Judaeo-Islamic; the discourse would have been unintelligible to either non-biblical religions or non-monotheists.

Judaism in particular. Some of these critiques have emerged from secular academic disciplines, like sociology and anthropology, while others have come from within religions themselves and have produced reformist movements that adapted traditional religious values to the changing realities of modernity. As I mentioned at the outset of this paper, this reform has produced a backlash of retrenchment within all three monotheisms. These camps perceive the public arena itself as a threat to their core religious ways and values and therefore they often do not participate in the type of rational discourse that Erlewine proposes. Rather, they retreat to particularistic rhetoric, which they perceive as uniquely faithful to their tradition and which they feel preserves their sense of authenticity. The challenge thus becomes how and where do we, who are confident in the ability of rational public discourse to negotiate particularistic claims, engage these ultra-traditionalist particularists?

The task is easier in contexts where a public forum for reasoned dialogue already exists. The greater challenge lies in parts of the world where there are no such arenas. Rather than dismissing and condemning these folks as lunatics and radicals, my own tradition requires that I sit down and begin a conversation with them, or at the very least their allies and supporters, articulated as "seeking peace and purse it" (Ps 34:15: *bakkesh shalom v'rodfehu*).

WHERE TO GO FROM HERE: THREE RECOMMENDATIONS

To identify the challenge is only a first step. Given the challenge of this chasm between different approaches to religion, what should be the role of the religious voice in the twenty-first century? What are the next steps?

- First, religious practitioners must acknowledge that our own traditions contain the seeds for both paths, these being the path of peace and the path of conflict. Rather than dismissing the radical or fundamentalist wings of religion as "hijacking" the faith and distancing ourselves from them by denying any relationship between our own version of religion and that of religious fanatics, we need to take full responsibility for the harmful elements within our traditions without fear that those who oppose us will use our words against us. And we must be ever vigilant about these hateful aspects of our traditions. If religious leaders do not actively contain and manage the more hostile and adversarial strains within our traditions, then the potential for adherents to draw on these strains to justify their destructive goals will remain, particularly given the stresses of globalization, which is in the process of dramatically transforming our societies. Such vigilance requires that religious leaders not only offer a different model for dealing with those harmful elements of our religious traditions, but also that we teach our clergy, educators and lay leaders how to tame these elements in order to prevent their use for destructive purposes.[17]

- Second, religions need to learn how to express their core ethical values in non-particularistic language. It is no longer sufficient for religious institutions to rally their own constituents to vote a certain way or advocate a particular position in the public forum. That approach can result in the tyranny of the majority over minorities. Rather, a more just and effective approach is to enable constituents to bring their religiously-grounded convictions to bear on public discourse in terms that all citizens can understand. Multi-faith religious coalitions that can lobby politicians are more effective because they are more representative than individual religious groups and because they come already equipped to communicate their views in non-particularistic language.

- This is a relatively new understanding of evangelism, one that reinterprets what it means to be a "light to the nations" in moral rather than doctrinal or exclusivist terms. How will religions do this? In

---

[17] One approach to vigilance is to examine problematic scriptural and traditional texts. Consider Jewish polemics that regard Christians in extremely negative terms, like the Talmudic statement, "You are called human [adam], Gentiles are not called human" (b. *Yevamot* 61a, transl. Daniel Matt, *Zohar*, vol. 1, 156, note 380. For more contemporary use of anti-gentile polemic, see David Bar-Chayim, "Yisrael Nikraim Adam [Jews Are Called 'Man']," in *Tzfiyah*, v. 3 (1989), 45–73). We can dismiss these kinds of statements as harmless since they were uttered by a powerless, persecuted people. Yet, how do we Jews ensure that these texts are not revived by contemporary Jews in Israel (who have political and military power) and used as pretexts for attacking Christians?

Christians might consider how to deal with texts like that written by Paul to the church of the Thessalonians (1 Thess 2:14–16): "For you, brothers and sisters, became imitators of the churches of God in Christ Jesus that are in Judea, for you suffered the same things from your own compatriots as they did from the Jews, who killed both the Lord Jesus and the prophets, and drove us out; they displease God and oppose everyone by hindering us from speaking to the Gentiles so that they may be saved. Thus they have constantly been filling up the measure of their sins; but God's wrath has overtaken them at last." How is *ioudaioi* best translated? How should this text be preached? This passage and others have been construed as Jews being a deicide race by such leading Church Fathers as Justin Martyr (*Dialogue with Trypho* 16.2–4), a view that contributed to anti-Semitic attitudes and acts over the centuries. One could equally suggest examining liturgical texts.

addition to requiring that our leaders and teachers gain a secular education, they need basic knowledge of world religions. This has been the approach of the Reform, Reconstructionist, Conservative and some Modern Orthodox Jewish seminaries. Yet, speaking from my own Jewish experience, the approach of these courses is too often apologetic, that is, from the point of view of how other religions relate to one's own particularistic religious truth, how to refute them, or how to defend one's own tradition against them. If these curricula are to elicit true interreligious understanding and mutual respect, they will need to put aside apologetic rhetoric and adopt a different approach, one that allows students to imagine themselves as adherents of those other religions and invites them to experience aspects of the other's religious life through either participation or observation. This includes all wings of those religions, as well as the most distant wings within our own tradition. This approach also requires that religious institutions embrace the ethic of hospitality (and not hostility), which can be found in the biblical tradition but was rare in subsequent centuries of the Jewish-Christian relationship. Grounds for this approach within the monotheistic traditions are found in the Jewish, Christian, and Muslim interpretations of Abraham welcoming the three visitors into his tent at Mamre.[18]

- Third, religious institutions need to find new, practical ways to help alleviate the challenges of modern life for the neediest members of society. The old ways of feeding the poor, housing the homeless, educating the uneducated and disaster relief still play a crucial role in society, so I am not suggesting they be abandoned. These services need to be expanded to underserved, remotely-located populations most vulnerable to radical religious influence. We are all keenly aware

---

[18] *Genesis Rabbah* 48.9. Jerome connects Mamre shrine activity in his own day to a belief in Abraham's ancient demonstration of hospitality (filoceni/a *filoxenia*; see Jerome, *De situ et nominibus locorum Hebraeorum*, transl. of Eusebius, *Onomasticon* 7.18-23). He commented that worshippers visited Mamre because (*eo quod*) of this belief. According to Jerome, this belief was what shrine adherents of all three religious backgrounds held in common. Even John Chrysostom, who is otherwise famous for his efforts at Christian triumphalism vis-à-vis Judaism, argued that the primary lesson to be learned from the visitation at Mamre was Abraham's generous hospitality (John Chrysostom, *hom in Gen* 41.8-10, 13-15, 21-22, 25-26; 43.10, 12. See especially 43.18: "He surpassed all the standards of hospitality!" [transl. Robert C. Hill, *Fathers of the Church* 82, 445], who dates the Genesis series of homilies to 385, when Chrysostom was still a deacon].) See Qur'an: Surah 11.69-76, for the Muslim reading.

that the modern world brings new challenges that often fall through the cracks of current social institutions, and religious communities are uniquely positioned to take up the slack; challenges like childcare, healthcare and eldercare, like job retraining, non-violent conflict resolution education, after-school and after-work youth activities, minority culture-preservation and micro-loan allocation. Many Christian, Jewish and Muslim relief organizations are already doing these things, but we need to keep looking for new ways to patch the holes in the social fabric of the countries in which we are not so firmly situated.

Religious leaders will get nowhere by drawing lines in the sand. While there is a time and a place for prophetic pronouncements and admonitions, these are not what is most needed to solve the problems of the twenty-first century. Today's problems call for extreme empathy and radical hospitality. This approach demands care and caution, lest empathy lead to side-taking and reinforce the oppositional structures that perpetuate hostility and violence between religious groups. Religious leaders have to be willing to sacrifice dearly-held truth-commitments and be ready to venture into unknown and unstable territory, both figuratively and literally. This is a risky venture that requires participants to leave their comfort zones and overcome fears, yet it is my conviction that this is what the twenty-first century is calling religious voices and persons to do and be.

III. Memory, Tradition and Revelation

Scripture and Revelation in the Jewish Tradition

David Fox Sandmel

Prologue

In my library is a complete set of Talmud, twenty, large, leather bound folio-sized books. It was printed by the Rom Press in Vilna, in 1922. I believe my grandfather purchased it and at some point gave it to my father. I inherited it from my father, and plan to pass it on to my daughter, herself now a student of Talmud. Jewish tradition teaches that Torah, of which Talmud is a part (as will be explained below), has been faithfully passed from teacher to student and parent to child ever since God revealed it to Moses on Mt Sinai and as he taught it to his student, Joshua.

Avraham Sutzkever was a Jewish poet. During the Second World War, he lived in the Vilna ghetto before escaping to the forests to become a partisan. In the following poem, written on 12 September 1943, Sutzkever describes melting the lead plates from the Rom Press in order to make bullets for the resistance to fight the Nazis.

> The Lead Plates at the Rom Press
> Arrayed at night, like fingers stretch through bars
> To clutch the lit air of freedom,
> We made for the press plates, to seize
> The lead plates at the Rom printing works.
> We were dreamers, we had to be soldiers,
> And melt down, for our bullets, the spirit of the lead.

At some timeless native lair
We unlocked the seal once more.
Shrouded in shadow, by the glow of a lamp,
Like Temple ancients dipping oil
Into candelabrums of festal gold,
So, pouring out line after lettered line, did we.

Letter by melting letter the lead,
Liquefied bullets, gleamed with thoughts:
A verse from Babylon, a verse from Poland,
Seething, flowing into the one mold.
Now must Jewish grit, long concealed in words,
Detonate the world in a shot!

Who in Vilna Ghetto has beheld the hands
Of Jewish heroes clasping weapons
Has beheld Jerusalem in its throes,
The crumbling of those granite walls;
Grasping the words smelted into lead,
Conning their sounds by heart.[1]

For us as Jews, faith, tradition and history with all their vicissitudes, are inseparable. This is what we transmit from generation to generation.

INTRODUCTION

In the following essay, I will explore the concepts of Scripture and revelation as they are understood in classic rabbinic thought. Rabbinic Judaism is the tradition that emerged after the destruction of the Second Temple by the Romans in the year 70 CE. This event brought to an end what is known as the Second Temple period (approx. 536 BCE–70 CE), the latter part of which, at least, was marked by great religious diversity among the Jews, both in the land of Israel and in the diaspora.[2] Despite this diversity, most Jews shared certain core beliefs, including that the people of Israel had a unique covenant with God, who had given them the land of Israel and commanded them to worship in the Jerusalem Temple.

---

[1] "Vilna Ghetto," 12 September 1943. Translated by Neal Kozodoy, at **www.tabletmag. com/jewish-arts-and-culture/books/24528/three-poems-by-avrom-sutzkever**
[2] For an overview of the Second Temple Period, see Lester Grabbe, *A History of the Jews and Judaism in the Second Temple Period* (London: T & T Clark International, 2004–2008).

The response to the tragedy of the destruction of Judaism's central and only shrine, as well as the loss of sovereignty in the land, required the creative transformation of Judaism—a renewal. Something had to replace the sacrificial worship and rituals that most Jews at the time considered to be essential components of the Jewish people's covenantal responsibility to their God. Into this breach stepped a group of leaders who came to be known as the rabbis.[3] They continued to view the Temple cult as the ideal form of worship and taught that, at the eschaton, God would return the people to the land and the Temple would be rebuilt. At the same time, they also taught that Torah, God's revealed word, contained an entire system for maintaining the covenant even without the Temple and regardless of where one lived, as can be seen in the following passage from rabbinic literature:

> God foresaw that the Temple would be destroyed, and He said, "While the Temple exists, and you bring sacrifices, the Temple atones for you. When the Temple is not there, what shall atone for you? Busy yourselves with the words of Torah, for they are equivalent to sacrifices, and they will atone for you. [Tanhuma (Buber) Acharei Mot, 35a]

Though it took several centuries, rabbinic Judaism eventually became the dominant expression of Judaism from the early medieval period until the dawn of modernity. The main part of my essay, therefore, will focus on how the rabbis understood Torah. I will also examine how classical conceptions of Torah have been reimagined and renewed in light of the challenges of modernity.

What is Torah?

The word "Torah" is best translated as "instruction" or "teaching" or "revelation." Historically, it has also been translated, primarily by Christians, as "law." This is a problematic and narrow rendering of the word,[4] which actually conveys multiple levels of meanings. The word "Torah" can refer specifically to the Pentateuch, the five books of Moses, which describes the

---

[3] For an overview of the transition from the Second Temple period to the rabbinic period, see Shaye J. D. Cohen, *From the Maccabees to the Mishnah* (Louisville, KY: Westminster John Knox Press, 2006, 2nd edition).

[4] As part of the classic Christian polemic against Judaism, Torah as "law" has been contrasted with the gospel. The "law" was considered restrictive, oppressive and spiritually deadening, while the gospel was portrayed as liberating, life-giving and suffused with God's love.

relationship between God and the people of Israel. It begins with the creation of the universe and ends with the death of Moses. While substantial parts of it are legislation, it also contains narrative and poetry. In synagogue ritual, "Torah" refers to the scroll (Sefer Torah, a book of Torah) which is housed in an Aron Kodesh, a "holy ark," a specific reference to the ark in which the tablets of the covenant God gave to Moses on Mt Sinai were stored (Ex 25:10). This scroll is handwritten according to ancient custom; as a ritual object it has a sanctity that a printed book of the Torah does not. In the synagogue ritual year, the Torah is read from the scroll sequentially from beginning to end in weekly portions. Thus Torah refers to a specific collection of literature as well as to specific ritual object. As we will see below, there is a wider definition of Torah that includes not only the Pentateuch, but by extension the TaNaKh as a whole and the entirety of rabbinic literature.

According to the rabbinic tradition, God revealed the Pentateuch in its entirety to Israel at Mount Sinai. It is the direct, perfect and authoritative Word of God. Exodus 19–20 describes the moment of revelation and Israel's acceptance of Torah. In many ways, this is the central, climactic moment of the entire Pentateuch. Everything that occurs before it is a prelude leading to this event. Much of what follows in the subsequent chapters of the Torah are the laws that, in Exodus 19–20, the Israelites commit to fulfill.

In terms of Jewish sacred Scripture, most scholars agree that the Torah was generally recognized as a unit no later than the fourth century BCE. And there seems to have been a consensus about a second collection of literature known as the Prophets no later than the second century BCE. However, in addition, during the Second Temple period there existed a plethora of Jewish religious writings in Hebrew, Aramaic and Greek that were considered "scriptural" by some Jews but not by others. This lack of a precisely defined canon reflected the varieties of Judaism (or as some prefer, "Judaisms") that characterized the Second Temple period as represented by groups including (but by no means limited to) the Pharisees, Sadducees, Essenes and the Qumran sect associated with the Dead Sea Scrolls. One of the primary differences between these groups was which writings were held to be sacred and authoritative, as well as how the Torah, which most Jews considered sacred, was properly interpreted and applied to daily life. However, as its name suggests, the primary focus of Second Temple Judaism was the Temple in Jerusalem and the sacrificial worship that was conducted there under the leadership of the high priesthood. In this regard, it is fair to say that it was the Temple rather than Scripture that united the Jewish community in antiquity; it was seen as the essential mechanism for maintaining the covenant between the Jewish people and their God.

With the destruction of the Temple and the increased emphasis on studying and interpreting God's Word, it makes sense that an authoritative canon became a desideratum, and some scholars date the closing of the Jewish canon of Scripture to the early rabbinic period, specifically to the first part of the second century CE. To the collections of the Torah and Prophets, already known in the Second Temple period, the rabbis delineated a third collection, known as the Writings, consisting of some, but by no means all, of Jewish sacred literature in circulation during the Second Temple period.[5]

The most common word that Jews today use for this anthology of sacred writings is TaNaKh, an acronym for Torah/Pentateuch, Neviim/Prophets and Ketuvim/Writings.[6] According to the rabbis, the Torah is the direct Word of God and it includes all the commandments, the 613 *mitzvot* that govern Jewish life. The prophetic writings contain the Word of God. Other books, such as Psalms, are considered to have been written by human beings inspired by God. TaNaKh, then, is the most common Hebrew word for Bible, though *miqra*, related etymologically to the Arabic Qur'an, is also used, as is *ha-katuv*, literally, that which is written, or, better, scripture.

In adapting to a post-Temple world, the rabbis built upon scriptural, interpretational and ritual traditions already known in the late Second Temple period and combined them with innovations that preserved the centrality of the idea of the Temple while substituting for it something that would enable Judaism to survive without what had once been considered its heart. Whereas sacred Scripture had been important for but not central to Second Temple Judaism, Scripture, or, more precisely, Torah, now became the focus and defining essence of rabbinic Judaism. Indeed, the word "rabbi" means "master" or "teacher," or, better, a master teacher of Torah.

Classical rabbinic Judaism focuses more on what God does and what God requires of Jews than on a systematic theological or philosophical understanding of what God is. This is often expressed in terms of creation, revelation and redemption. God created and sustains the world. God revealed God's commandments to Israel at Mt Sinai, and God will ultimately redeem Israel and all of humanity, just as God redeemed Israel from Egyptian slavery as described in the book of Exodus. Creation occurred in the past; the final redemption will take place in the future. Jewish tradition teaches Jews to be grateful for the former and wait in hope for the latter. In the meantime, God's revelation—Torah—teaches them to live in the world in right relationship with God and other human beings.

---

[5] Some of those works not included in the final canon of Jewish Scripture are considered canonical by some Christians (see the chart referenced in the following footnote).

[6] A chart listing the books of the TaNaKh in order and comparing Jewish Scripture to various Christian traditions of ordering the Bible can be found, at **http:// catholic-resources.org/Bible/Heb-Xn-Bibles.htm**

THE RABBIS AND THE TWO-FOLD TORAH

The rabbis consider the Torah to be a universal document; its norms are universal and it is available to all who would seek it out. It was given in the wilderness, rather than in the land of Israel, and was offered to all the nations of the world, as is seen in the following passage that stresses the universality of the Torah:

> "They encamped in the wilderness." (Ex 19:1) The Torah was given in public openly and in a free place. For had it been given in the land of Israel, the Israelites could have said to the nations of the world: you have no share in it. But now that it was given in the wilderness publicly and openly and in a place free for all, everyone wishing to accept it could come and accept it. One might suppose that it was given at night, but Scripture says: and it came to pass on the third day when it was morning (v. 16). One might suppose that it was given in silence, but Scripture says: when there were thunders and lightning (ibid.). One might suppose that they could not hear the voice, but Scripture says: and all the people saw the thunder and the lightning" (Ex 20:15) and "the voice of the Lord is full of majesty, etc. (Ps 29:4). Balaam the evil said to all the people who stood around him: the Lord is giving strength unto his people (ibid., V. 11). And they all opened up their mouths and said: the Lord will bless his people with peace.
>
> (Mechilta of Rabbi Ishmael, Parashat Yitro, Bachodesh 5)

According to the rabbis, the revelation of Torah at Mt Sinai was a corporate event witnessed by the entire people of Israel. At the same time, however, revelation was also individual. God addressed the people as a whole and each individual personally at one and the same time:

> 25. Another comment on "I am the Lord thy God." (Ex 20:2) Rabbi Hanina bar Papa said: the Holy One appeared to Israel with a stern face, with an placid face, with a friendly face, and with the joyous face: with a severe face appropriate for the teaching of Scripture – when a man teaches Torah to his son, he must impress upon him his own awe; with an placid face appropriate for the teaching of Mishnah; with a friendly face appropriate for the teaching of Talmud; with a joyous face appropriate for the teaching of Haggadah.[7] Therefore the Holy One said to them: though you see me in all these guises [I am still one] – I am the Lord thy God.
>
> Rabbi Levi said: the Holy One appeared to them as though He were a statue with faces on every side, so that though a thousand men might be looking at the statue, they would be led to believe it was looking at each one of them. So, too, when the Holy One spoke, each and every person in Israel could say, the Divine Word is

---

[7] For a definition, see below.

addressing me. Note the Scripture does not say, "I am the Lord your [plural] God," but "I am the Lord your [singular] God." (Ex 20:2) Moreover, Rabbi Yosi bar Rabbi Hanina said, the Divine Word spoke to each and every person according to his particular capacity. And so do not wonder at this. For when manna came down for Israel, each and every person tasted it in keeping with his own capacity – infants in keeping with their capacity, young men in keeping with their capacity, and old men in keeping with their capacity. Infants in keeping with their capacity: like the taste of the milk that an infant sucks from his mother's breast, so was the taste of manna to every infant, for it is said: "it's taste was like the taste of rich cream" (Num 11:8); young men according to their capacity, for of the manna they ate it is said: "my bread also which I give you, bread, and oil, and honey" (Ez 16:19); and old men according to their capacity, as it is said of the manna that they ate: "the taste of it was like wafers made with honey" (Ex 16:31). Now each and every person was enabled to taste manna according to his particular capacity, how much more and more with each and every person enabled according to his particular capacity to hear the Divine Word. Thus David said: "the voice of the Lord is in its strength" (Ps. 29:4) – not the voice of the Lord in his strength but the voice of the Lord in its strengths – that is, in its strength to make itself heard and understood according to the capacity of each and every person who listens to the divine word. Therefore the Holy One said: do not be misled because you hear many voices. Know that I am He who is one and the same: "I am the Lord thy God."

(Pesikta d'rav Kahana, Ch. 12)

Key to the rabbinic understanding of Scripture and revelation is the concept of the two-fold Torah. When God revealed the Torah to Moses on Mt Sinai, the rabbis teach, it consisted of both a written Torah (*torah she-bichtav*) and an oral Torah (*torah she-b'al peh*). Although the written Torah is always given pride of place, as the following passage shows, without the oral Torah the written Torah cannot be properly understood. Thus the written Torah and oral Torah are parts of an inseparable whole. In the next passage, oral Torah is equated with Mishnah, Talmud and Haggadah.[8]

The Mishnah is the foundational work of rabbinic Judaism, codified in the early part of the third century CE under the authority of Rabbi Judah the Patriarch. The Mishnah is a compendium of law and legal arguments that describe a life of sanctification. Though it does not follow the text of Torah in order, it is essentially a commentary on the Torah, elucidating and expanding the Torah's laws. It is worth noting that while the Mishnah

---

[8] For an introduction to rabbinic literature, see Charlotte E. Fonrobert and Martin S. Jaffee, *The Cambridge Companion to the Talmud and Rabbinic Literature* (Cambridge: Cambridge University Press, 2007).

describes a way of life in a world with no Temple, a significant portion of it deals precisely with the Temple rituals as if it were still in existence.

The Talmud consists of the Mishnah and a commentary on the Mishnah known as the Gemara that was composed in the rabbinic academies between the time of the codification of the Mishnah and the end of the sixth century CE. There are, in fact, two versions of the Gemara: one composed in the land of Israel and the other in Babylonia. For a number of reasons, it is the Babylonian Talmud that eventually became the primary version of the Talmud for the vast majority of the Jewish world.

While Mishnah and Talmud refer to specific works, the term Hagaddah is much broader and refers to a vast literature of rabbinic biblical commentary including both legal and homiletic works. All of the rabbinic literature, this oral Torah, is considered to have been revealed to Moses at Mt Sinai:

> "Write these words" (Ex 34:27). It is written, "If I write for him so many things of My Law, they are accounted as a stranger." (Hos 8:12) When God revealed Himself at Sinai to give the Torah to Israel, He communicated it to Moses in order: Bible, Mishnah, Talmud, and Haggadah, as it says, "And God spoke all these words." (Ex 20:1) Even the question a pupil asks his teacher God told Moses at that time. After he had learnt it from God, He told him to teach it to Israel. Moses said: "Lord of the Universe! shall I write it down for them?" God replied: "I do not wish to give it to them in writing, because I foresee a time when the heathen will have dominion over them and take it away from them, and they will be despised by the idol-worshippers; only the Bible will I give them in writing; but the Mishnah, Talmud, and Haggadah I will give them orally, so that when the idolaters enslave them, they will remain distinct from them." He said to the prophet: "If I write for him so many things of My Law, they are accounted as a stranger. I will, therefore, give them the Bible in writing; but the Mishnah, Talmud, and Haggadah will I give them orally." "Write"- refers to the Bible; "For after the tenor of these words" applies to the Mishnah and Talmud which keep Israel distinct from the idolaters.
>
> (Exodus Rabbah 47)

The term "oral Torah" can be confusing. Originally this literature was, indeed, oral; it was not committed to writing but, rather, was memorized and transmitted from one generation to the next. This served two purposes. The first was, as the passage above suggests, to prevent its dissemination beyond the rabbinic circles in which it originated. The second was to maintain a distinction between it and the written Torah. Eventually, however, even the oral Torah came to be written down. Until that time, however, this oral Torah was faithfully passed from one generation to the next, as is illustrated in the opening lines of a section of the Mishnah known as *pirkei avot*, the chapters of principles.

1:1. Moses received the Torah from Sinai and gave it over to Joshua. Joshua gave it over to the Elders, the Elders to the Prophets, and the Prophets gave it over to the Men of the Great Assembly. They [the Men of the Great Assembly] would always say these three things: Be cautious in judgment. Establish many pupils. And make a fence around the Torah.

1:2. Simon the Righteous was among the last surviving members of the Great assembly. He would say: The world stands on three things: Torah, the service of God, and deeds of kindness.

1:3. Antigonos of Socho received the tradition from Simon the Righteous. He would say: Do not be as slaves, who serve their master for the sake of reward. Rather, be as slaves who serve their master not for the sake of reward. And the fear of Heaven should be upon you.

2:1 Rabbi would say: What is the straight path which a person should choose for himself? Whatever is an ornament to the one who follows it, and an ornament in the view of others.

"Rabbi," in 2:1, is Judah the Patriarch, under whose authority the Mishnah was codified. The full passage, then, charts an unbroken and, according to tradition, a completely reliable chain of tradition from Moses at Mt Sinai to the Mishnah, and by extension to the entire rabbinic tradition. In this regard, it is telling that Moses is often referred to as *Mosheh Rabbeinu*, Moses our Rabbi/Teacher, thus underscoring the rabbis' belief that the traditions they were teaching, even if Moses could not have imagined them, were given to Moses at the moment of revelation. The Babylonian Talmud (Menahot 29b) acknowledges that later rabbinic teaching, even if unknown to Moses, was nonetheless revealed to him on Sinai.

In addition, the rabbis, and the rabbis alone, are the authoritative interpreters of Torah. In the following passage, neither the performance of miracles nor even direct communication from God can overrule the judgment of the rabbis.

[...] Rabbi Eliezer declared it clean, and the Sages declared it unclean; and this was the oven of 'Aknai [...]. It has been taught: On that day Rabbi Eliezer brought forward every imaginable argument, but they did not accept them. He said to them: "If the halachah agrees with me, let this carob-tree prove it!" Then, the carob-tree was torn a hundred cubits out of its place (others even say four hundred cubits). "No proof can be brought from a carob-tree," they answered. Again he said to them: "If the halachah agrees with me, let the stream of water prove it!" At that moment, the stream of water flowed backwards. "No proof can be brought from a stream of water," they rejoined. Again he urged: "If the halachah agrees with me, let the walls of the schoolhouse prove it," and the walls inclined to fall. But Rabbi Joshua rebuked them (i.e. the walls), saying: "When scholars are engaged in a halachic dispute, who are you to interfere?" Hence they did not fall, in honor of Rabbi Joshua. But neither did they resume the upright, in honour of Rabbi Eliezer. So to this day, they are still standing inclined. Again he said to them: "If the halachah agrees with me, let it be proved from Heaven!" Whereupon a Heavenly Voice cried out: "Why do you dispute with Rabbi Eliezer, seeing that in all matters the halachah agrees with him!" But Rabbi Joshua arose and exclaimed: 'It is not in heaven!" (Deut 30:12) What did he mean by this? Rabbi Jeremiah said: "[He meant that] the Torah had already been given at Mount Sinai. We pay no attention to a Heavenly Voice, because You have written in the Torah at Mount Sinai: 'After the majority must one incline.'" (Ex. 23:2) Rabbi Nathan met Elijah and asked him: "What did the Holy One, Blessed be He, do in that hour?–He laughed! He replied, saying, 'My sons have defeated Me, My sons have defeated Me!'"

(Babylonian Talmud, Baba Metzia 59a-b)

Finally, Torah as revealed to Moses at Mt Sinai contains the answer for any question that may arise about fulfilling God's law. This is already hinted at in the passage above from Exodus Rabbah: Even the question a pupil asks his teacher God told Moses at that time. A similar point is made in the passage from the Babylonian Talmud in which Moses could not follow the discussion between Rabbi Akiba and his disciples. And a passage from *Pirke Avot* 5:22 states: "Turn it over again and again, because everything is in it." Torah, here understood broadly to encompass both the written and oral Torah, contains the answers to all legal questions that might confront a rabbi at any time. Proper study and application of previous legal decisions and principles can elucidate what the law is, even in a situation that could not have been imagined either by Moses or by the rabbis. Whether it is bio-medical ethics (e.g., stem cell research or in vitro fertilization) or intellectual property in the age of the internet, not only does Jewish law have something to say about it, what it has to say was already revealed to Moses at Mt Sinai. The contemporary Jewish legal scholar may come up with a new interpretation to address a new problem, but that interpretation was in the original revelation, in a sense, waiting to be applied when needed. Even when scholars disagree about the meaning of a particular biblical text or the details of Jewish law, if the intention is to understand Torah, conflicting opinions are both "the words of the living God" (Babylonian Talmud, Eruvin 13b).

Thus, for the classical rabbinic tradition, Torah, both written and oral, was revealed to Moses at Mt Sinai. The rabbis are the authoritative transmitters and interpreters of Torah. Torah contains all relevant knowledge for the fulfillment of Israel's covenantal obligations, even for situations that could not have been conceived of by previous generations.

THE CHALLENGES OF MODERNITY

For all intents and purposes, all Jews accepted this understanding of Scripture and revelation until the dawn of modernity. The Enlightenment, however, brought with it challenges to religious authority in general, and the authority of revealed Scripture in particular. The Jewish community responded to these challenges in a variety of ways. Some Jews continued to accept the classical teaching about Scripture and revelation and along with it the authority of the rabbinic tradition; this position came to be known in the Jewish community as orthodoxy. Others sought to adapt Jewish teaching to modernity by redefining Torah; the primary expressions of this are the Reform and Conservative movements.[9]

The Reform movement in the USA traces its roots to Germany in the early 1800s. Over the last 130 years, its rabbinic body, the Central Conference of American Rabbis (CCAR), has attempted on four different occasions to offer a definition of Torah that affirms its centrality to the Jewish tradition while, at the same time, reflecting the modern critique of revealed religion. The first of these dates from 1885 and is known as the Pittsburgh Platform. It states:

1. We recognize in every religion an attempt to grasp the Infinite, and in every mode, source or book of revelation held sacred in any religious system the consciousness of the indwelling of God in man. We hold that Judaism presents the highest conception of the God-idea as taught in our Holy Scriptures and developed and spiritualized by the Jewish teachers, in accordance with the moral and philosophical progress of their respective ages. We maintain that Judaism preserved and defended midst continual struggles and trials and under enforced isolation, this God-idea as the central religious truth for the human race.

2. We recognize in the Bible the record of the consecration of the Jewish people to its mission as the priest of the one God, and value it as the most potent instrument of religious and moral instruction. We hold that the modern discoveries of scientific researches in the domain of nature and history are not antagonistic to the doctrines of Judaism, the Bible reflecting the primitive ideas of its own age, and at times clothing its conception of divine Providence and Justice dealing with men in miraculous narratives.

---

[9] Reform and Conservative Judaism are specific movements, each with its own institutional body; in that sense, there is one "address" for each. Orthodoxy, on the other hand, consists of a variety institutions, and includes Hassidic and non-Hassidic movements as well as ultra-Orthodox and modern Orthodox movements. For an overview of modern Judaism, see N. R. M. de Lange and Miri Freud-Kandel, *Modern Judaism: An Oxford Guide* (Oxford: Oxford University Press, 2005).

> 3. We recognize in the Mosaic legislation a system of training the Jewish people for its mission during its national life in Palestine, and today we accept as binding only its moral laws, and maintain only such ceremonies as elevate and sanctify our lives, but reject all such as are not adapted to the views and habits of modern civilization.
>
> 4. We hold that all such Mosaic and rabbinical laws as regulate diet, priestly purity, and dress originated in ages and under the influence of ideas entirely foreign to our present mental and spiritual state. They fail to impress the modern Jew with a spirit of priestly holiness; their observance in our days is apt rather to obstruct than to further modern spiritual elevation.[10]

Two key points in the Pittsburgh Platform bear noting. The first is that the Torah, while a "potent instrument of religious and moral instruction," is not the perfect and authoritative Word of God of the classical rabbis. It is, rather, the product of its historical moment; it contains "primitive" elements that can be rejected. Second, perhaps not as obvious from the text above, is a clear distinction between the Bible, that is, between the TaNaKh, and the rabbinic literature. The early Reformers rejected the idea of the two-fold Torah, relegating the rabbinic literature to a decidedly secondary position.

In 1937, the Reform rabbinate again addressed the concept of Torah. In "The Guiding Principles of Reform Judaism," popularly known as the Columbus Platform, the idea of revelation as "continuous" is introduced, as opposed to the classical rabbinic view of the uniqueness of the revelation at Sinai and the belief that all knowledge was contained in that initial revelation. In the passage below, the distinction between written and oral Torah implied in the earlier document has been replaced by a reference to, and reverence for, both the written and oral Torah. At the same time, this statement also holds that both written and oral Torah, while historically conditioned and, in some cases, no longer binding, remain central to Jewish self-understanding.

> *Torah.* God reveals Himself not only in the majesty, beauty and orderliness of nature, but also in the vision and moral striving of the human spirit. Revelation is a continuous process, confined to no one group and to no one age. Yet the people of Israel, through its prophets and sages, achieved unique insight in the realm of religious truth. The Torah, both written and oral, enshrines Israel's ever-growing consciousness of God and of the moral law. It preserves the historical precedents, sanctions and norms of Jewish life, and seeks to mold it in the patterns of goodness and of holiness. Being products of historical processes, certain of its laws have

---

[10] At **http://ccarnet.org/rabbis-speak/platforms/declaration-principles/**

lost their binding force with the passing of the conditions that called them forth. But as a depository of permanent spiritual ideals, the Torah remains the dynamic source of the life of Israel. Each age has the obligation to adapt the teachings of the Torah to its basic needs in consonance with the genius of Judaism.[11]

In "Reform Judaism: A Centenary Perspective from 1976," the CCAR speaks in more general terms about Torah as an ongoing process using the language of relationship. While privileging "the earliest confrontations" between the Jews and their God, in its reference to "rabbis and teachers, philosophers and mystics, gifted Jews in every generation" (which should be understood as self-referential), it significantly expands the classical definition of Torah. Gone are explicit references to "primitive" ideas or the "products of historical processes."

> *Torah*–Torah results from the relationship between God and the Jewish people. The records of our earliest confrontations are uniquely important to us. Lawgivers and prophets, historians and poets gave us a heritage whose study is a religious imperative and whose practice is our chief means to holiness. Rabbis and teachers, philosophers and mystics, gifted Jews in every age amplified the Torah tradition. For millennia, the creation of Torah has not ceased and Jewish creativity in our time is adding to the chain of tradition.[12]

In 1999, the CCAR once again attempted to define Torah, in a document entitled "A Statement of Principles for Reform Judaism." The positive tone of the 1976 platform is continued in the passage below, which is not concerned with defining what Reform Jews do not accept as was the case in the 1885 platform. Instead, it embraces Torah and calls for a reengagement with its texts as well as with all the ritual and ethical commandments.

> 1. We affirm that Torah is the foundation of Jewish life.

> 2. We cherish the truths revealed in Torah, God's ongoing revelation to our people and the record of our people's ongoing relationship with God.

> 3. We affirm that Torah is a manifestation of עולם אהבת (*ahavat olam*), God's eternal love for the Jewish people and for all humanity.

---

[11] At **http://ccarnet.org/rabbis-speak/platforms/guiding-principles-reform-judaism/**

[12] At **http://ccarnet.org/rabbis-speak/platforms/reform-judaism-centenary-perspective/**

4. We affirm the importance of studying Hebrew, the language of Torah and Jewish liturgy, that we may draw closer to our people's sacred texts.

5. We are called by Torah to lifelong study in the home, in the synagogue and in every place where Jews gather to learn and teach. Through Torah study we are called to מצות (*mitzvot*), the means by which we make our lives holy.

6. We are committed to the ongoing study of the whole array of מצות (*mitzvot*) and to the fulfillment of those that address us as individuals and as a community. Some of these מצות (*mitzvot*), sacred obligations, have long been observed by Reform Jews; others, both ancient and modern, demand renewed attention as the result of the unique context of our own times.

7. We bring Torah into the world when we seek to sanctify the times and places of our lives through regular home and congregational observance. Shabbat calls us to bring the highest moral values to our daily labor and to culminate the work-week with קדושה (*kedushah*), holiness, מנוחה (*menuchah*), rest and ענג (*oneg*), joy. The High Holy Days call us to account for our deeds. The Festivals enable us to celebrate with joy our people's religious journey in the context of the changing seasons. The days of remembrance remind us of the tragedies and the triumphs that have shaped our people's historical experience both in ancient and modern times. And we mark the milestones of our personal journeys with traditional and creative rites that reveal the holiness in each stage of life.

8. We bring Torah into the world when we strive to fulfill the highest ethical mandates in our relationships with others and with all of God's creation. Partners with God in תקון עולם (*tikkun olam*), repairing the world, we are called to help bring nearer the messianic age. We seek dialogue and joint action with people of other faiths in the hope that together we can bring peace, freedom and justice to our world. We are obligated to pursue צדק (*tzedek*), justice and righteousness, and to narrow the gap between the affluent and the poor, to act against discrimination and oppression, to pursue peace, to welcome the stranger, to protect the earth's biodiversity and natural resources, and to redeem those in physical, economic and spiritual bondage. In so doing, we reaffirm social action and social justice as a central prophetic focus of traditional Reform Jewish belief and practice. We affirm the מצוה (*mitzvah*) of צדקה (*tzedakah*), setting aside portions of our earnings and our time to provide for those in need. These acts bring us closer to fulfilling the prophetic call to translate the words of Torah into the works of our hands.[13]

---

[13] At **http://ccarnet.org/rabbis-speak/platforms/statement-principles-reform-judaism/**

The Conservative movement has also attempted to define Torah. The following citation is from "Emet Ve'Emunah: Statement of Principles of Conservative Judaism" of 1998.

Revelation

Conservative Judaism affirms its belief in revelation, the uncovering of an external source of truth emanating from God. This affirmation emphasizes that although truths are transmitted by humans, they are not a human invention. That is why we call the Torah torat emet. The Torah's truth is both theoretical and practical, that is, it teaches us about God and about our role in His world. As such, we reject relativism, which denies any objective source of authoritative truth. We also reject fundamentalism and literalism, which do not admit a human component in revelation, thus excluding an independent role for human experience and reason in the process.

The nature of revelation and its meaning for the Jewish people, have been understood in various ways within the Conservative community. We believe that the classical sources of Judaism provide ample precedents for these views of revelation.

The single greatest event in the history of God's revelation took place at Sinai, but was not limited to it. God's communication continued in the teaching of the Prophets and the biblical Sages, and in the activity of the Rabbis of the Mishnah and the Talmud, embodied in Halakhah and the Aggadah (law and lore). The process of revelation did not end there; it remains alive in the Codes and Responsa to the present day.

Some of us conceive of revelation as the personal encounter between God and human beings. Among them there are those who believe that this personal encounter has propositional content, that God communicated with us in actual words. For them, revelation's content is immediately normative, as defined by rabbinic interpretation. The commandments of the Torah themselves issue directly from God. Others, however, believe that revelation consists of an ineffable human encounter with God. The experience of revelation inspires the verbal formulation by human beings of norms and ideas, thus continuing the historical influence of this revelational encounter.

Others among us conceive of revelation as the continuing discovery, through nature and history, of truths about God and the world. These truths, although always culturally conditioned, are nevertheless seen as God's ultimate purpose for creation. Proponents of this view tend to see revelation as an ongoing process rather than as a specific event.[14]

---

[14] At **www.icsresources.org/content/primarysourcedocs/ConservativeJuda-ismPrinciples.pdf**

The Conservative movement positions itself in between Reform and Orthodoxy, as is seen in its references to relativism and fundamentalism. However, both the Conservative and Reform definitions of Torah reflect the desire to preserve the centrality of Torah while remaining open to contemporary critical biblical scholarship. In practical terms, this position presents challenges to religious authority and therefore to maintaining standards of belief and practice within both the Reform and Conservative communities. Nonetheless, Torah study remains a central activity in both Reform and Conservative synagogues, and each movement has, in recent years, produced significant commentaries on the Torah, specifically for use in synagogue worship and study.

Finally, a significant portion of those who identify as Jews today do not consider themselves religious. Jewish identity is defined by membership in the Jewish people as a result of having been born a Jew (though one can become Jewish through a process of conversion), rather than by a profession of faith. Some "secular" Jews, even while rejecting the sanctity of Torah, its divine origins and its authority, continue to view it as a record of Jewish origins, a repository of Jewish culture, a source of Jewish values and something worthy of study.

When speaking of renewal and identity, another important response to the challenges posed by modernity was the emergence of Zionism, the national liberation movement of the Jewish people. Zionism in not monolithic—it has both secular and religious interpretations, as well as Communist, socialist and other iterations. And each has its own approach to Scripture and revelation. Even for many of the secularists, traditional Jewish literature—especially the TaNaKh and to a lesser extent the Talmud and the midrashic literature—if not religiously authoritative, is nonetheless the embodiment of the history and culture of the Jewish people, a source of identity, values and pride.

The return to sovereignty by the Jewish people in 1948—especially in light of the Shoa—has ushered in a new period of renewal and reinterpretation of identity. One of the most challenging aspects of this focuses on political power. What had been, for almost two thousand years, an academic or intellectual subject, suddenly became concrete and had real world significance. The implications of this are still being worked out.

Finally, notions of identity have undergone profound changes in the last couple of generations. What was once considered a given (religion, nationality, gender) is increasingly being viewed, especially by younger people, as both a construct and a choice.

Despite, or perhaps because of these changes, there remains a deep interest in text study, both Talmud and Torah—often engaged in by Jews who would not describe themselves as religious (or might identify as avowedly secular). Indeed, as part of a range of projects consciously designed to renew Judaism in the contemporary world, creative models of Torah study are being developed, rooted in traditional methodologies and texts while incorporating non-traditional modes of reading and/or texts. For example, in Chicago, Rabbi Benay Lappe has founded *Svara*, A Traditionally Radical Yeshiva.[15] Its website explains:

> SVARA is named for the Jewish concept that moral intuition informed by serious Jewish learning is a source of Jewish law that can "trump" Torah. SVARA's work follows the direction of the Rabbis of the Talmud, who were willing to make radical moves—sometimes overturning the Torah itself—to make Judaism more meaningful, compassionate, and responsive to the human condition. Through rigorous short- and long-term Talmud learning programs, SVARA: A Traditionally Radical Yeshiva builds and activates a radically inclusive and interpretive community of 'players' who seek to restore Judaism to its radical roots so that it might once again be a voice of courageous moral conscience in the world and reflect the truest possible vision of what it means to be human.
>
> SVARA's commitment to the Queer experience means that people who have traditionally experienced Judaism as an outsider—in any conceivable way—can find a home, learn to give voice to their narrative from within the Jewish story, and gain the necessary text skills and halachic (Jewish legal) expertise to enrich, push, and contribute to the evolving Jewish tradition. Through short and long-term learning, those who were once outsiders become trustworthy, courageous, and authentic transmitters of the tradition.[16]

> Mastery of Talmud confers a legitimacy and confidence in one's leadership that cannot be gained otherwise. Through traditional methods of study in the original Aramaic and Hebrew, SVARA develops and empowers innovative Jewish change agents who are then learned, empathetic, and experienced in both worldly and Jewish sources, thereby creating a dynamic, inclusive, and accessible tradition.

And in Israel, where the majority of Jews self-identify as "secular," an organization called BINA describes itself as "the leading organization at the intersection of Jewish Pluralism & Social Action in Israel. BINA strives to strengthen Israel as a democratic pluralistic society, by emphasizing Judaism as a culture, through Jewish values of Tikkun Olam (Hebrew: "repairing the world")."[17] One of its programs is the Secular Yeshiva.

---

[15] Yeshiva is the Hebrew name for a place of Torah study.
[16] At **www.svara.org/about-svara/**
[17] At **www.bina.org.il/en/about**

The BINA Secular Yeshiva is the only non-orthodox institute of its kind in Israel today. Young adults intensively study Jewish texts and Jewish culture from sources ranging from the Bible and Gemara to classic Israeli literature and Zionist history. Students learn with renowned experts from their fields of academia, Jewish scholarship and social activism. Students engage in local community action and organize Jewish cultural events and holidays. This format fosters a long-term commitment to Jewish study, social action and Jewish expression, encouraging students to interpret the sources in a meaningful and personal way.[18]

The ongoing development of the Jewish tradition can be described in terms of continuity and change. Jews see themselves as part of an ancient people with its own sacred literature and traditions. Changing circumstance, both political and intellectual, have forced Judaism to change and adapt, even as Jews understand themselves to be part of an unbroken chain that reaches back three millennia and more. Its remarkable ability to renew itself, to redefine what it means to be a Jew, has enabled it to survive in an often-hostile world.

---

[18] At **www.bina.org.il/en/programs/yeshiva/about**

The Role of Memory in the Formation of Early Christian Identity

Binsar Jonathan Pakpahan

Introduction

Identity is always connected with memory and its formation cannot be separated from remembering the past–a process which can be either personal or communal. Identity is formed in relation to a wide range of personal, communal, national or even regional memories (and sometimes myths).[1] These compete internally within us, so that one particular memory seems more important than another at any given moment. In short, memory plays an important role in the development of our identity.

Recent research in psychology, sociology, philosophy, medicine and anthropology has affirmed the importance of memory. The factors that play a role in how memories are shaped compete with one another, with context, culture and politics. In this, individual and communal factors are of varying importance. Today's technologies allow us to store vast amounts of data, which has created problems in terms of how we actually deal with memories.[2]

---

[1] See current discussions on Yael Zerubabel, *Recovered Roots: Collective Memory and the Making of Israeli National Tradition* (Chicago: The University of Chicago Press, 1994); Mary S. Zurbuchen (ed.), *Beginning to Remember: The Past in the Indonesian Present* (Singapore: Singapore University Press, 2005). Chiara Bottici and Benoit Challand, *Imagining Europe: Myth, Memory, and Identity* (New York: Cambridge University Press, 2013); and Paul Fussell, *The Great War in Modern Memory* (New York: Oxford University Press, 2000).

[2] I have extensively dealt with the problem of memory of past hurt, in Binsar J. Pakpahan, *God Remembers: Towards a Theology of Remembrance as a Basis of Reconciliation in Communal Conflict* (Amsterdam: VU University Press, 2012).

Religious identity is partly based on memory. Remembering the saving acts of a specific deity is important in the formation of a religious community and the story of most religious communities is based on the memory that has been handed down over generations. For instance, Christians base their identity on the remembrance of God's saving act in Jesus Christ.

The Bible is in itself a book of memory, consisting of the recollections of those who encountered God in their lives and who were inspired to tell and write down their stories, thus passing them down to future generations. In the following, we will look at the role of memory in the formation of Christian identity by examining how biblical communities perceived remembrance and how they treated their memory.

This essay will draw on recent social memory theory in order to understand how remembrance is used in the Old and the New Testaments. Furthermore, I shall analyze how biblical communities understand memory in their contexts and, by using two different methods, hopefully establish the function of memory in the formation of Christian identity.

The role of memory is more active than the mere recollection of certain events that occurred in the past. This essay will demonstrate how the recent exploration of social memory in the biblical communities has shaped their identity. For Israel and the early Christian communities, the act of remembering the past is connected with action. Remembrance takes place in the community that preserves the memory of the event and reactualizes it every time it celebrates the memory. For Christians, the command to remember is deeply rooted in the Eucharist. While celebrating the Eucharist, memories of Jesus remind us of the past pain while, at the same time, possibly providing a redemptive memory.

MEMORY AS A BATTLEFIELD

The first theologian comprehensively to deal with memory was Augustine, who regarded memory as a dynamic, active and continuous notion that helps us to recognize God. According to Augustine, memory is "a great field or a spacious palace, a storehouse for countless images of all kinds which are conveyed to it by the senses."[3] At first sight, we might surmise that Augustine implies that memory is like the hard disk of a computer on which a certain set of data can be stored. Memories can then be retrieved whenever needed, each through its own gateway. Nonetheless, although Augustine compares memory to a storehouse, he believed that one can never fully control what is actually stored nor control the ability to recall the content whenever desired.

---

[3] Augustine, *Confessions* (Harmondsworth: Penguin, 1961), Book X, 8.

Augustine's theory of memory is connected to his theory of time. For him there are three different times: a present of past things (memory), a present of present things (perception) and a present of future things (expectation).[4] He believes there to be no real present except our present perception of what the past was, what the present is and what the future will be. What has happened to us will be stored in our memory and used to recognize our present and future.

The feelings that in part make up our memories change over time. Thus, my feelings toward something are kept in my memory and can be retrieved whenever I want. However, once recalled it will not exactly correspond to what I felt when I experienced the original feeling. Augustine refers to memory as the stomach of the mind and to feelings as food. Sad feelings (food) that are digested in my memory (stomach) stay in my memory but the "food" no longer tastes the same as it did when it first entered the "stomach."

Remembering is the dynamic process of reinterpreting our memories. Memories are reexperienced when the one who remembers gives meaning to them. This is why the process of forgetting is an interesting phenomenon. According to Augustine, "When I remember memory, my memory is present to itself by its own power; but when I remember forgetfulness, two things are present, memory, by which I remember it, and forgetfulness, which is what I remember."[5] Forgetting is actually the act of remembering that we have forgotten something. We do not realize that we have forgotten something if we have no memory of it in the first place.

Augustine suggests that memory is always present but that we cannot fully control it. Remembering the past involves reinterpreting an event and giving meaning to it. Feelings are not an integral part of memory. Rather, what we remember is the "taste" of an emotion rather than the emotion itself. Remembering always involves giving another meaning. Augustine's theory of memory captures the difficulty of understanding the role played by memory in the formation of Christian identity.

Recent philosophical studies have further explored Augustine's memory theory and defined different categories of memories.[6] The memory of an event is different from the memory of the emotion experienced. A person can remember what happened during a football match—who scored, where the match was played, how many people attended the match, etc.—and subsequently recall the memory ten years later. Meanwhile, however, the emotions will have changed. While, at the time the match was played, one might have been happy that one's team won, ten years later, one will re-

---

[4] Ibid., Book XI, 20.

[5] Ibid., Book X, 16.

[6] See John Sutton, "Memory," in *The Stanford Encyclopedia of Philosophy* (Summer 2010 Edition), at **http://plato.stanford.edu/archives/sum2010/entries/memory/**

member that one had been happy without necessarily feeling this happiness. While the memory of the event stays the same, the emotion has changed.

In the construction of memory and identity, the memory of the emotion can also be passed on. The passed on memory of the emotion could take its original form, be strengthened or lessened according to the need of the formation of identity, especially communal identity. A community needs emotion to strengthen the bond between individuals. It is often the memory of the emotion that brings individuals together instead of the memory of the actual event. A group of people who played football together have bonded because of the shared memory of the emotion instead of the event. They feel connected because of the memory of the tears and joy experienced during the matches. After ten years, they might still remember how happy they were as a team while having forgotten the details of how they won. It shows that the relationship between memory of an event and memory of an emotion is a dynamic one.

In the formation of religious identity, the memory of the emotion plays a more important role than the memory of what actually took place. Such distinctions and categories provide helpful perspectives when examining how Christian identity has been shaped by the social memory of the biblical communities.

THE FORMATION OF SOCIAL MEMORY

With reference to social memory theory, some Bible scholars have argued that the Bible consists of a web of stories, delivered by different storytellers, rooted in their respective community and with differing opinions as to how memory should be delivered and preserved. The study of social memory began as a philosophical and social analysis research methodology that attempted to look at how the social environment of the storyteller or writer shaped the memories that were included in the texts.[7]

Phillip Davies, an Old Testament scholar, acknowledges the recent interest in cultural or collective memory. He recognizes Maurice Halbwach's, Jan Assmann's and Paul Ricoeur's contributions to the field of biblical social memory.[8] For him, the purpose of social memory as a methodology

---

[7] See Mark S. Smith, *The Memoirs of God: History, Memory, and the Experience of the Divine in Ancient Israel* (Minneapolis: Fortress Press, 2004), 133. He argues that most of biblical scholars have been directing their attention towards the social power in the production of the texts. For a short history of the social memory process in biblical society, see Dennis C. Dulling, "Social Memory and Biblical Studies: Theory, Method, and Application," in *Biblical Theology Bulletin* 36 (2006), 2–4.

[8] See Maurice Halbwachs, *On Collective Memory*, ed. and transl. Lewis A. Coser (Chicago: University of Chicago Press, 1992); Jan Assman, *Religion and Cutural Memory: Ten Studies*, transl. Rodney Livingstone (Stanford, California: Stanford

is not to ascertain what precisely happened in the past, but "rather as a narrative of the past that makes sense of (and in) the present and for the future. Hence, it is a constitutive function of ethnicity, the *ethnos* being in this case the group bonded by the shared 'memory' of the past."[9]

In biblical research, the concept of social memory is used to analyze how groups influence the writer in delivering the memory that was later passed on in the form of narratives, texts, images or even rituals. This is why the study of social memory particularly encourages us to move away from a mere historical approach of finding out what truly happened in the story, to moving toward what we remember and how we remember it.[10] Social memory emphasizes "the importance of history for understanding and interpreting the context that gives shape to social memory as it is encountered in literary texts. Material remains, diaries, letters, and the like."[11]

Hearon established that stories of the past can indeed become a group's social memory if they speak to the people, and their relevance is being emphasized by the storyteller. Most of the time, the story of God's saving power in the past is being transferred as the hope that God will intervene in the present and the future. Hope gives certain stories their power and durability in social memory. Stories can also function as acts of resistance toward the present and foster hope for the future.

An analysis of the social memory takes into account the context within which a story was produced as well as the social powers that might have influenced the way in which the writer remembered and delivered the story. As we explore what remembrance means in terms of biblical theology, or how communities in the Bible understood the terms "memory" and "remembrance" and what they meant for them, we must first comprehend how memory and context shaped the society and how important their cultural memory was. Thus, we seek to establish what remembering means in a biblical context, and to what extent remembering influenced the forming of the identity of the people at the time the text was written and in the future.

We must bear in mind that, for certain reasons, some memories have been preserved while others have not. Usually, memories have already travelled far—from an oral to a written tradition. Fully to comprehend

---

University Press, 2006); and Paul Ricoeur, *Memory, History, Forgetting*, transl. Kathleen Blamey and David Pellauer (Chicago: The Chicago University Press, 2006); Philip R. Davies, *The Origins of Biblical Israel* (New York: T & T Clark, 2007), 31.
[9] Davies, ibid., 32.
[10] See Holly Hearon, "The Construction of Social Memory in Biblical Interpretation," in *Encounter* 67 no. 4 (2006), 348. See also Holly Hearon, "The Art of Biblical Reinterpretation: Re-Membering the Past into the Present," in *Encounter* 66 no. 3 (2005), 343–59.
[11] Hearon, "The Construction of Social Memory …," ibid., 349.

the complexities of social memory in the biblical context implies trying to perceive the narratives within the horizon in which they were written or remembered.[12] In the biblical context, remembering and forgetting are social actions related to hearing and choosing a story so that it becomes the community's definitive story in terms of identity formation.

Despite the different environments and the great time span over which the Bible was written, its narratives share the same basis. One thing that social memory theory clearly establishes in biblical research is that the basic memory that underlies the whole remembrance in Israel, and later in Jesus' time, is the purpose of remembering God's saving action. While the defining moments when and where God saved God's people are remembered in different ways, the purpose always remains the same, namely, never to forget how great God's saving action is to the people of the covenant. The command to remember is then being translated into written narratives about what to remember.

THE ROLE OF MEMORY IN THE BIBLE

The Old Testament notes that the commandments to remember and behold played a very important role with regard to Israel's identity.[13] Israel was asked to remember God's saving act from Egypt to the land of Canaan. Israel is told to remember and pass on the memory of God's saving action through generations (Deut 11:19).

The Hebrew word for remembrance connotes an activity of more than just an activity of the mind. As we see in the Old Testament, God's remembrance is strongly connected to actions such as blessings (e.g., Ps 132:1; cf. also Ps 20:3; 2 Kings 20:3; Isa 38:3) and punishment (Hos 7:2; 9:9; 8:13; Jer 14:10). If Israel is being punished, they will ask God not to remember their

---

[12] For an argument that defended the visibility of understanding the story of the past, despite the different contexts and understanding in looking at the context, see Philip Francis Esler, *New Testament Theology: Communion and Community* (Minneapolis: Augsburg Fortress, 2005), 67–87. He uses intercultural communication arguments to understand how specific contexts understand their narratives, and how we can use those findings in understanding that context from a distant time span. He thinks that by using four factors, culture, groups and social roles, the individual and the environment, we can interpret a document in its context or in its social memory.

[13] In the Old Testament, the word that is translated with "remember" has the root זכר (zkr), which is a verb common masculine singular construct and means to think (about), meditate (upon), pay attention (to); remember, remembrance, recollect; mention, declare, recite, proclaim, invoke, commemorate, accuse, confess. See Brevard S. Childs, *Memory and Tradition in Israel* (London: SCM Press, 1962). Also see Craig Dykstra, "Memory and Truth," in *Theology Today,* vol. 44, no. 2 (July 1987), 159–63.

iniquities (Isa 64:9). For Israel, the memory of God's saving acts is not about what really happened, but about the testimony of how they encountered God. These memories of encounters will be looked at from a new perspective. The memory renews and changes them over generations[14] and each event becomes relevant for each subsequent generation.[15]

In the New Testament, Jesus asked the disciples to remember him in the institution of the Eucharist. Jesus took over the remembrance of the Passover and continued the celebration in remembrance of him. God's past saving action is now being actualized in the remembrance of God's saving act in Jesus' life, work, death and resurrection. The remembrance of the memory of Jesus is also active. When we remember Jesus in the Eucharist, we know that it is not only about remembering what happened in the past but that Jesus is present with the celebrants.[16]

THE ROLE OF MEMORY IN THE EARLY COMMUNITIES IN JESUS' TIME

In the New Testament, memory plays an important role in the forming of Christian identity. Early Christian communities preserved their memory of Jesus in oral form. New Testament scholar Werner Kelber posits that Jesus' teaching was subsequently represented through storytelling for present needs.[17] This tradition of preserving the past is carried on through repeated patterns of oral transmissions. The problem that can arise is that the repetition of the message by the second storyteller is perceived as if the story were told for the first time. The audience regarded the stories they were told as original while the storyteller always tried to keep the structural core of the original.[18] Thus, memory is preserved through the repetitive mode of memory transmission in the form of its structural core.

---

[14] Gerhard von Rad, *God at Work in Israel* (Nashville: Abingdon, 1980), 13.

[15] Gerhard von Rad, *Old Testament Theology*, vol. II: *The Theology of Israel's Prophetic Traditions* (Edinburgh: Oliver and Boyd, 1967), 104.

[16] Martin Luther holds that Jesus is really present in the tasting the bread and drinking of the wine. The remembrance in the Eucharist is an active one, the event is re-actualized every time it is celebrated.

[17] Werner H. Kelber, "The Generative Force of Memory: Early Christian Traditions as Processes of Remembering," in *Biblical Theology Bulletin* 36 (2006), 15. See also Werner H. Kelber, "The Works of Memory: Christian Origins as Mnemohistory," in Alan Kirk & Tom Thatcher (eds), *Memory, Tradition and Text*, Semeia 52 (Atlanta: Society of Biblical Literature, 2005), 221-48.

[18] Kelber uses Crossan's theory of *ipsissima structura* (structural core), John Dominic Crossan, *In Fragments: The Aphorisms of Jesus* (San Francisco: Harper and Row,

The action of preserving the memory of the past was motivated by the urge to keep the message alive for the present. Tradition is based on the stories and the actions to preserve those memories in the communities. The traditions are not accepted as such, rather, as Hendel claims, "tradition can—and must be—revised in order to retain its truth,"[19] because what matters most is the interpretation and revision of the past instead of truth or fiction. The remembered and reinterpreted social memory in the tradition will then form the identity of the new communities that received it. The purpose of remembering is "as a functioning social memory, e.g., as a continual process of commemorative activities, intent on commitment to the past and serving social relevance and identity in the present."[20] Precisely because of this mode and purpose of transmitting social memory, it comes as no surprise that memory was a strong force in the forming of the early Christian communities.

In these communities, memory was a powerful force behind the preservation of the tradition. Memory was more than a mere recalling of an event that had occurred in the past. Rather, remembrance served to relive and reexperience Jesus' teachings and make them relevant to the present context. Within the context of the early Christian communities, memory and the order to remember were vital in order to continue the tradition.

In *Jesus Remembered*,[21] James D. G. Dunn discusses the impact of the Jesus tradition. He is convinced that, during Jesus' time, remembrance in the oral tradition was so powerful that his teachings were remembered so vividly by his disciples and passed on to others as if the memory of Jesus were Jesus himself.[22] The memory of Jesus' teachings that was passed on through oral traditions was considered as valid as Jesus' teaching. Dunn agrees with Kelber that memory transmission, especially through the oral tradition, is intended to transmit the message rather than the actual facts. According to him, "in oral transmission a tradition is performed, not edited."[23] The essence of the memory lies in the core of the story and not in the detail.

1983). According to this, the community in Jesus' time preserved the tradition through a repetition of the structural core of Jesus' story.

[19] Ronald Hendel, *Remembering Abraham: Culture, Memory, and History in the Hebrew Bible* (Oxford: Oxford University Press, 2005), 98.

[20] Kelber, "The Generative Force of Memory," op. cit. (note 17), 21. He continues, "At this point, one can agree with the observations of Kirk and Thatcher that "every act of tradition is an act of remembering" (39) so that " 'tradition' is in fact the substance of 'memory'. " (40).

[21] James D.G. Dunn, *Jesus Remembered* (Grand Rapids: Wm. B. Eerdmans. 2003).

[22] See also Samuel Byrskog, "A New Perspective on the Jesus Tradition: Reflections on James D.G. Dunn's Jesus Remembered," in *Journal for the Study of the New Testament* 26.4, 461.

[23] Dunn, op. cit. (note 21), 248–49.

However, free interpretation does not mean that the story of Jesus can be interpreted in whatever way. Dunn believes that in the New Testament, Jesus' earliest community and followers passed on the tradition in a controlled manner. Dunn refers to Kenneth E. Bailey, a New Testament scholar specialized in Middle Eastern life, who identifies three types of oral traditions in the Middle East that were used during Jesus' time: formal controlled, informal controlled and informal uncontrolled.[24]

When tradition is transmitted via an informal, uncontrolled oral tradition the community does not express an interest in preserving or controlling the tradition. One example of this type of oral tradition is the spreading of gossip. He argues that Rudolf Bultmann's view on the synoptic tradition belongs to this type.

> Bultmann does not deny that there is a tradition stemming from Jesus, but asserts that it has, for the most part, faded out. The community, he feels, was not interested in either preserving or controlling the tradition. Furthermore, the tradition is always open to new community creations that are rapidly attributed to the community's founder.[25]

The second model is the formal controlled oral tradition.

> It is *formal* in the sense that there is a clearly identified teacher, a clearly identified student, and a clearly identified block of traditional material that is being passed on from one to the other. It is *controlled* in the sense that the material is memorized (and/or written), identified as "tradition" and thus preserved intact.[26]

The defender of this model is the Scandinavian Riesenfeld and Gerhardson school.[27] An example of this tradition is the memorization of the Bible,

[24] See Kenneth E. Bailey, "Informal Controlled Oral Tradition and the Synoptic Gospels," in *Asian Journal of Theology* (April, 1991), 34–54; "Middle Eastern Oral Tradition and the Synoptic Gospels," in *Expository Times* 106 no. 12 S (1995), 363–67. See also Dennis Ingolfsland, "Jesus Remembered: James Dunn and the Synoptic Problem," in *Trinity Journal* 27 NS No. 2 (Fall 2006), 187–97.

[25] Bailey, ibid., 38. Bailey quoted Bultmann to show his argument when Bultmann wrote, "I do indeed think that we can now know almost nothing concerning the life and personality of Jesus, since the early Christian sources show no interest in either, are moreover fragmentary and often legendary, and other sources about Jesus do not exist." See Rudolf Bultmann, *Jesus and the Word* (New York: Charles Scribner's Sons, [1934] 1958), 8.

[26] Bailey, op. cit. (note 24), 38.

[27] See Birger Gerhardsson, *Memory and Manuscript: Oral Tradition and Written Transmission in Rabbinic Judaism and Early Christianity* (Copenhagen: Ejnar Munksgaard, 1961, 1964).

hymns or the Qur'an as a way of preserving the content. Jesus used the mnemonic techniques of preserving the Torah when teaching his disciples. The church also recited Jesus' teachings under the guidance of the apostles. Until today, this tradition has survived in the Middle East where people recite and memorize the Qur'an or the Bible.

Bailey argues that while the gospels are too similar to be the result of uncontrolled oral tradition the fact that they are not exactly the same proves that this tradition is not fully formally controlled.

According to Bailey, the third model, which he calls the informal controlled type, is the model of oral tradition most likely to have been used during Jesus' time. The retelling of Jesus' story was informal in the sense that there was no "one correct story," but they were controlled in the sense that the stories had to be within certain more or less strict limits. What is important is that the core of the memory remains the same, while the way in which the stories were told could differ. It is the content not the detail that is crucial in the transmission of memory.

An example of this model is a gathering called *haflat samara* (a party for preservation), which until today still takes place in mainly isolated communities in the Middle East. The stories told in the form of *haflat samara* involve three levels of flexibility. During the first level, which includes poems and proverbs, not a single word can be changed and the public will correct the reciter should they make a mistake. This is a question of honor and no one wants publicly to recite poems or proverbs unless they are sure that they have accurately memorized entire passages. During the second level, the core of the story must not be changed but the way in which the story is told is subject to the storyteller's style. This level of flexibility applies to historical stories and parables that are of importance for the identity of the community. The third level gives the greatest flexibility and is used for telling jokes and sharing daily news or reporting on inter-communal violence.[28]

According to Bailey, at one point the stories about Jesus had to be preserved accurately. Yet, the different accounts of the story show that the informal controlled tradition is the best explanation for the oral tradition in preserving Jesus' teachings. James Dunn refers to Bailey's third model and concludes that Jesus' followers were careful to preserve and pass on the Jesus tradition, but because of the nature of the oral tradition in storytelling, the dialogue and oral interpretation may change slightly while the core essentially remains the same. The only realistic way to understand Jesus is to understand the way in which Jesus is being remembered.

---

[28] See Kenneth E. Bailey, "Informal Controlled Oral Tradition and the Synoptic Gospels," in *Asian Journal of Theology*, vol. 5, no. 1, 1991, 40–42; Kenneth E. Bailey, "Middle Eastern Oral Tradition and the Synoptic Gospels," op. cit. (note 24), 364, 366.

Although Dunn did not describe exactly how Jesus was being remembered, or what remembrance means for a society at the time of the storytelling, we can assume that what he was describing is how collective memory or social memory worked at the time of the early New Testament communities.

In Jesus' communities we sense a strong element of the Old Testament tradition of remembrance since the apostles were familiar with this tradition. The call to remember is also actively connected with a sense of identity. In the early Christian communities, memory was preserved orally in order to remember, recognize and to give a sense of communal identity.

THE EUCHARIST AND THE COMMAND TO REMEMBER

Our exploration of remembrance in the New Testament leads us to the Eucharist, celebrated to remember Jesus. Jesus himself institutes the command "to remember" in the Eucharist. The Eucharist is not a whole new tradition that Jesus created; it is indeed a continuation of remembrance expressed in the Passover meal. The past deliverance of Israel is retrieved for the present moment by making present Christ's redemptive act, and is to be remembered for the future. Jesus is the paschal lamb that is to be sacrificed on the cross, and his sacrifice is a unique, one-time event of lasting impact.

The Eucharist provides the opportunity together to celebrate the memory of the past, including one's own. The liturgy or the Eucharist is the place to celebrate the memory of Jesus' life, ministry, death, resurrection, ascendance and his promise to return. This memory is experienced as if Jesus himself were present in the celebration. This is what the disciples understood when they were celebrating it after Jesus returned to his Father. The Eucharist therefore functions as a safe place of communal remembrance. This remembrance can be used to heal other memories as well. The memory of God's saving act in Jesus helps the community to receive and change the emotion of the memory that they have.

One of the factors in the Eucharist is the forgiveness of sins during the communal meal. When forgiveness happens around the table, then the memory of the event can be preserved with a different meaning. It is not a memory of pain alone, but more: it has become a memory and a life story, a life lesson for the entire community. They will be enabled to give new meaning to what had happened in light of God's love for and forgiveness of all involved. The past is still there as is the story. Yet, personal remembrance can diminish when the person realizes that the community has remembered their pain. Then the memory is not only a memory of pain but is on the way of being transformed into a memory of healing, for both victims and perpetrators.

Three theologians have contributed their thoughts on the importance of memory in the Eucharist. First, Johann Baptist Metz, a Catholic theologian, reminds us that in the Eucharist we also remember the suffering of Christ, or *memoria passionis*. The remembrance of the suffering can be translated into remembrance of the past hurt. Thus, what Metz proposes is a theological basis for the remembrance of past hurt. Second, Alexander Schmemann, an Orthodox theologian, brings the Eucharist to the fore as the most important sacrament because of its communal aspect. Schmemann also reminds us of the centrality of the Eucharist in worship and theology. Because of its central place, we should be aware of any hidden motives for using the Eucharist for one's own purpose. And third, Miroslav Volf, a Protestant theologian, states that we should remember for the sake of embrace and reconciliation. His plea to remember truthfully is not only addressed to the victims and perpetrators but the entire community. There is a quasi handing over of personal memory to communal memory that is based on the theological premise that Christ will enable us to remember truthfully in love.

In the liturgy of the Eucharist we remember the suffering. If the perpetrators feel the pain of shame and regret about that which cannot be undone this implies that they recognize that they are in need of healing and forgiveness. The Eucharist invites and embraces us to come together as one and offers a safe place to let go of negative memories toward people who do not want to remember the past because it is too painful. At the same time, the Eucharist also offers a place of remembrance so that the memory of the past will not be lost.

MEMORY THAT DEMANDS

The formation of Christian identity was based on the preservation of the memory of Jesus. Recalling those memories demands that we act out our identity. Although in the oral tradition the remembering of details of a given event is not entirely unimportant, it is the emotional connection and the feeling of connectedness to the story that count. The memory of God's saving action is being re-actualized and re-member-ed, thus involving and claiming everyone who celebrates it.

The contribution of the three theologians have advanced the concept of active memory by saying that the remembrance of God calls us to remember the suffering (Johann Baptist Metz), to embrace everyone including those who have wronged us (Miroslaf Volf) and to produce a theology that is responsible to its context through the liturgy of the Eucharist (Alexander Schmemann). The concept of an active memory helps us to provide a theological foundation for remembering past hurt and the possibility to change the memory of the emotion. This is an idea that we need further to explore in the theology of remembrance and memory.

The elements of redemptive memory in the liturgy of the Eucharist will help people to reconcile with the painful past. In the new culture of remembrance, memory will most likely stay entrapped. Eucharistic redemptive memory gives us fresh hope that our remembrance of the past will not be a negative one. It encourages us to remember and deal with our past. When past hurt is being remembered, it will be transformed into a redemptive memory of God's remembrance.

Sacred Text, Revelation and Authority: Remembering and Transmitting the Word

Nelly van Doorn-Harder

When you read the Bible as a personal message to you from God, the words find their way to the depths of your conscience and spiritual sensitivity. You read with a spiritual awareness, your heart being open, receptive and ready for obedience and joy. Like living and distinct fingerprints of God's will and pleasure, they move, form and impress their divine, effective impact. In response, the deadened conscience revives [...]. Father Matta el-Miskeen (1919-2006).[1]

Introduction

Pondering the question of what makes a text sacred, I realized how my reading on the Orthodox churches has not only influenced my understanding of Scripture but also given me renewed appreciation for the way in which Martin Luther approached the Bible. My fieldwork among Coptic Orthodox Christians of Egypt opened new vistas on understanding how Christians throughout the ages have transmitted and interpreted the Bible in relation to the ongoing and living tradition of interpretations and extra biblical stories. This tradition started during the first centuries of Christianity and has become an inherent part of Orthodox Christian faith and practice. Furthermore, my research on Islam in Southeast Asia led me new levels of

---

[1] www.spiritualite-orthodoxe.net/vie-de-priere/index.php/matta-el-meskeen-
-orthodox-teachings/how-to-read-the-bible-matta-el-meskeen

understanding for the deep respect Muslims have for the sacred text of the Qur'an in its oral and aural forms and the powerful impressions reciting the text leaves on those reciting and those hearing it.

Religious texts become sacred and gain religious authority through the individual and communal responses of those who believe it to contain messages from the Holy. Christians believe the Bible to convey God's words and teachings and its text remains sacred and meaningful as, throughout the ages, communities of believers continue to read, recite and interpret it.

In this day and age, many might disagree with this specific interpretation of what makes a religious text sacred. Living in post-Enlightenment times, the influence of the historical-critical method, propagated by the German theologian Adolf von Harnack at the beginning of twentieth century, still influences our ways of thinking. To them the text was a historical source and speculating about God's will was seen as "unscientific." When the famous theologian Karl Barth threw a wrench in this approach, he was branded a "neo-Orthodox."

In retrospect I realize that the teachers who taught the theology classes I took at the University of Amsterdam, also worked along opposing paradigms. Nobody ever positioned themselves, however, and they seemed simply to present the texts as they saw fit. So we were treated to inspiring classes about the Old Testament where the teachers spoke about the Psalms as divinely inspired poetry, and mind-numbing hours on the New Testament. The New Testament professor went through one of Paul's letters by way of his stack of filing cards, ripping the text apart word for word. The fact that I cannot remember which epistle we studied is ominous at best. All that has stayed in my mind is that we spent days discussing the Greek equivalent of the word "orphaned," as in people feeling orphaned after Paul had left their community.

My scholarly work on Coptic Christianity and Islam, took me on a journey into the unknown. In some ways it was akin to what the Protestant poet Kathleen Norris experienced when she became a lay member, an oblate, of a Benedictine community. Her book *The Cloister Walk* is based on this experience and she describes, for example, how attending the daily liturgies opened her eyes to the relevance and immediacy of the Psalms: "In expressing all the complexities and contradictions of human experience, the Psalms act as good psychologists. They defeat our tendency to try to be holy without being human first."[2] Following the Benedictine rhythm of chanting or reciting the Psalms three times a day, Norris cannot but agree with the observation that "God behaves in the Psalms in ways he is not allowed to behave in systematic theology."[3]

---

[2] Kathleen Norris, *The Cloister Walk* (New York: Riverhead Books, 1996), 96.
[3] Norris is quoting British Benedictine Sebastian Moore, ibid., 91.

Norris's reminder that sacred texts are also liturgical texts that not only need to be read but also heard, allows many of us to gain a deeper appreciation and respect for the role the Torah and the Qur'an play in the lives of Orthodox Jews and Muslims. In fact, reading the text in silence is a rather recent phenomenon.

THE ORAL AND THE AURAL

In his by now classic study, *Beyond the Written Word,* William Graham suggests that "in most major religious traditions, sacred texts were transmitted orally in the first place and written down only relatively recently."[4] Although we tend to think of the Bible as the printed word, the oral dimension of the biblical text remains relevant today as it continues to be transmitted in sermons, meditations, poems and hymns. As Graham points out, at the heart of the Protestant Reformers' emphasis on Scripture as "writ" "was a vivid sense of the living, spoken Word of God that is communicated both in Christian preaching and in the reading of Scripture."[5]

In the sometimes hours-long chanted Orthodox liturgies we can observe a keen awareness of the importance of carrying and performing the biblical text. At the same time, they place the Bible within the context of an ongoing tradition that reaches back to the first centuries when the church as an institution was still developing. Deep study of the views and visions of the early Christian fathers continues to guide their practice of the faith and the ways in which they look at Scripture. The Orthodox approach has often been called "mystical" since it does not sharply distinguish between personal experience of the divine mysteries and the church's dogmas. However, mystical should be understood as a form of human awareness that is within every believer's reach. The nineteenth-century Russian Orthodox Metropolitan Philaret of Moscow, described this reality as: "none of the mysteries of the most secret wisdom of God ought to appear alien or altogether transcendent to us, but in all humility we must apply our spirit to the contemplation of divine things."[6]

In this essay I will focus on the voice of Egyptian Coptic Orthodox theologian Father Matta el-Miskeen or Matthew the Poor (1919–2006). Infusing the voices of Christians throughout the centuries into teachings for our time, his

---

[4] William A. Graham, *Beyond the Written Word. Oral Aspects of Scripture in the History of Religion* (Cambridge: Cambridge University Press, 1987), 4.

[5] Ibid., 143.

[6] Vladimir Lossky, *The Mystical Theology of the Eastern Church* (Crestwood, NY: St. Vladimir's Seminary Press, 1976/1998), 8.

internationally acclaimed book, *The Communion of Love,* among others, reflects on how the Bible remains relevant and vital for living in the twenty-first century. Based on sermons preached in the desert monastery of Saint Macarius during the 1970s, Matta el-Miskeen conveys a radical God-centered message that challenges our tendencies for human-centeredness and trusts in the ongoing working of the Holy Spirit to guide Christians on their life journey.[7]

While these teachings are often labeled as mystical, I shall argue that Father Matta el-Miskeen's vision would have appealed to Luther. After all, Luther fully believed that the Holy Spirit guided his readings of "the unitary and consistent Word of God," that to him was a whole that should be "read diligently in any of its parts."[8]

When reading Christian writings my studies of Islam insert themselves in as far as the Muslim understanding and treatment of the Holy Text are concerned. Finding similarities or interesting approaches to the Qur'an enriches our own considerations of what makes a text sacred and grants it religious authority.

As is the case in most Orthodox churches, Father Matta el-Miskeen's reflections on the Word of God were heavily influenced by the early fathers. In order to illustrate some of the language early Christian writers used to express their ponderings on the Divine, I will start the section below with the words of Hilary of Poitiers, Basil the Great and other great teachers of the church.

In search of the Divine

Despite having raised in the religion and values of the Roman Empire, Hilary, later Bishop of Poitiers, found purpose and meaning when he discovered the Old Testament that preached the living God "who transcends all things yet is present in them, outside everything yet inside, the ex-centric center, the 'author of beauty' disclosed in the beauty of the world."[9] Quoting the Psalm of David (Ps 139:7-10), Hilary expressed his sense of wonder about God's omnipresence:

> Where can I go from your Spirit?
> Where can I flee from your presence?
> If I go up to the heavens, you are there;

---

[7] Matthew the Poor, *The Communion of Love* (Crestwood, New York: St. Vladimir's Seminary Press, 1984). Father Matthew or Matta el-Miskeen, was the abbot of the Egyptian Monastery of St. Macarius.

[8] Graham, op. cit. (note 4), 146.

[9] Olivier Clément, *The Roots of Christian Mysticism. Text and Commentary,* transl. Theodore Berkeley, O.C.S.O. and Jeremy Hummerstone (NY: New York City Press, 1993), 18.

If I make my bed in the depths, you are there
If I rise on the wings of the dawn,
If I settle on the far side of the sea,
Even there your hand will guide me,
Your right hand will hold me fast.

When Hilary discovered the opening words of the Gospel of John, "In the beginning was the Word, and the Word was with God, and the Word was God" (Jn 1:1), his intellect "overstepped its limits," as at that point he learned more about God than he ever expected.[10]

Moved by the holy signs and words of God, St Basil the Great (330–379 CE), Bishop of Caesarea, summed up the history of salvation in the liturgy that continues to be sung in Orthodox churches across the globe:

> You visited [humanity] in various ways, in the loving kindness of your heart, You sent prophets. You performed mighty works by Your saints who in every generation were well-pleasing to You. You spoke to us by the mouth of Your servants, the prophets, who foretold to us the salvation which was to come. You gave us the law as a help. You appointed angels as guardians. And when the fullness of time had come, You spoke to us by Your Son Himself [...].[11]

This text reflects how the early church fathers understood the Word of God to have been embodied in three degrees that all led to Christ. The very existence of the cosmos that led ancient religions to deep spiritual understandings, the Divine revelation that provided the law and the history of those worshipping the One and Only God, and finally the Word incarnated. This final word, according to their understanding, gave meaning to the cosmic and the legal expression of the Divine: "freeing the former from the temptation to absorb the divine 'Self' in an impersonal divine essence, and the latter from the temptation to separate God and humanity."[12]

Contemplating the mystery of Christ as revealing the mystery of the living God moved the early Christians to tears and resulted in poetic outpourings such as the second-century Jewish-Christian text of *The Odes and Psalms of Solomon*:

> His love for me brought low his greatness.
> He made himself like me so that I might receive him.

---

[10] Ibid., 20.

[11] For the entire text, see **www.stlukeorthodox.com/html/orthodoxy/liturgicaltexts/divineliturgybasil.cfm**

[12] Clément, op. cit. (note 9), 35.

> He made himself like me so that I might be clothed in him.
>
> I had no fear when I saw him,
>
> For he is mercy for me.
>
> He took my nature so that I might understand him,
>
> My face so that I should not turn away from him.

Humanity could communicate with the Word of God through Scripture. Embodying the Word, Scripture then was an aspect of the incarnation. As a result, the early Christians considered the entire Bible to be one continuous moment of incarnation, representing the union between the Divine and human beings in the form of the Word that was brought to us by Christ. The Old Testament foretells what the New Testament declares and understanding the words happens in circles of initiation or levels of understanding. As Gregory the Great commented, "The mysteries of God are unveiled in one and the same language throughout all its writings."[13]

The leaders of the early church firmly believed that the Bible text was always alive. Through the work of the Holy Spirit, knowledge and understanding were not simply passed down but constantly renewed in persons and adapted to place and time. Origen compared the Scripture to an almond: the bitter rind is the literal letter that kills and numbs the mind and thus should be rejected. The protecting shell holds the teachings concerning ethics; this part requires a process of going into greater depth and a level of obedience and humility. To reach the third layer, one has to purify one's mind since it is the kernel that is the spiritual part; the part that matters and feeds the soul with the mysteries of the divine wisdom.[14] Matta el-Miskeen and Luther call on us, through the first two layers, to desire penetrating the third that is waiting to be found by all who try.

Understanding Scripture and translating it into our own historical context was a life-long endeavor that could not succeed when approached as pure science but needed the insights of the heart that only came with fervent prayer and deep humility. "Reckon prayer to be the key that opens the true meaning of the Scriptures," Isaac of Nineveh taught his disciples. And Gregory the Great taught that:

> Reading one and the same word of Scripture, one person is nourished by history only, another looks for the typical [from *typos,* the "figure" of Christ] meaning, another by means of this same meaning reaches towards the contemplative meaning. Most often, these three dimensions are found there at the same time... In this way the words of God advance at the pace of the reader.

---

[13] Ibid., 102.

[14] Ibid., 99.

> Sacred Scripture [...] tests the strong with its more obscure sayings and gives satisfaction to the simple by it concrete language, [...] it is intelligible to readers who have little culture, and educated people continually find new meanings in it.[15]

In the twentieth century, after many years of reflection and meditation on the Scriptures, Father Matta el-Miskeen equally stressed the fact that the Bible is not just a book about historic events. While describing events that convey the actions and words of God as well as the acts of humans who followed or rejected God's Word, the true goal of the text in Matta el-Miskeen's view is to "reveal the living God Himself in our own selves."[16] Matta el-Miskeen saw a single divine plan guiding the Scriptures as they were transmitted to us. Luther equally considered the Old and the New Testaments to convey God's plan in unison, seeing them as "an indissoluble, consistent whole, the ultimate purpose of which was to proclaim and to disclose the Christ."[17]

PRESERVING AND TRANSMITTING THE TEXT

In understanding the Scriptures and appreciating the value of the text by itself I remain deeply indebted to the Islamic tradition of memorizing the Qur'an. Across the globe, Muslims of all ages strive to learn parts of the Holy Scripture by heart, or to memorize the entire text. The prerequisite of any engagement with the Qur'an is the firm belief that it represents the Word of God. As one of the many handbooks on reciting the Qur'an states, "the reciter has to believe in the words of the Qur'an and fully accept its messages."[18]

The text itself is considered sacred and sanctifies the reciter and their environment by the mere act of chanting the words out loud. Remembering how he learned to recite the Qur'an recitation as a child, Imam Jamal Rahman writes:

> The sounds penetrate the Muslim body and soul even before they reach the mind. As a child I loved to recite from the Qur'an because I was told that God hides in its verses so that, as you recite them, God can kiss your lips [19]

---

[15] Ibid., 102.

[16] Matthew the Poor, op. cit. (note 7), 41.

[17] Graham, op. cit. (note 4), 146.

[18] Muhammad Ibrahim H.I Surty, *The Science of Reciting the Qur'ān* (Nairobi, Kenya: the Islamic Foundation, 1988/2000), 31.

[19] Imam Jamal Rahman, *Spiritual Gems of Islam. Insights & Practices from the Qur'an, Hadith, Rumi & Muslim Teaching Stories to Enlighten the Heart & Mind* (Woodstock,

Not only Muslims learn the text by heart but also Orthodox Jews memorize and recite the Torah, while Orthodox Christians still strive to memorize and recite the Psalms and parts of the gospel. Early Christianity equally relied on transmitting and preserving the stories about the teachings of Christ. The transmission of the eyewitness stories was an important part of spreading the new message that came to be written down in the gospels. When the authors of the gospels codified the oral transmission they believed that the Holy Spirit guided them.

During the 1970s, a Belgium Benedictine monk asked Matta el-Miskeen how he read the Bible and was told that one should take a passage and repeat it until it merges with the heart and mind. If necessary, one should read the text out loud for hours or days without end until one moved from hearing with the ears to hearing with the heart in order for the word to take root.[20]

Luther equally stressed the importance of reading and hearing the text until it took root:

> Secondly, you should mediate, that is, not only in your heart, but also externally, by actually repeating and comparing oral speech and literal words of the book, reading and rereading them with diligent attention and reflection, so that you may see what the Holy Spirit means by them. And take care that you do not grow weary or think that you have done enough when you have read, heard, and spoken them once or twice, and that you then have complete understanding. You will never be a particularly good theologian if you do that, for you will be like untimely fruit which falls to the ground before it is half ripe.[21]

Since the 1960s, The mystical or contemplative approach to reading the Scriptures as found in the Benedictine practice of *lectio divina* has made a comeback in the Catholic Church. This method equally sees the Scriptures as the living word that one has intimately to engage with. It consists of four steps: first taking a bite (*lectio*), then chewing on it (*meditatio*). Next is the opportunity to savor the essence of it (*oratio*). Finally, the word is digested and made a part of the body (*contemplatio*).[22]

Pope Benedict XVI stressed the role of the Holy Spirit in this method of studying the Scriptures, which he applied in his meetings with priests to let their discussions be guided by Scripture:

VT: SkyLight Paths Publishing, 2013), 4.

[20] Matthew the Poor, op. cit. (note 7), 29.

[21] Martin Luther, "Preface to the Wittenberg Edition of Luther's German Writings, 1539," in Helmut T. Lehmann (ed.), *Luther's Works*, vol. 34 (Philadelphia: Muhlenberg Press, 1960), 286.

[22] Gervase Holdaway, *The Oblate Life* (Collegeville, MN: Liturgical Press, 2008), 109.

One condition for *lectio divina* is that the mind and heart be illumined by the Holy Spirit, that is, by the same Spirit who inspired the Scriptures, and that they be approached with an attitude of "reverential hearing."[23]

READING THE TEXT

Luther as well as Matta el-Miskeen stressed the importance of how we approach the Scriptures. For most of Christian history, the teaching of the Scriptures was aimed at initiation into the sacred texts and practices of the church not just at finding information.[24] In this context, Father Maximos, the Greek Orthodox bishop of Cyprus, told a group of twenty-first-century pilgrims that "rationalists and fundamentalists fail to understand the spiritual meaning of sacred texts and the purpose for which they were written."[25]

According to Father Matta al-Miskin, when reading the Bible "we aim at understanding and not at research, investigation or study, for the Bible is to be understood, not investigated."[26] He discerned two ways of reading the text. Following the first way, one reads and puts oneself in control of the text, trying to subject its meaning to one's own understanding and then comparing it with the understanding of others. In the second way of reading, one places the text on a level above oneself and tries to bring one's mind into submission to its meaning.[27] According to him, the ultimate goal is spiritual understanding, not intellectual memorization:

> Spiritual understanding centers on the acceptance of a divine truth, which gradually reveals itself, rising on the horizon of the mind till it pervades all. If the mind and its reactions are brought into willing obedience to that truth, the divine truth continues to permeate the mind even more and the mind develops with it endlessly.[28]

Father Matta el-Miskeen considered approaching the text with one's intellect as an unproductive exercise since it "weakens the divine truth, and

---

[23] Cindy Wooden, "Chapter and verse: Pope uses Bible reflection to address 'his' priests," at **www.catholicnews.com/services/englishnews/2012/chapter-and-verse pope-uses-bible-reflection-to-address-his-priests.cfm**

[24] Tjeu van den Berk, *Mystagogie. Inwijding in het symbolisch bewustzijn* (Zoetermeer: Uitgeverij Meinema, 1999/2007), 23.

[25] Kyriacos C. Markides, *Gifts of the Desert. The Forgotten Path of Christian Spirituality* (New York, London: Doubleday, 2005), 92. The bishop referred to as Maximos is in fact Bishop Athanasius of Limassol.

[26] Matthew the Poor, op. cit. (note 7), 17.

[27] Ibid., 16.

[28] Ibid., 17.

strips it of its power and breadth."[29] "There is no intellectual means of entering into the gospel, for the gospel is spiritual. It must be obeyed and lived through the Spirit before it can be understood."[30] The ultimate goal is not to look for particular or tangible results, but to develop a relationship with God. The writers of the gospel did not produce:

> A meticulous text of a precise history that related things concerning a man named Jesus, but– quite to the contrary–to relate the living reality that stood before their eyes and hearts (i.e. the reality of the Lord Jesus Christ, the Son of the living God who filled their being, emotions, and faith) which had been recorded in their memory in utmost fidelity and precision.[31]

The early church leaders equally taught that mere understanding of Scripture was useless unless one obeyed its injunctions. This insight was the foundation that transformed Luther from an original thinker into an influential church reformer. According to Heiko Oberman, it was because Luther was prepared to test his observations and discoveries "against the Scriptures and ultimately to anchor it there."[32]

The early fathers compared the holy text to an ocean that we can never fully explore. According to Isaac of Nineveh:

> The soul marvels at the novelties it meets on the ocean of the mysteries of the Scripture. Even if the understanding that swims on the surface of the waters – the ocean of the Scriptures– is able to dive into the full depth of the meanings hidden in them, [...] study, provided it so desires, suffices for it to become firmly attached to the unique thought of the mystery.[33]

This metaphor of the Scripture as an ocean was also used by the great Muslim mystic and theologian Al-Ghazali (1058-1111 CE) who called his book on Qur'an recitation and interpretation *The Jewels of the Qur'ān*.[34] He refers to the Qur'an as a fathomless ocean and urges those reciting the text to sail to its midst in search of the jewels of its meanings. It will lead the seeker to a deeper appreciation of the text and move them from the

---

[29] Ibid., 18.

[30] Ibid., 20.

[31] Ibid., 59.

[32] Heiko A. Oberman, *Luther. Man between God and the Devil,* transl. Eileen Walliser-Schwarzbart (New York, NY: Doubleday, 1992), 153.

[33] Clément, op. cit. (note 9), 101.

[34] Al-Ghazālī, Abū Hamīd Muhammad ibn Muhammad al-Tūsī, *The Jewels of the Qur'ān: al-Ghazālī's Theory. (Kitāb Jawāhir al- Qur'ān),* transl. Muhammad Abul Quasem (London: Kegan Paul International, 1977).

apparent meaning (*zahir*) to the inner meaning (*batin*). This notion of the inner and the apparent meaning of the text resembles Origen's idea of the different layers of the Scripture that he compared to an almond. According to Origin, "The divine meaning of the Scriptures has to be gleaned from the letter of it and beyond the letter, through contemplation guided by the Spirit."[35]

Matta el-Miskeen's insistence that when reading, heart and mind should be connected, can be seen as a form of contemplative reading. For many centuries this contemplative reading of the Bible was part of a Western form of spiritual theology that countered scholasticism.

However, to attain deep understanding of the Scriptures, one also has to approach the text with an attitude of humility and obedience that allows for the heart to be touched. Only when we are prepared to submit to the truth can we reach a level of spiritual understanding that according to Matta el-Miskeen "expands with the knowledge of the truth, and the truth, in its turn, opens up into 'all the fullness of God' (Eph 3:19), to infinity."[36]

We continue to wrestle with questions about how to translate the ancient message into our present circumstances. Luther preached about the difficult process of "finding the thin line between using and abusing" the Scriptures:

> Whoever wants to read the Bible must make sure he is not wrong, for the Scriptures can easily be stretched and guided, but no one should guide them according to his emotions; he should lead them to the well that is to the cross of Christ, then he will certainly be right and cannot fail.[37]

In 1934, Bonhoeffer was firmly convinced that only a church that had "an intimate connection with Christ and was dedicated to hearing God's voice and obeying God's commands, come what may, including the shedding of blood," could withstand the Nazi regime.[38]

CONCLUSION

I have tried to provide some main points of discussion concerning questions about the relationship between sacred text and revelation and what

---

[35] Clément, op. cit. (note 9), 99.
[36] Ibid., 18.
[37] *WA* 1, 52, cited in Oberman, op. cit. (note 32), 173.
[38] Eric Metaxas, *Bonhoeffer. Pastor, Martyr, Prophet, Spy* (Nashville, TN: Thomas Nelson, 2010), 249.

makes a text sacred. Indirectly I have addressed the question about who the custodians of the revelation are. I drew a line from the early church leaders to more recent voices. My main argument was that the text to those who believe in it, who have dedicated their time and energy to transmitting and preserving it, agree on the premise that this is not an ordinary text that we can mine for historic, archeological and anthropological knowledge. These individuals consider themselves to have become its custodians who can interpret its sacred meanings. Being a custodian then not only includes being a specialist of the text, but also to take its message seriously and to apply it in daily life.

Father Matta el-Miskeen wrote that the academic type of reading, understanding, exposition and teaching has gained precedence in Christian churches throughout the world. He saw this reality as a sign that

> The Gospel has been reduced to a source from which one may quote verses or prove principles, and the ideas it contains have become academic points to support sermons and articles. So the Gospel has become a reliable way of gaining fame, academic degrees, and the admiration of the world.[39]

While bemoaning the "academification" of interpreting texts, Father Matta commits them into the hands of ordinary people who take them seriously since the gospel still has to be lived in daily life.[40] Luther was convinced that Christians are to engage in deep study, commit time and effort and trust that the Holy Spirit will guide their efforts in interpreting the Scriptures. From his own experience, he knew that such engagement can lead to deep transformation:

> The "Gates of Paradise" were opened to him and a flood of knowledge swept over him once he had succeeded in grasping the passage (Romans 1.17) in which Paul quotes the prophet Habakkuk: "The just shall live by faith" (Habakkuk 2.4). "I am not good and righteous, but Christ is."[41]

In our time, Father Matta el-Miskeen equally reminds us that we should approach the Scriptures with respect and the right attitude and raise questions from the divine perspective, not our own. To him, "any search for inner or outer peace outside of God" is bound to fail.[42] In his foreword to

---

[39] Matthew the Poor, op. cit. (note 7), 23.
[40] Ibid., 25.
[41] Oberman, op. cit. (note 32), 153.
[42] Matthew the Poor, op. cit. (note 7), 10.

The Communion of Love, Henri Nouwen writes that Father Matta's spiritual writings helped him to

> discover the true space: that "objective" space in which I can freely walk, raise the right questions concerning God's Love, and search for answers that gradually grow in me as I dwell in that holy space. These writings pull me out of my subjective rumination and introspection and lead me into a new and open space where God dwells and invites me to dwell with him.[43]

---

[43] Ibid., 10, 11.

IV. Case Studies: Twenty-first-century Formation of Community

Forming Roots in the Midst of Rootlessness: Religious Identity in the Pacific Northwest

Catherine Punsalan-Manlimos

I was raised in such deeply Christian cultures that my religious identity is an inextricable part of my self-understanding. The Philippines is one of only two predominantly Christian countries in Asia, boasting of almost ninety-five percent of the population being Christian with eighty-six percent Catholic. While I had a three-year experience of attending Sunday school at a Protestant church in my childhood, I was raised in a culturally Catholic context. While aware of the existence of other religions, until my move to the Pacific Northwest, I was immersed in contexts where some form of the Christian faith was always part of the air people breathe. Even my theological education brought me to a Catholic university whose student body's religious affiliation was not statistically different from that of the Philippines.

In such contexts, I could assume some shared vision of the human person, of the world and of God. While there are two millennia of different theologies and a still growing number of denominations in the Christian tradition, there are nevertheless shared stories and shared beliefs. Often, the points of contention among Christians are the implications of these beliefs for the concrete way people ought to live their lives and order communities. I taught Christian, particularly Catholic, theology largely by challenging people's common understanding of shared Christian beliefs. Critique and question served to strengthen people's understanding of what it means to claim to be Christian.

A little over a decade ago, I came to the Pacific Northwest region of the USA to teach at a Jesuit Catholic university. My experience of religious identity formation, which came from largely religiously monolithic contexts, hardly prepared me for the religious diversity I would encounter. Simply to question and critique the Christian faith in such a context would only serve to affirm the preconceptions of many rather than invite critical thought about religious identity. As director of Seattle University's Institute for Catholic Thought and Culture, one of my key roles is to create opportunities for people to learn about Catholicism and the Catholic intellectual tradition. In this paper, I share some learnings from this role. I begin with a few notes about the religious landscape in the USA in general and the Pacific Northwest in particular. I proceed to describe two programs at Seattle University and what they taught me about how to become more deeply rooted in my faith in the midst of what appears to be religious rootlessness.

A DIFFERENT RELIGIOUS CONTEXT: DIVERSITY AND NON-AFFILIATION

According to Robert Putnam and David Campbell, religious innovation and creativity can be found throughout the USA. Religious toleration and religious flexibility are descriptive of many parts of the country today. In *American Grace: How Religion Unites and Divides Us,* they argue that American religious life has always been characterized by innovation.[1] Such creativity and innovation are even more necessary in light of the uptick of North Americans who identify as religiously unaffiliated.[2] At the same time, sociologist José Casanova notes that the increased number of the religiously unaffiliated should not be read to mean that North Americans have become less religious. Instead, more North Americans are foregoing affiliation with traditional religious communities or groups.

Putnam and Campbell identify what they call a shock and two after-shocks to explain the current US religious landscape. The cultural revolution of the 1960s constitutes the shock with the rise of religious conservatism in the 1970s and 1980s and the youth's disaffection from religion in the 1990s and 2000s as the aftershocks. And it seems, we are still reeling from this second aftershock today.[3] The increase in non-affiliation appears to be less of a reflection of people's beliefs in God and more of a rejection of

---

[1] Robert Putnam and David Campbell, *American Grace: How Religion Unites and Divides Us* (New York: Simon & Schuster, 2010), 161–79.

[2] "Growth of the Nonreligious," Pew Research Center: Religion & Public Life, 2 July 2013, at **www.pewforum.org/2013/07/02/growth-of-the-nonreligious-many-say-trend-is-bad-for-american-society/**.

[3] Putnam and Campbell, op. cit. (note 1), 91–133.

religious organizations that are seen as "too concerned with money and power, too focused on rules and too involved in politics."[4]

The authors note that the major shift is not only towards non-affiliation but also religious tolerance. They posit that religious toleration has increased in the USA because the nation is becoming more religiously diverse. It is now more likely that one has a neighbor, a friend or a coworker from a different religious tradition.[5] At the same time, people become "spiritual but not religious." Casanova suggests that they embrace "different forms of "Sheilaism," the idea of an individualistic religious expression.[6] People move away from institutional religion but not from some form of religious faith. The exercise of individual freedom in the choice of religions happens not only in the denominational marketplace of religions but also in the choice of very individualized religious or spiritual expression. So, while there is an increase among the unaffiliated among North Americans, the USA remains a very religious country.

The direction of the shift in the religious landscape observed in the country has long been characteristic of the Pacific Northwest. In *Religion and Public Life in the Pacific Northwest: the None Zone,* historian and theologian Patricia Killen, along with her co-author, Mark Silk, describe the distinctiveness of the Pacific Northwest's religious landscape. Of the region they say:

> The Pacific Northwest is an open religious environment. This place is alternately indifferent or inviting to religion, an obstacle or opportunity, a refuge or revelation. Here, more than in other regions of the United States, weak religious institutions and the absence of a dominant institutional religious reference group allow for a highly elastic religious reality. This is a religious environment where boundaries and identities are fluid, where energy and movements coalesce and then dissolve... This physical and spiritual environment confronts all who enter the region with a set of religious tasks that involve clarifying individual religious identity, constructing social relationship, and making sense of the land itself. As they negotiate these tasks, individuals both adopt and exhibit the Pacific Northwest's religious ethos or style.[7]

---

[4] "Religion and the Unaffiliated," Pew Research Center: Religion & Public Life, 9 October 2012, at **www.pewforum.org/2012/10/09/nones-on-the-rise religion/**, para. 4.

[5] Ibid., 548-50.

[6] Casanova quotes one woman's description of her way of being religious: "I believe in God. I'm not a religious fanatic. I can't remember the last time I went to church. My faith carried me a long way. It's Sheilaism. Just my own little voice." José Casanova, "The Religious Situation in the United States 175 Years After Tocqueville," in Miguel Vatter (ed.), *Crediting God: Sovereignty and Religion in the Age of Global Capitalism* (Bronx, NY: Fordham University Press, 2011), 260.

[7] Patricia O'Connell Killen and Mark Silk, *Religion and Public Life in the Pacific Northwest: the None Zone* (Landham, MD: Rowman and Littlefield, 2004), 10–11.

Seattle University is a Jesuit Catholic University situated in the Pacific Northwest of the USA. Thus, it is no surprise that religious diversity, including non-affiliation or a non-traditional approach to religions, is found among the faculty and staff of Seattle University. Under these circumstances, an institution that is religiously affiliated and draws its mission and identity from this affiliation needs to create space for genuine, open dialogue about religions. The institution has to maintain fidelity both to its roots and also to the diverse commitments of those who advance its mission. Opportunities must be created where both those who embrace the Catholic faith and those who do not can express their particular religious or faith commitments or non-commitments. Anecdotally, some of those who identify as Catholic are reticent to be open about their religious affiliation for fear of either not being taken seriously as academics by their colleagues or for fear of being somehow misunderstood. On the other hand, those who are not Catholic are often suspicious of efforts by the university explicitly to promote its Catholic identity, fearing relegation to second-class status at the university. Yet, the response has been very positive when opportunities for genuine learning about Catholicism are offered and creative spaces for dialogue around it are made available.

A proactive effort to engage faculty in dialogue around religion for a religiously affiliated university, I believe, is critical. Many embrace the university's mission in general. While a number are aware of the religious roots of the university, and consequently its mission, the commitment to mission does not necessarily mean an embrace of the religious commitment that is at the heart of this mission. The opportunity to understand and unpack the religious roots of the university in a dialogical manner is crucial for a university that hopes to remain faithful to its identity as a Catholic university, while providing an opportunity for faculty and staff to explore the roots of their own commitment to the shared mission. The various programs offered at Seattle University that allow for learning about Catholicism have often also served as opportunities for participants to examine their own religious commitment or non-affiliation.

PROGRAMMING FOR ROOTING IN ROOTLESSNESS: THE CASE OF SEATTLE UNIVERSITY

Data is not available regarding the religious affiliation or non-affiliation of university employees. Nevertheless, various roles at the university have provided me with the opportunity to gather a sense of my colleagues' diverse religious commitments. At the same time, I have had the opportunity to participate in the creation of various programs aimed at both deepening the commitment to the mission in general and to the Catholic character of the university in particular. A sense of the university's religious landscape, of the various attitudes towards Catholicism in particular and Christianity in general is helpful in designing such programs.

To help illustrate the importance of sensitivity to an institution's religious landscape, let me describe two programs that have been implemented over the past five years at Seattle University. The first of these is the Women in Jesuit Mission (WJM), which is currently overseen by the Office of Mission and Identity. The second is the Summer Faculty Study Group, run by the Institute for Catholic Thought and Culture. Women in Jesuit Mission began as a gathering of Catholic women at Seattle University who desired to explore their vocation as women in the Catholic Church. The intention of the original group was to deepen their commitment to their work at the university by situating it in light of their identity as Catholic women in a shared mission. But as the group began to embrace a discerned need to move beyond the core group and offer an opportunity for other women working at the university to deepen their understanding and commitment to their work, the kinds of programs offered had intentionally to take into account the diversity of religious commitment or non-affiliation of the women on campus. They had to be aware of the religious diversity among the group that would explore a shared commitment to the university and its mission. At the same time, the impetus for the original group could not be disregarded in this broader religious space. What emerged under the leadership of Marilyn Nash, campus minister for Ignatian Spirituality and Jennifer Tilghman-Havens, assistant director of the Office of Mission and Identity, is a series of offerings that includes: retreats for women that is informed by the *Spiritual Exercises of St Ignatius*[8] but tailored to the spiritual and religious diversity of the women who choose to participate, and liturgies and prayer gatherings informed by a Catholic sacramental vision that invites "seeing God in all things" but executed in a manner where all feel invited and welcomed. The leadership style of these women is such that it allows for participants to take leadership in the group at various times, bringing in the particularity of the latter's experiences and expertise.

A second example is the Summer Faculty Study Group. The study groups are created to bring together primarily faculty to discuss the intersection of the Catholic intellectual tradition and a salient issue of discourse in public life. In its first years, the study group has taken up issues related to gender and sexuality, economic justice and violence, and

---

[8] "The Spiritual Exercises are a compilation of meditations, prayers, and contemplative practices developed by St Ignatius Loyola to help people deepen their relationship with God." See more at **www.ignatianspirituality.com/ignatian-prayer/the-spiritual-exercises**

the environment and social justice. A group composed primarily of faculty with various disciplinary expertise gathered for eight half-days of study and dialogue. Their task is to dig deeply into the various philosophical, biblical and doctrinal roots of contemporary Catholic teachings related to the topic for a given summer. They wrestle with how these teachings impact or might influence current discussions. The intent is to create a space wherein authoritative teachings from the tradition are presented, while inviting participants to identify the value and offer critique of these teachings in light of their expertise and experiences. By bringing together differing voices that represent diversity in terms of disciplinary expertise, religious identification, ideological commitments and life experiences, the study group provides an opportunity for a rich learning. Integration of the intellectual and personal, of the mind and heart, invites trust and genuine dialogue. Participants are able to identify shared and divergent assumptions. Subject matter experts on contemporary issues as well as the theological and philosophical foundations of the Catholic Church's teachings contribute their knowledge to the conversation. Participants have an opportunity to articulate constructive critiques of Catholic teachings in light of a deeper understanding of these as well as the expertise shared by colleagues. They are encouraged to bring their own disciplinary expertise as well as personal experience into the conversation. What is created is a space for personal, yet academic and well-informed dialogue.

It is also an opportunity for faculty of diverse religious commitments to learn about Catholic teachings and find those points of resonance and dissonance with their worldview. While intended to invite faculty into a deeper understanding of the religious tradition at the foundation of the institution, it also serves as an opportunity for them to bring their personal faith commitment to enrich the learning. Faculty participants point to both solid content and genuine dialogue as characteristic of these study groups. Most notably, the study groups model the university's goal of educating the whole person with faculty drawing not only on their academic expertise but personal experience as they dissect Catholic thought in relation to pressing current issues. Each iteration of the study group has led to increased intentionality in the inclusion of ritual and spiritual practice to inform the intellectual discourse. Doing so allows for an experiential introduction to the participants of the integration of the intellect and the affect.

A take away: Non-dominant bodies in leadership

While several things are noteworthy about these two programs there is one point I would like to highlight: the importance of non-dominant bodies in leadership.

Catholicism is hierarchical and patriarchal. While a global religion with the majority of adherents in the global South, it came to these places in most cases on the ships of colonizers. Not surprisingly, it has, until very recently, been deeply Euro-centric. The easiest symbol to recognize for the Catholic Church in the USA is probably the older, white male wearing a liturgical vestment presiding over Mass. The authority vested in such a figure has the potential to curtail creativity and dialogue and invite deference and submission.

While some Jesuits, those belonging to the priestly order that founded the university, have been involved in the programs I describe, the initiative and leadership have come from elsewhere. Women have been largely at the helm. The approach has been collaborative and invitational. I would argue that such leadership contributes to the atmosphere of openness to dialogue and open engagement with Catholicism. I suspect that the fact that I am a mid-career, Catholic woman of color has contributed to the receptivity of colleagues to my invitation to study and engage Catholicism. I do not carry in my body the markers of dominance that are associated with religion in the USA. I am not a vowed religious. I am not white. I am not male. I do not carry with me any unearned power due to ordination, color/race nor gender. Instead, I am, like most of my colleagues, a person of faith who seeks to grow in understanding of my tradition in conversation with others. I, too, as evidenced by the body that I bring to the table, have many critical and pointed questions to ask of this same tradition. I know I can learn from those with different faith/religious commitments, ethnic roots, sexual orientation, life experiences and disciplinary expertise. I happen to be a trained Catholic systematic theologian whose transcultural experiences lead me more to ask questions and seek ways to find answers than to offer them.

To create opportunities for shared leadership is empowering. To recognize the authority of disciplinary expertise and personal experience in studying Catholic teachings and contributing to Catholic thought is liberating. What is created is the possibility of dialogue and mutual learning. What it offers is a safe space to engage and consider what might be worthwhile in the Catholic and Christian intellectual tradition, its roots in the wisdom and knowledge of the past and its implications and potential for engagement with concerns of the present. It allows Catholicism to be engaged as a living faith tradition that simultaneously can be reverenced and questioned, as all traditions ought to be.

CONCLUDING REFLECTION

I have described the expanding effect of trying to remain rooted in a religious tradition in a religiously plural context. I discovered that dialogue with persons of other faith commitments has deepened and enriched my understanding and commitment to Catholicism. While it was the move to the Pacific Northwest that taught me this, Catholics today are receiving the call to dialogue from the head of the Catholic Church, Pope Francis, who has demonstrated a humble openness to learning from the laity, from the Catholic churches throughout the globe, from other Christian communities, people of other faiths and people of no faith. He humbly acknowledges those areas where he is no expert and seeks dialogue with those who are, so that the problems of our world, especially the condition of the most vulnerable and neglected, can be addressed. He does this by humbly embracing his authority while acknowledging the authority of others. Inspired by his Catholic faith, he humbly honors the faith commitments of others and invites all people to share in the common project of caring for our world.

The Renaissance that Never Happened: Considering the Institutional Challenges of Judaism in Germany

Paul Moses Strasko

Introduction

On 14 September 2006, the headlines in Germany proclaimed the arrival of what was once an unthinkable renaissance—a living, vibrant Judaism in the land that once had nearly decimated this same people and religion. The occasion of the headlines was the ordination of three liberal rabbis at the Abraham Geiger Kolleg of the University of Potsdam. This ordination served as a coming of age for post-Shoah Judaism in the land where the continuation of the religion was once anything but self-evident.

"The Miracle from Potsdam" read *Die Zeit* and quoted then president of Germany, Horst Köhler: "[This is a g]ift for our country for which scarcely anyone dared hope."[1] Other headlines focused on precedence[2] or that is was "an important sign"[3] while others more soberly called it merely "The First Step" and wrote:

> Was this ordination a sign of the much-vaunted normalization of Judaism in Germany? "To say so would be premature," answered Walter Homolka [the rector

---

[1] "Religion: Das Wunder von Potsdam," at **www.zeit.de/2006/37/Rabbi-37**
[2] "3 Rabbis Ordained as Judaism Re-emerges in Germany," at **www.nytimes. com/2006/09/15/world/europe/15rabbis.html?fta=y&_r=0**
[3] "Erste Rabbiner-Ordination ist ein wichtiges Zeichen," at **www.linksfraktion. de/pressemitteilungen/erste-rabbiner-ordination-wichtiges-zeichen/**

of the Abraham Geiger Kolleg]. And Dieter Graumann [current president of the *Zentralrat der Juden in Deutschland*] believes, "Normalization occurs only when you no longer have to discuss it." This event was a source of joy. Nevertheless, Graumann warned against too much euphoria. [He] cautioned: "Three rabbis do not make a Jewish summer. We need at least thirty times three."[4]

In addition to the hope and symbolism of this and subsequent ordinations, a plethora of books and articles published from the mid-nineties until the first years of the 2010s trumpeted this miracle of resurgent Judaism to the point that this author was quoted in *Die Zeit* as saying there is *"kein besseres Land für Juden."* There is no better place for Jews to live than Germany.[5]

Recently the emotional high has begun to fade in the wake of troubling signs. Non-Orthodox graduates of the rabbinical schools in Germany have begun to leave central Europe while others are un- or underemployed even with empty pulpits still in Germany—some empty after public disputes between community leadership and rabbis including lockouts and lawsuits. Previously disenfranchised members of the former Soviet Jewry majority began winning more board elections across the country, at times displacing all German-speaking leaders of previous administrations. One troubling incident, a physical altercation in the Senate of the Jewish Community of Berlin over financial issues, was captured on YouTube, showing the world the fraying seams.[6] Additionally, no amount of optimistic reporting could cover up the ever-more empty synagogues and lack of religious involvement across almost every community. This does not even begin to mention the effects of recent surges in anti-Semitism. On the one hand, there are groups such as Chabad, Limmud and the Jahrestagung der Liberalen Juden in Deutschland that sell out their tickets or fill their seats disproportionately to the visible reality of the majority of formal synagogues. Yet, there are community synagogues with thousands of members on their rolls that need to pay members to show up in order that a *minyan* be present for all services—ten men.[7]

Although these challenges are quite specific to the rebuilding and sustaining of a viable Judaism in Germany, they point to universal problems of evolving cultural needs, marketing, secularism, fundamentalism,

---

[4] "Der erste Schritt," at **www.juedische-allgemeine.de/article/view/id/6463**
[5] "Kein besseres Land für Juden," at **www.zeit.de/2012/15/DOS-Rabbiner**
[6] "Brawl breaks out among Berlin Jewish community," at **www.jpost.com/Jewish-World/Jewish-News/Brawl-breaks-out-among-Berlin-Jewish-community-314360**
[7] The idea of a paid *minyan* is not new to Germany, but was historically used to ensure the presence of ten men during weekday services that mourners could say *Kaddish*. The fact that paid *minyanim* would be required in even extremely large (more than a thousand) members on Shabbat is not only troubling, but also indicative of the dearth of attendance.

politics and daily relevance that are truly not that different from many of those that affect other religions inside and outside of Germany.

In this essay I shall focus on one aspect of the languishing Judaism in Germany: the failure of these formal structures built after the Shoah. Although arguments could be made for multiple points of failure, the primary argument here is that institutions built to support post-war German Jewry, namely the Zentralrat der Juden in Deutschland (ZJD) and the system of community synagogues or *Einheitsgemeinde*[8] and the assumptions and thought processes underlying these institutions, are woefully inadequate to address change and deal with a type of diversity that did not exist in 1950.

BUILDING INSTITUTIONS

In 1990 there were 30,000[9] Jews in Germany. Miraculous after the annihilation of Jews during the Nazi era, the 30,000 still represented an aging population with limited Jewish resources and opportunities. The decision of the German government in 1991 to open up the floodgates to Jews from the former Soviet Union (FSU), however, transformed Germany from a tragic backwater of Judaism to the fastest growing Jewish population and suddenly the ninth largest population of Jews in the world.[10]

Before this explosion, the previous fifty years had seen formal movement towards rebuilding from the ashes left behind after the Shoah. The ZJD[11] was founded in 1950 to allow for the continued integration and rein-

---

[8] The *Einheitsgemeinde* is not an invention of the post Shoah era, rather of the *Haskalah*. For a full treatment of the origins of the *Einheitsgemeinde* and its contrast to the evolution of Jewish communities in the USA at the same time, see Karlheinz Schneider, *Judentum und Modernisierung* (Frankfurt/Main: Campus Verlag, 2005).

[9] The 30,000 figure is an often misunderstood demographic figure, as it does not represent surviving German Jewry. The remnant of German Jewry rather could be more easily found in Israel through the "Yeckish Aliya" of the 1930s or the much greater number that fled to the USA.

[10] Although the 119,000 Jews in Germany represented still only a fraction of the 523,000 in 1933, the explosion of German Jewry gave not only the impression on paper that Judaism was once again alive, but also that there was a "raw material" with which to create vibrant communities. The 119,000 included children and young adults, young married couples and, especially in earlier waves, highly educated professionals—all the raw materials of new life. This number represents the number of "registered" Jews, or German residents that listed their religion as "Judaism" for tax purpose. This number does not include in many cases Jews of patrilineal decent or non-practicing Jews that chose "no religion" in registration for tax or anonymity purposes, among others.

[11] Translated as the Central Council of Jews in Germany and named such as opposed to the Central Council of German Jews. The new organization acknowledged

tegration of the 37,000 Jews living there at that time, and to aid the West German government in its effort to support rebuilding the infrastructure that had been decimated.

At the community level, the buildings meant to support a 100–200 person membership could no longer service the new multitudes that arrived in the 1990s. New buildings had to be built, new personnel hired to aid in social and integration work[12] and new rabbis and cantors brought into the country. The ZJD had been formed essentially to deal with a completely different Jewish demography, culture, history, language and even self-identity than the one standing on the doorstep speaking Russian.

This led to two immediate problems: programming and *halachik* (legal) status. Regarding Jewish status, while Jewish legal identity was determined either through matrilineal descent or through legal conversion, national identity in the FSU was passed through father and Jewish identity was a stamp in the passport that said "Jewish" under the heading "nationality." As some immigrating FSU Jews tried to gain enfranchisement in Germany, often the first questions asked were if they could prove their Jewish status. After three generations of forced secularism this often was not possible. With the overwhelming amount of functioning Jewish communities led by Orthodox rabbis, Jews that had been persecuted for the stamp in their passport were now told that they were not Jewish.[13]

With this immediate rift between the existing Jewish infrastructure and the newly disenfranchised Jews, potential numbers that could bolster the renaissance were lost immediately to disappointment.[14] A common attempt at a solution was to turn the *Einheitsgemeinde* into integration offices.

---

in 1950 that the majority of Jews remaining in Germany at that time came from "displaced persons" camps as opposed to groups of returning German Jews.

[12] The German government essentially outsourced certain integration work for the masses of Soviet Jews through the communities to which they had been sent. This included German language instruction, vocational instruction and social integration help. For an example of how this manifests, for the Jewish community of Duisburg, Mülheim/Ruhr and Oberhausen in North Rhine Westphalia there was roughly a membership of 200 in 1990 which swelled to 2700 in the 2000s. In order to support the new numbers, a new synagogue and community center were built in 2000 along with satellite offices in three other locations, each with a full-time social worker or integration specialist.

[13] Paperwork that would act as "proof" could include Jewish marriage documents (*ketubah*) of the mother or maternal grandmother, for example. Such paperwork, however, requires a functioning religious community, including leadership to execute the documents and constituents wishing to participate in the religious traditions.

[14] Although there are no figures or studies to determine just how many were turned away from synagogue life in these early days, that damage can at least minimally be extrapolated from the number of FSU Jews that choose no religious affiliation

Instead of focusing on rebuilding Jewish knowledge and identity, communities moved away from religion as a primary raison d'etre, focusing instead on paying for social workers, integration workers, funding chess clubs and FSU cultural specific parties and dances in the hope that the attendees of the FSU social gatherings would somehow spill over into greater religious attendance.[15] This focus was further supported by the ZJD and the German government's specific funding of integration activities such as language classes. In reality, the social activities seldom translated into a significant increase of service attendance.

Yet, the sudden appearance of at least numerically enough Jews to warrant hope of a viable Jewish life led to new efforts in the 1990s and beyond to build diversity into religious life in addition to institutions to support the diversity and by default challenge the institutions of the status quo.[16] Lauren Rid, president of the progressive community in Munich, articulated the outreach intentions behind this diversity in addressing issues of contemporary Jewry: "Because we are such a new community, we reach people that self-identify as *'jung und jüdisch'* [young and Jewish] who in reality possess few roots in the old-fashioned Orthodox world of Munich or outside Germany."[17]

Progressive[18] communities began to fight not only for existence but state recognition, including an attempt to build a progressive rabbinical seminar to aid in building leadership for these communities if not implicitly

---

in Germany. As mentioned earlier, 119,000 are members and between 250,000 and 270,000 Jews or people of Jewish descent live in Germany.

[15] Further to demonstrate the absurdity of the crossover, across nearly all Jewish communities in Germany, without exception, the most attended and celebrated "holiday" is 9 May, the day of the victory of the red army over Germany. In the Jewish Community of Duisburg (JGD) in 2013 there were 390 attendees and in 2014 just over 400. (Source: JGD security logs)

[16] For a comprehensive treatment of the rise of Progressive Judaism in Germany from a journalistic perspective, see Heinz-Peter Katlewski, *Judentum im Aufbruch* (Berlin: Jüdische Verlagsanstalt Berlin, 2002), 105–50.

[17] Ibid., 113.

[18] Terms such as "Reform," "Liberal" and "Progressive" are not used consistently in this presentation, reflecting the inconsistency and lack of understanding of the terms in Germany. Generally speaking, although Reform began in Germany in the nineteenth century, it is considered an American phenomenon and the term is usually substituted with "Progressive" to reflect the international body of Reform Judaism, the WUPJ or the World Union of Progressive Judaism. "Liberal" is at times used interchangeably with "Progressive," but can also refer to the radically different German Liberalism of the thirties as reconstituted in communities such as Pestalozzi Strasse in Berlin—such communities are not egalitarian and are "Liberal" in that they have a choir and organ. Conservative Judaism in Germany is gener-

for the purpose of combatting the tacit Orthodox nature of post-war German Judaism. Outside Germany, however, formal organs of Judaism from various streams had been loath to give support to Jewish institutions in Germany, a situation not aided by infighting among the small handfuls of leaders in Germany.

Yet Rabbi Walter Homolka continued his efforts, battling for official acknowledgement of non-Orthodox Judaism, founding the Abraham Geiger Kolleg rabbinical seminary and ordaining the first rabbis educated in Germany since the Shoah, eventually founding the AGK Cantorial School, the Ernst Ludwig Ehrlich Studienwerk (ELES)[19] and the Zacharias Frankel College.[20] In addition, he ensured the solidification of ties between these efforts in Germany and the World Union of Progressive Judaism, Hebrew Union College and the Rabbinical Assembly as well as being instrumental in founding the Jewish School of Theology at the University of Potsdam, the first state funded School of Jewish Theology in Europe.[21]

The reality nonetheless remained that the vast majority of Jews in Germany, based on location, old definitions of membership and simple inertia, did not shift their support to the newer WUPJ congregations and few of the new, German-educated rabbis outside of Orthodoxy, have been able to obtain or maintain positions in an *Einheitsgemeinde* or find other means of full-time rabbinical employment inside Germany. The new institutions simply seemed not yet a part of the old way of doing business.

CASE STUDY: DUISBURG

The Jüdische Gemeinde Duisburg, Mülheim/Ruhr, Oberhausen (JGD) with 2,700 members boasts the second largest membership registry in North Rhine Westphalia and the seventh largest in Germany.[22] Before the nineties, the total membership barely topped one-hundred after the reformation

---

ally referred to as "Masorti" and Synagogues that call themselves "Conservative" generally mean anything from "more conservative than Liberal" to "Orthodox."

[19] ELES was founded in 2008 in order to provide financial support to Jewish students at high school and university levels in Germany and throughout Europe.

[20] Frankel was founded in 2013 in partnership with the Ziegler School of Rabbinical Studies in Los Angeles, a Masorti (Conservative) institution related to the Jewish Theological Seminary in New York. Although the Frankel School shares the same administrative umbrella as AGK, the course of study, policies and directorium are separate.

[21] "The School of Jewish Theology," at **www.juedischetheologie-unipotsdam.de/index/information-in-english.html**

[22] "Gemeinden," at **www.zentralratdjuden.de/de/topic/59.gemeinden.html**

of the community in the fifties by either returning or surviving German Jewish families.[23] The hall in Mülheim/Ruhr where they met had become obsolete with FSU immigration and the community eventually built a new synagogue (1999) on land in Duisburg in an industrial wasteland that slowly became prime real estate in the 2000s.

The growing pains with such a numbers and culture shift became apparent in how the community proportioned its funding. In 2013, JGD paid three full-time social workers[24] in addition to one business manager and one administrator. All cantorial, rabbinical and educational duties were performed by a single rabbi with the exception of kindergarten through fourth grade education.[25] In addition to this, JGD paid a private security firm, comprised primarily of FSU community members, to staff the bullet-proof glass security booth at the synagogue entrance as well as providing "minijobs" to other FSU members.

When I took over the position of rabbi of JGD in July, 2012, the previous two rabbis had left only after court battles with the JGD board. After years of infighting between "Russian" Jews and "German" Jews,[26] between rabbis and JGD boards and even between different factions of FSU Jews, service attendance had dwindled to less than fifteen per service, eight to twelve of whom were "paid" *minyan* members.[27]

There was an initial dramatic increase of attendance,[28] mostly due to an influx of families from the surrounding region that wished to attend

---

[23] For a comprehensive history, see Barbara Kaufhold, *Juden in Mülheim an der Ruhr* (Duisburg: Salomon Ludwig Steinheim-Institut für deutsch-jüdische Geschichte, 2004).

[24] Often given titles such as "Integration Manager" in order to be eligible for certain state funding.

[25] A Jewish community of similar size in the USA, for example, might pay 2-5 rabbis, 1-2 cantors (in addition to rabbinical and cantorial students), a full-time educator in addition to other paid teachers plus a full-time business manager and administrator as well as building maintenance, janitorial services, etc.

[26] Even though these two terms are the most common used in Germany to describe the polarity in German Jewish Communities, it is important to remember, as noted earlier, that the "Germans" comprise of a mix of descendants of Jews from all over Europe left behind in displaced persons camps in addition to some surviving or returning German Jews, while the "Russian" Jews in truth came from Russia, the Ukraine, Lithuania, Latvia, Moldova, Georgia, Armenia, Azerbaijan, Kyrgyzstan and Kazakhstan, among others.

[27] JGD did not offer cash payments to its "paid" *minyan* as is often the case but, rather, provided a monthly 2 zone transit pass for the VRR regional transportation authority of the Ruhrgebiet. (Source: Personal Journal).

[28] Over the course of the first six months, service attendance doubled and then tripled on average reaching a peak of 45–60 per service, before slowly decreasing over the next year. (Source: Personal Journal).

a synagogue other than their own *Einheitsgemeinde*. The new numbers included primarily Progressive Jews without a non-Orthodox option in the region—religious Jews looking for a viable religious community. The institutional models of membership, however, slowly reduced most of the gains back to nearly zero, leaving once again little more than the paid *minyan*.

As opposed to a system such as in the USA or Switzerland, where membership is based on application and donation or dues, the mingling of church and state in Germany means that the membership rolls are solely determined by the number of residents of a specific district that check "Jewish" on their registration forms. Although it varies by state, generally nine percent of the total tax burden is collected as a "church tax." The "church" that receives these funds depends on registration. Those paying no taxes, such as those on social welfare, are required to pay five Euros a month as *Kultusgeld*[29] to the house of worship of their chosen faith in their administrative district.

What this meant for the JGD was that of the 2,700 people that had checked "Jewish" on their registration forms, eighty to eighty-five percent were on welfare and contributed no significant financial support. A total of less than 600 were active in synagogue life.[30]

As can be seen with Duisburg, the German membership model also leads to a lack of choice. The ZJD explicitly works via the *Einheitsgemeinde* system where with few exceptions there is no competition. The American Jewish Yearbook describes the problem:

> Owing to the historical development of church-state relations in Germany, Jewish communities were always organized as *Einheitsgemeinde*, in which religious, social, and financial services were administered under a single institutional roof. The *Einheitsgemeinde* were thus the sole recipients of financial support from the state. As the example of Berlin demonstrated, this arrangement could accommodate a pluralistic religious community. More often, however, the religious life within the *Einheitsgemeinde* was dominated in the postwar era by Orthodox rabbis.[31]

If you live in a city, you can only be a member of that synagogue. If you go elsewhere in search of a more fitting community, regardless of how often you attend and how much you donate, you cannot be a member of that community or be otherwise enfranchised unless you move your place of

---

[29] Literally, ritual funding.
[30] Less than 600 voted in the 2014 elections, roughly 300 attend the Hanukah and Purim balls, the largest social events in the community. (Source: Personal Journal).
[31] David Singer et al. (eds), *American Jewish Yearbook, 1999* (New York: American Jewish Committee, 1999), 150.

domicile to that city.[32] In this system, there is no effective competition under the auspices of official Judaism, and only outside groups with alternative funding such as Chabad have had any viable success in challenging the dominant paradigm.

Out of the nearly seventy rabbis listed in the two rabbinical conferences in Germany, more than two out of three are Orthodox, and out of the non-Orthodox, less than twenty serve as full- or part-time community rabbis, five of whom serve as sole rabbis in an *Einheitsgemeinde*.[33] The reality of Judaism is that although it is possible for non-Orthodox to lead more traditional services and to cater for many of the Orthodox needs, the same is simply not the case in reverse. The end result is a basic lack of any choice whatsoever for the vast majority of (mostly secular) Jews living in Germany where only an *Einheitsgemeinde* exists. It could therefore be argued that Orthodox Judaism is the de-facto state sponsored Jewish denomination of Germany with very few actually Orthodox Jews living in Germany.

IMPACT AND LESSONS

With the Duisburg experience as an example of normativity in Jewish Germany today it would be fair to assume that the infrastructure building itself had been a flawed enterprise. Yet, any formal expression of religion requires an educated clergy, spaces and materials, funding to pay for infrastructure and salaries and communication and integration between the organs of the religion—the exact services offered through the *Einheitsgemeinde* and sponsored by the ZJD. Formal religion with these elements has at least a chance of survival.

---

[32] There are few exceptions. The Berlin *Einheitsgemeinde* functions as an umbrella organization that supports Sephardic and Ashkenazi Orthodox synagogues in addition to Masorti (Conservative), Reform and German Liberal. In Frankfurt am Main there is an egalitarian community that meets in a side chapel in the main Westend Synagoge under the auspices of the Frankfurt *Einheitsgemeinde*. The other synagogues partially or completely independent of *Einheitsgemeinde* system, including the twenty-four that are members of the World Union of Progressive Judaism (see www.liberale-juden.de/gemeinden/), have had various degrees of success in securing federal/tax funding, but as a whole still represent about 4000 total members out of the 119,000 total registered Jews in Germany.

[33] Both the *Orthodoxe Rabbinerkonferenz* (clearly meant for Orthodox members) and the *Allgemeine Rabbinerkonferenz* (for Reform, Masorti/Conservative, Renewal, Reconstronctionalist and other) are official organs of the ZDF. See the membership rolls and biographies for the two rabbinical conferences, at **http://a-r-k.de/rabbiner/** and **www.ordonline.de/rabbiner/**

When the FSU Jewry began the mass immigration of the nineties, the disparity between the assumptions and practices of the mostly Orthodox institutional rabbinate and the secular Jews from the FSU has created an immense rift. Yet there are exceptions. Groups like Chabad have had unparalleled success in spite of their epitomizing the religion that so many in Germany reject. This is not an attempt to glorify Chabad, rather to point out that working outside formal structures has produced results that are simply not the reality in the *Einheitsgemeinde*. The very concept of an *Einheitsgemeinde*, where all streams and philosophies must somehow exist under one administrative roof, contradicts diversity or any ability to search for a better fit, be it Chabad or a Progressive community.

Indeed, organizations and events like Limmud and the Jahrestagung that like Chabad draw disproportionate numbers can be explained in contrast to the seemingly unchangeable reality of the *Einheitsgemeinde*: there you can meet a diversity of Jews and have a choice as to what types of services to attend and which lectures or panels to visit.

The universal message that springs forth from this tale of pathos seems to be that religion remains relevant, but that the best intentioned structures that support religion doom it to failure if they are not willing to divest themselves of the hindrances to relevancy. There are simply too many choices and religious audiences are no longer captive. The universal human expressions that gave us religion now need to compete with more pervasive and exciting idolatries of secular marketing and technology. Germany and its Jewish renaissance are not ready to be relegated to a cautionary tale as long as communities still exist and those that are within the community search for relevance in spite of the challenge of governing organizations.

The Changing Face of Religions in Southern Africa

Herbert Moyo

Introduction

In Africa today religion does not appear to be threatened by secularization and/or the natural sciences. Instead, we can observe considerable growth, mainly in Christianity and Islam. Africans are becoming increasingly religious, with the majority practicing a form of religious syncretism between African Traditional Religions (ATRs) and either Christianity or Islam. While to my knowledge there has never been a time in the history of Africa that people were not religious, the increasing religiosity of the African people raises the question as to what the role and future of the church in Africa are and who authenticates whether the religious voice is truthful or diabolical.

This essay will discuss contemporary trends in the church's ministries such as the performing of miracles, spiritual healing and advocacy in the quest for improving the socio-economic, political and religious spheres of human life. I shall demonstrate the dynamics between church traditions in the light of miracles, spiritual healing and interventions in the socio-economic and political conditions of society.

Background

Christianity has existed in parts of North Africa since the first century CE.[1] According to the *Atlas of World Christianity*, African Christianity has

---

[1] Thomas C. Oden, *How Africa Shaped the Christian Mind. Rediscovering the African Seedbed of Western Christianity* (Downers Grove, IL: InterVarsity Press, 2007);

experienced rapid growth: from less than ten percent in 1910 to nearly fifty percent in 2010, with over seventy percent in sub-Saharan Africa. These figures have been corroborated by the 2011 Pew Research Foundation Report on Global Christianity according to which Africa has seen the fastest numerical (sixty-fold) growth of Christianity between 1910 and 2010.[2] In the twentieth century, Africa went from a majority of ATR followers to being predominantly a continent of syncretic Christians and Muslims.

Given these immense growth rates and the significance of African Christianities there is more than one reason to emphasize the strategic relevance of the African churches in terms of social and political development, good governance and human rights in Africa. Christianity plays an important role in civil society in the areas of peace and conflict resolution and the protection of human rights. In the twenty-first century, African Christianities have increasingly become subject to transformation processes for justice, education and human rights. It will be crucial for the future of African Christianities to develop a new understanding of their own historic role—on the continent as well as globally—and to develop a better concept of how the complex issues and demands of African identity, unification and the challenges of peace, reconciliation and ecological disasters on the continent can be answered by the fellowship of African churches in collaboration with other progressive religious movements.

AFRICAN CHRISTIANITIES AND THE MINISTRY OF HEALING

In Africa, religion is premised on the realm of the supernatural. In the face of death, incurable disease, bad luck and spiritual challenges, people from all walks of life turn to religion in situations that are beyond human control. This applies to people from all religions—ATRs, Christianities and Islam. Religion is viewed as the key to that which human beings cannot unlock.

In the realm of the supernatural, the most common reference is made to sickness and prosperity. Healing is central to the quest for religious intervention. In the pursuit of healing and prosperity many Africans are happy to belong to more than one religion as, according to the ATRs, belonging to multiple religions is not a problem. Since the different gods of the various religions one belongs to are powerful, this gives increased powers to those who adhere to different religions. Contrary to Judaism, Christianity and Islam, ATRs are not monotheistic.

Thomas C. Oden, *The African Memory of Mark. Reassessing the Early Church Tradition* (Downers Grove, IL: InterVarsity Press, 2011); http://earlyafricanchristianity.com/
[2] **www.pewforum.org/Christian/Global-Christianity-exec.aspx**

The future of Christianity lies in its ability to respond to the socio-economic and healing needs of the African people and it is challenged to respond to diseases such as HIV-AIDS, TB, malaria and many waterborne diseases. Churches experiencing exponential growth are founded on healing. They perform miracles and spiritual healing in the name of Jesus and miraculous healing crusades, camps and sessions are held where people profess to have been miraculously healed. For example,

> on many television channels across sub-Saharan Africa, images of people living with HIV being "miraculously healed" are being aired. In some instances, people living with HIV form their own queue carrying placards that indicate their specific health challenge. The "man of God" will then touch the person living with HIV and declare them delivered in "the name of Jesus."[3]

In many instances people are given holy water or holy pieces of strings of wool to use as tangible sources of healing.

In Zimbabwe, popular church leaders such as Makandiwa, Uebert Angel and Johanne Masowe attract thousands of people seeking healing. Many Africans value the services that are being offered and therefore do not mind paying to access these church leaders. In South Africa, there are also several miracle healers such as Motseneng Mboro and Pastor Chris, and those church leaders who do not promote miraculous healing do not attract a large following.

For Christianity to be comfortable in Africa it has to resonate and inculturate with ATRs. "The beliefs and practices of ATRs seek to secure health and eliminate pain and suffering. Salvation in ATRs is to a very large extent earth-bound: health, prosperity and longevity in this world."[4] Similarly, according to Laurenti Magesa,

> [...] from beginning to the end, from birth to death, African religion stresses and orients its adherents, directly or symbolically, towards the abundance of life' motif. Thus birth, all the rites of passage marking different stages in the development of the vital force, and indeed earth itself as the culmination of life, receive special attention in African Traditional Religious activity.[5]

---

[3] Ezra Chitando and Charles Klagba, *In the Name of Jesus! Healing in the Age of HIV* (Geneva: WCC Publications, 2013), 2.
[4] Ibid., 6.
[5] Laurenti Magesa, *African Religion: The Moral Traditions of Abundant Life* (Nairobi: Pauline Publications Africa, 1997), 250.

The rates of growth between mainline churches, Pentecostals and African initiated (independent) churches (AICs) vary with AICs growing extremely quickly because of their healing crusades. The liturgy is based on healing and problem solving. Some movements are called hospitals to explain the centrality of healing.

The growth of the Pentecostal churches and AICs can also be explained by the spiritualization of materialism. In Zimbabwe, prophets such as Emmanuel Makandiwa of the United Family International Church, Uebert Angel of Spirit Embassy and Walter the Magaya of Prophetic Healing Deliverance (PHD) Ministries perform miracles for material gain. There is popular money miracle where the prophet prays that a church member gets money and the following day there is money on the church member's bank account. Prophets pray for people to have homes, money, cars, businesses, designer clothes and employment. In the case of witchcraft, the prophets are said to cast away evil spells in the name of Jesus.

HEALING AND RELIGIOUS IRRESPONSIBILITY

In their healing ministries the churches have shown a considerable level of irresponsibility. Discouraging the taking of tried and trusted forms of medication constitutes a criminal act on the part of the church. For example, some people have stopped taking antiretroviral drugs claiming to have been miraculously healed; this has resulted in drug resistant strains of HIV. The government has thrown doubt on the healing practices of the church and the question of who authenticates the voice of the church in its ongoing healing mission needs urgent attention.

CELEBRATING THE GOD OF LIFE AND STANDING UP FOR DIGNITY AND JUSTICE

As one of the key players in civil society, African Christianities significantly contribute to the continent's social and political development. Africa is riddled with corruption, partisan politics, political violence, rigged elections, genocides, tribalism and wars, all of which negatively impact the socio-economic sphere and result in the abuse of human rights, economic meltdown and the mass movements of people as refugees.

The mainline churches are usually the conscience of society, with individual pastors as well as certain Christian institutions prophetically advocating against questionable political developments. Despite the fact that many Southern African countries are secular, Christianity is respected by about seventy percent of the people. The voice of the church is respected as the voice of God. Christians are responsible for being concerned about the structures of society as well as the morality of individuals who make up society.

In light of the violent African political landscape, the church is called to be society's conscience and to bring about tolerance, consensus and cooperation in order positively to influence the quality of life on earth. The church should use its wealth and heritage of ethical teachings to speak prophetically in defense of human dignity and human rights.

The church can dialogue with political leaders, government representatives and community organizations on issues concerning the welfare of society. In Africa the church continues to deliver services that should be provided by the government. For example, through its diaconal ministry the church responds to the government's failure to provide hospitals, schools and hospices. The church contributes certain values, such as equity for example, to the earthly kingdom and is called to continue to be the voice of the voiceless.

The responsible participation of the church in politics brings its own challenges. In most cases, the AICs are happy with the status quo. They are the campaign grounds of the ruling political parties such as the Madzibaba in Zimbabwe and Shembe in South Africa. Pentecostal churches, on the other hand, claim neutrality with regard to earthly matters concentrating rather on the kingdom of heaven. The church's failure to speak with one voice can lead to confusion. Which church voice should society listen to?

Some governments have created pro-government Christian councils to speak on behalf of government and in opposition to councils that are critical of the government. The pro-government associations are given ample space in the partisan government media to speak positively about the government in religious and theological terms. There is no authority that has a mandate to authenticate these religious voices.

THE ROLE OF AFRICAN CHRISTIANITIES IN NATION BUILDING

Despite the multiple voices of African Christianities the church has a role to play in nation building. This is justifiable because over seventy percent of the population in Africa south of the Sahara are Christian. Nation building is the process of reinforcing the common bonds among the people of a nation state, region and continent for general stability and prosperity.[6]

---

[6] Béla Harmati, *Church and Nation Building* (Geneva: Lutheran World Federation, 1983), 7.

African Christianities in the twenty-first century should be fostering moral and ethical values such as rectitude, honesty, love, tolerance, joy, reconciliation, forgiveness, righteousness and self-criticism. African Christianities should be visible in contexts of social development and speak the truth there where a transcendent voice is needed.

In communities, pathologically divided according to ethnicity, gender, linguistic, tribal, cultural and economic structures that hinder nation building, Christianity can provide an example by being unified in diversity. Christianity can bring together people from diverse backgrounds, worshipping the same God and fostering common values, common symbols, a common sense of progress, common participation in decision making, equality before the law, mutual respect for others and mutual tolerance. Moreover, by providing explicit theological and ethical foundations for nation building, grounded in biblical references, it can be a constructive, credible force in society safeguarding the human dignity of all people.[7] The authentic voice of the church must choose the path of dialogue and cooperation rather than confrontation, while denouncing injustices.

Christianity can build a nation by holding the community together through communal rituals that emotionally and psychologically bind people together as one family. This is done by providing religiously sacred norms and values as moral foundations for social organization.

Christianity is also used to legitimate governments in Africa and some presidents are sworn in by bishops. The presence of the Bible authenticates and ritualizes the ceremony and if the church and the Bible are used in the swearing in, society seems to respect such a government as the legitimate authority.

SACRED TEXTS IN THE AFRICAN CONTEXT

In Christianity, sacred texts are viewed as symbols of truthfulness and holiness and are respected as authentic, even if their message can be used for diabolical purposes. Once a statement or "voice" can be traced to a sacred text, Africans accept the voice as legitimate. The Bible is referred to as the Word of God and doubting it is tantamount to doubting God. This is so despite the fact that sacred texts, such as the Bible, do not speak with one voice. An uncritical acceptance of the Bible does not take into consideration that there is no monolithic understanding of biblical verses and narratives. The Bible, a symbol of the truth, is used in courts of law where those testifying place their hand on the Bible and say "...so help me

---

[7] Ibid., 9.

God."[8] A religion that uses a sacred text as a source of its message relies on the sacred text to authenticate its voice.

The religious voice is not always life affirming and since it is an authority onto itself it can be dangerous to society if it transmits information. An example of this is when the religious voice advocates miracle healings rather than the use of tried and tested medication such as ARVs. Courts of law and scientific societies should have the right to sanction the religious voice in such cases. Christianities and Islam continue strongly to impact people's lives and substantially contribute to human development and nation building. God does not only speak to us through the church and theology but calls us to use our reason and knowledge e.g., the natural sciences and medicine.

---

[8] David Popenoe, B. Boult and P. Cunningham, *Sociology* (Cape Town: Prentice-Hall, 1998), 325.

V. Intersection of Identities

Ummah at the Intersection of Identities

Celene Ibrahim-Lizzio

Identity and critical theory

Over the last sixty years, trends of knowledge production in the academy have ushered in increased consciousness about how vectors of identity, such as class, gender, ability, ethnicity, religion and others, shape experience and prime humans to understand and interpret their social world in varying ways. Identity has become a phenomenon that is regularly discussed and analyzed within the humanities and social sciences, in particular. In this discursive sphere, identity is not merely about our patterns of social belonging that influence the ways in which we cooperate—or not—with one another on the basis of shared aims and values. Since the mainstreaming of psychoanalytic methods, it is possible to speak about the "socially structured field within the individual,"[1] wherein various identities exist simultaneously and prompt humans to feel, think and act—sometimes in contradictory ways or according to "unconscious" desires. Hence, identity can be a based on physiology, or circumstances beyond individual choice or control, such as ethnicity or dis/ability, but identity is simultaneously a social identification that can be actively aspired to, such as membership in a socioeconomic group or a social distinction that is cultivated with great dedication and expenditure. The patterns of behavior that reinforce identity

---

[1] David Ohad and Daniel Bar-Tal, "A Sociopsychological Conception of Collective Identity: The Case of National Identity as an Example," in *Personality and Social Psychology Review* 13, no. 4 (2009), 354–79.

can be referred to as an individual's habitus, to evoke the sociological term popularized by Pierre Bourdieu.

Identities shift as individuals encounter one another, change locale and acquire new knowledge, new languages and new conceptual systems. Hence, processes of identity formation constitute fertile ground for interdisciplinary and critical scholarship. In this vein, the effects of popular culture and media on identity formation emerged as a robust field. With the relative ease of global travel and connectivity for large segments of the population, new identity groups are regularly brought about or consolidated through technological innovation. Technological connectivity itself has shifted the possibilities of what constitutes an identity. Enhanced interconnectivity and the online presence of countless interest groups enable individuals readily to form identity groups around hobbies and social causes. Here, identity entails a sense of self or uniqueness, but it simultaneously connects individuals to larger social networks.

Different identities are laden with social capital such that the consequences of holding a particular identity—intended or unintended, material and immaterial—can be quite profound for the so-identified individuals. The degree of identification with socially valued collectives influences quality of life intangibles, such as self-worth, self-confidence and sense of life satisfaction. Conversely, individuals with socially devalued identifications can be readily isolated on the basis of this identity, as has historically been the case with identities that coalesce around skin tone. This potentially isolating effect is also an acute experience for individuals with identities that challenge historically dominant identity paradigms, as has been the case with sexual identity. In this way, socially constructed paradigms create axes of normal—to—aberration, and desired—to—undesirable. This insight is at the heart of much of feminist and queer theory's attempts to point out the significance of gender hierarchies.

Particularly since the rise of feminist, gender and queer studies, academics have produced a plethora of studies on social hierarchies and privilege. Here, identity is not only about physiology, sense of self and life choices, but it is about how larger human collectives regulate the distribution of resources and capital. Liberation theology also combines this observation about resource distribution with the conviction that theology should be worked out from the perspective of the poor and oppressed as the frame of the theological picture. Such politics of identity production, regulation, suppression, inclusion and exclusion are perhaps most overt in the case of national identities, where the "in groups" and the "out groups" or the dominant groups and the subservient groups are made to be distinct vis-à-vis documentation, fences, policing and the resource distribution of the state, corporations and other powerful actors. Postcolonial studies, and its proponents in theological circles, have helped bring these dynamics to the forefront of academic conversations.

At the level of governance, politics often begin and end with the dynamics of identity inclusion and exclusion. Acquiring control over the distribution of resources and gaining ever greater access to wealth, and in turn life's luxuries and comforts, is often at the core of the many global conflicts that pit one identity group, religious, national, ethnic and others, against another. In the face of such conflicts, the core insight of theologies of pluralism is that religious identity, belief and practice should never—in an ideal world—be used as a mechanism of domination and control. This conviction is, in fact, at the heart of secular-liberal aspirations for the ideal public sphere, where individuals are (ideally) at liberty to choose a religious identity, but they are also (ideally) at liberty to desist. This modern modality for the conceiving of religious identity—alongside the historic failure of large religious collectives to act according to the values they proclaim—has generated large numbers of individuals who happily identify as "nones" (people of no religious affiliation), who sometimes identify as "spiritual but not religious," or who are humanists that engage in interreligious discourses.

Transnationally, the relationship between religious identity and governance is a pressing affair, particularly as governments engage in legal and electoral struggles to establish "freedom of religious expression" and to determine where the protections and entitlements offered to identity groups begin and end. Debates over women's veils in public institutions and debates over hate speech verses free speech are such instances. This tension between identity-based rights and the reach of secular law is also clear in the arena of biopolitics. Debates over abortion, access to birth control, who is eligible to marry whom and other matters, bring debates over personal liberty and the greater good into sharp focus. Legislation on these matters sparks passions of religious coalitions and identity groups on all sides of the issues. This is merely one way in which religious identities become embroiled in electoral politics. At times, the intensity of public debates can cause religious identity groups dramatically to rupture into sub-identities. The spectrum of Jewish perspectives on Israeli government policies, and the various, competing coalitions that have been generated as a result, is an example of one such rupture.

In the spirit of this overview that attempts to capture the many dimensions at play in a discussion of identity, and religious identity in particular, my paper addresses core theological questions from a practical, applied theological perspective: What is God's vision for the world? What is the human response to God's vision? What is the place and purpose of religion in human life? From my perspective, within Islamic theological studies, the questions are fairly straightforward and have clear answers within the Qur'an and prophetic Sunna: God is self-sustaining, but humans are utterly dependent on God. God created humans so that God could be known; it is human's purpose to stretch their capacity, to strive to the furthest extent of their ability, by performing strange rituals, by abiding by laws, by training their desires, all to "know" God. Most humans fail to do this—some fail miserably. The purpose of religion is to help us not to fail miserably.

The theology is simple—until it becomes embodied and embedded in the experiences of actual religious communities who are, at their best, struggling to live up to their standards of piety and devotion, striving to take clues for how to best do so from their scriptures and exemplified by their prophetic forebears and their saints. Rather than think about religious identity in a contextual vacuum, I draw my insights and examples primarily from the North American context. I explore the intersection of Muslim religious identity with other markers of identity, including national identity and gender identity. In this process, I point to instances were identities are brought together in distinctive, revealing ways, such as in the case of interreligious marriage and religious conversion. I probe these essential questions in a way that highlights the experience of religious communities that strive to be relevant, inclusive, adaptable and simultaneously true to their core ethical principles and theological convictions.

MUSLIM IDENTITY AND NATION

References to "the Muslim world" or "the Muslim community" are commonplace in the discourse of scholars, politicians and policy makers. My anecdotal evidence suggests that the phrase is also a common one among congregants, merchants, taxi-drivers and spirited adolescents who make up the quintessential "street" in any given local. Yet, however much this term "the Muslim world" makes for quick an easy reference, it is a nebulous term. What is meant by this phrase? All Muslims globally? A collective of Muslim-majority societies? A combination of the global Muslim-majority societies and societies boasting substantial Muslim populations? What, then, counts as a substantial Muslim population? India? Nigeria? Perhaps, France? What about smaller minority populations? Are Muslims in America, Tennessee, Brooklyn, or Seattle part of "the Muslim world?" Do these Muslims make up an entity that can be called the Muslim nation? What does it mean to have a religious nation in the era of nation-states?

As someone who may be considered part of this "Muslim nation," and as someone who came to the community as an Anglo-American convert, I am continually amazed at the intra-Muslim diversity, a diversity that defies any homogenizing descriptor. Even the identity descriptor Muslim itself reveals relatively little about a person's theological commitments and religious practices, and it speaks nothing to the range of other intersecting identities that a person may have. There is, in fact, a large assortment of theological ideas and devotional practices that shape and inform individual religious subjectivity, which all fall under the umbrella identity of Muslim. I have even met Muslims who prefer to describe themselves as "trying to be Muslim," i.e., trying to be in the state of being in submission and servitude. I have also met Muslims who self-identify as secular Muslims, and even Muslims who are Muslim merely on account that a birth certificate or other such document proclaims as much.

Beyond the arena of religious subjectivity and practice, diversity among Muslims in some ways reflects broader global categories, such as "white" or "colored," etc.; but there are identity categorizations too that are somewhat unique to local experience such as, in the American context, "indigenous Muslim" and "immigrant Muslim," categories whose meanings have shifted with the passage of time. North American Muslims are founding institutions that represent constituencies with blended identities, and so-called "third-spaces" are emerging that often deliberately seek to defy and transgress old identity categories. To bring this discussion to the theological level, the questions then become, What is the *umma?* What is the twenty-first-century *umma?* Who is included, who is excluded? And what are our mutual obligations across identity borders?

MUSLIM IDENTITY, UNITY AND COMMUNITY

In the North American Muslim context, and in other locales, one of the most important, current grassroots conversations involves how to make Muslim community centers, civic organizations, representative bodies and alternative collaborative spaces truly inclusive of the rich diversity of Muslims in America. Towards this end, in April of 2014, The Prince Alwaleed Bin Talal Islamic Studies Program at Harvard University in Cambridge, Massachusetts, in cooperation with the Institute for Social Policy and Understanding, hosted an auspicious two-day forum that drew together North American Muslim scholars, activists, artists, performers, community-builders, social entrepreneurs and thought leaders to brainstorm best practices and new avenues and for creating inclusive spaces, telling authentic stories, leading Muslim institutions and meeting the needs of North American Muslims. As a part of this collaboration, we brainstormed regarding both long-term aspirations and concrete, practical steps to make Muslim community centers and institutions inclusive to the breadth of Muslim identities, from secular to religious, Shi'ite to Sunni, African to Asian, female to male, first-generation to fifth-generation, gay to heterosexual, wealthy to economically underprivileged, socially liberal to conservative, etc.

In other places, very different questions face the Muslim *umma*. In the era of the disintegration of the institutions of the nation-state in many places, where basic services cannot be provided, where there is poverty and starvation, or where warfare abounds, what is the place of the religious nation? What is the meaning of *umma* vis-à-vis the push in various locales to establish an Islamic state? For Muslims living as minorities in economically prosperous nation-states, what is the right balance between supporting and fostering the establishment of Muslim cultural centers and foundations to promote community in these places on the one hand, and the broader, yet equally pressing obligation to think about community in more global terms, on the other? All of these questions are essential for exploring God's vision for the world, the human response to God's vision and the place and purpose of religion in human life.

MUSLIM IDENTITY AND COEXISTENCE

Amidst the plurality of transnational, cultural, doctrinal and intra-Muslim identity differences, there is a pragmatic need for cultivating a sense of unity, a shared identity that does not derive from uniformity, but from recognizing common aims and shared stakes, not only among Muslims but between Muslims and their neighbors of multiple faith and ethical and civic orientations. Providing a range of quality social services and having a unified front against prejudice and discrimination are two distinct areas where unity, these being intra-Muslim and interreligious, has been a priority. North American Muslim organizations, ranging from the Muslim Public Affairs Council (MPAC), now a quarter century old, to the newly founded Muslim Anti-Racism Collaborative (MuslimARC), attest to this ability for Muslims to organize around a common identity for pragmatic, political aims.

Collaboration between Muslim communities and other American faith and civic action communities has been building rapidly. Despite the devastation caused by criminal minds waving religious banners, and nation-states that claim religious identities but do not act upon their convictions, the success of intra-religious organizations (e.g. The New York City Muslim Consultative Network) alongside interreligious initiatives (e.g., the Sisterhood of Salaam Shalom), are particularly impressive and commendable. These partnerships and relationships have only become more robust in the face of severe adversity from contrarians and exclusivists, who see difference as threatening. Much progress has been made in terms of collaboration across religious identity borders and, at the same time, much work remains. What are the best strategies and practices for building coalitions to work to dispel injustice and hypocrisy?[2] How can human's best respond to the plurality of religious paths? How is religious plurality part of God's vision?[3] In the quest for renewal, these are essential questions.

MUSLIM IDENTITY AND SECULARISM

Another pressing aspect of religious identity is how to hold that identity in societies that are secularized or rapidly secularizing. One response is an artistic one. North American Muslims with blended identities and duel commitments to religion and country have catalyzed what may be seen as a new artistic movement, whose cultural products blend religious symbols and values with secular culture. The consumers of such artistic products are both Muslims integrating or already utterly integrated into the North American social fabric, as well as Americans who are skeptical of, or ignorant about, Muslim integration. In both senses, the artistic movement can be described as an initiative to bring about awareness of diversity and integration (unity not uniformity). This push includes individuals and artistic collectives such as country music artist Kareem Salaama, whose 2007 "A Land Called Paradise," directed by Lena Khan, featured a candid array of American Muslim voices. The controversial Mipsterz (Muslim Hipsters) 2013 video rendition of "Somewhere in America," by popular rap artist Jay-Z, also generated robust intra-Muslim dialogue on religious identity and assimilation, as did the video by Chicago-based Rayyan Najeeb, filmed to the smash hit song "Happy" by singer and producer Will Pharell. The video features an eclectic array of smiling and dancing American Muslims. Also noteworthy in the artistic and popular culture realm is the 2014 premiere of the character Kamala Khan as Ms Marvel by a team at Marvel Comics.

Such artistic collectives fuse expressions of Muslim identity with elements of mainstream North American culture in an artistic and cultural push to present Muslims in both their ordinary and extraordinary lives. These productions and others have been described as a "new Muslim re-

---

[2] For some preliminary observations, see Anna Halafoff, "Countering Islamophobia: Muslim Participation in Multifaith Networks," in *Islam and Christian-Muslim Relations* 22, no. 4 (2011), 451–67.

[3] An increasingly robust literature on Muslims and interreligious relations includes contributions by Jerusha Tanner Lampety, Hussein Rashid, Homayra Ziad, Jospeh Lumbard, and others.

naissance," and attest to the sense of flourishing that is made possible by intra-Muslim and interreligious, and artistic and civic collaboration.[4] On the other hand, salient fears about how much assimilation is too much are also fueling high-stakes debates that involve intergenerational dynamics and shake up the socially conservative/liberal fault lines that are pronounced within North American Muslim communities.

MUSLIM IDENTITY, CONVERSION AND RADICAL HOSPITALITY

Religious conversion can be another fraught topic because it entails a rejection of community or a turning away from a given theological conviction. For the community that is left, or for individuals that hold the theological conviction that is explicitly rejected, anger, worry or fear can readily be evoked. On the other hand, converts bring an influx of diversity, knowledge and experience into their new community and can serve—with some finesse and practice—as bridge builders between the new religious community-of-belonging to the previous one. Conversion is not merely rejection; conversion can be an invitation for expanded connectivity and the forging of new composite communities of belonging.

What does this look like on the ground? Muslim converts are integrating in—and contributing to—North American Muslim communities in growing numbers.[5] This has several implications, including making religious identity even more porous. It also means, in the North American context for instance, that any given non-Muslim is even more likely personally to know—and maybe even care for and about—a Muslim neighbor, friend, acquaintance, or even family member. The personal connections have the potential to humanize the religious and cultural other, or at least provide the impetus to learn a little more, or slowly to let down the intra-personal guards caused by unfamiliarity. From a theological perspective, it is an opportunity to cultivate love over fear, to open doors rather than to shut them. This is part of the ethic of hospitality that is found in multiple manifestations across multiple religious traditions: on the one hand, we must care for the traveler's in our midst and, on the other, we are all wayfarers in this world.

Religious conversion also brings up questions of hospitality in a different way. How can a host community be hospitable and supportive of the new members? As I see it, the essential needs and desires for new Muslims, and long-time con-

---

[4] Rabia Chaudry, "A New Muslim Renaissance is Here," in *Time Magazine* (April 2014).
[5] Ihsan Bagby, "The American Mosque 2011: Basic Characteristics of the American Mosque Attitudes of Mosque Leaders," in *Report Number 1 from the US Mosque Study 2011* (January 2012), 12-13 for information on conversion rates and demographics.

verts are quite similar to the needs of other members of Muslim communities: nurturing, supportive spaces to learn, probe, explore and bond with one another. New Muslims often enter the realm of faith with a steep learning curve; but what Muslim does not have more to learn about their faith? New Muslims often embark on their journey with only a little Arabic language capacity; but how many Muslims at large have travelled the full terrain of classical Arabic? New Muslims may be searching for direction with family or work relationships that have become strained on account of their religious conversion; but how many of us could not benefit from a map in our attempts to navigate these relationships more generally? New Muslims may need basic information on how to pray, but who among the seasoned Muslims has perfected prayer such that there is no more to learn? New Muslims may crave bonds with co-religionists, whose words and presence can further lead them on the path, but who out there is not, at heart, yearning for guidance and support? New Muslims may thirst for more of the intellectual stimulation that drew them to the faith, but what scholar can claim that they have drunk until dry the well of learning?

Dynamics of conversion are fraught with old questions that need new answers. For instance, should Muslim women's marriages with non-Muslims be recognized? What religion are children in a multireligious household? Perhaps most pressingly is the issue of conversion *away from* Muslim identity, an area in which much work remains to be done.

IDENTITY, BIASES AND BIGOTRIES

There are many Qur'anic commandments that instruct Muslims about how to live as individuals in a nation or community. Perhaps the most essential is to cultivate radical compassion, what many refer to as the "golden rule": cultivate virtue such that we wish for another human what we wish for ourselves. The Qur'an also suggests in that "getting to know one another" and "competing with one another in goodness" are essential aspects of God's vision for humanity. What is clearly not part of God's vision for humanity is identity-based biases and bigotries. Biases and bigotries are expressed in a myriad of forms and across cultural contexts. Biases and bigotries are carried from generation to generation; they rise—and are manipulated—in times of conflict and in the midst of power struggles for supremacy and where economic interests are at stake. Even, in times of relative peace, lingering biases are given expression in a myriad of cultural, political and artistic forms. Biases ebb and flow according to political circumstances; however, where bias occurs, even subtly, it is critical to confront it in compassionate ways, and to strive for better reconciliation between potentially conflicting groups, so that dignity can be protected and conflict assuaged.

This is clearly a fraught process, but it is one that can be well worth the effort when done with sincerity and persistence.

The biases are well known and studied, but they are also entrenched and persistent. Biases may not even be overt or intentional. Often they are a result of misinformation or over-generalization. As I find myself often repeating in the North American context that: "not all Muslims are Arabs—not even a majority of Muslims are Arabs—not all Arabs are Muslims, and not all Middle Easterners identify as Arab." On the other side of the biasline, I often find myself explaining: "Israel is a nation-state, and the collective Jewish civilization across the centuries, and an eschatological vision of hope." Or, I have to point out that: "Western can signify a geographic origin or a sociopolitical standpoint; it can sometimes be taken to be synonymous with Christendom; it cannot be simply assumed that something of Western origin is inherently superior." How we understand the Other is not merely an abstract academic question. Rather, it has direct bearings on organizing social institutions and enacting public policy.[6]

Biases and bigotries tend to minimize the nuances, the liminal spaces, the ambiguities and the incongruences. Biases and bigotries destroy our shared religious optimism for a future that is just, equitable and peaceful, an optimism that is at the core of many temporal and eschatological visions for the world. Biases and bigotries are an unserviceable means for understanding identity—religious or otherwise, and perhaps the most striking point about biases and bigotries is that we all have them—even when we say we do not.

Muslim identity and queerness

One of the most overt identity biases within the Muslim community is against queer identity. Particularly because it has the potential to be so divisive, the issue requires extended attention and contextualization.

In the latter half of the twentieth century, feminist critiques of religious texts and traditions facilitated and inspired a broader dismantling of such notions as gender complementarity and compulsory heterosexuality. Even as anti-queer religious coalitions fortified their positions to promote compulsory heterosexuality and an ideology of gender complementarity, considerable numbers of Jewish, Christian, and Muslim scholars employed historical and philological methods to highlight gender biases and formulate alternative interpretations of religious texts. Although un-reading religious proscriptions on female–female eroticism was one immediate objective of such feminist

---

[6] See Fathali Moghaddam, *Multiculturalism and Intergroup Relations: Psychological Implications for Democracy in Global Context* (Washington, DC: American Psychological Association, 2008).

scholarship, the results were further reaching, taking aim at the very forces of orthodoxy that stood to determine which sexualities and sex identities were included in more exclusive definitions of religious polity. In light of such feminist critiques, the rhetoric and attitudes toward non-cisgender and queer sexualities evolved within the fold of North American Jewish and Christian congregations and representative bodies from the 1970s to the turn of the twenty-first century. There are to some extent Muslim queer identity groups and mosque congregations that support queer identity, but they are not prevalent. It bears noting that stances regarding same-sex sexuality and sex identity within religious communities and representative organizations, are not only pertinent to members of a given community; religious coalitions frequently campaign and exhort influence in electoral politics, legal debates and wider policy circles. Realms of religion and civil governance are dynamically connected, particularly on the issue of marriage, which is a nexus where religious and civil authority converge.

Queer sexualities exist at a political, ritual and hermeneutic borderland, where the boundaries of what constitutes normativity are contested and renegotiated within the religious polity at multiple rhetorical sites. These include the definition of marriage and access to its benefits and privileges within the life of religious communities; the conception of personal autonomy and the policing of permissible forms of sexual engagement (e.g., who may exercise desires with or upon whom and how); the standards and processes by which community leaders are endowed with norm-setting authority, and the texts, traditions, rituals and ceremonies that serve to communicate that authority and legitimacy to congregations and wider constituent bodies.

Some religious polities have maintained highly fortified positions on same-sex sexuality and others are presently internally divided with regard to the acceptance of same-sex desire and expression. A number of sizable religious groups have gone through internal discursive processes and have, in gradualist steps over the course of several decades, shifted their own internal borders with regard to regulating sexuality. A number have come to take assertive stands against compulsory heterosexuality and particular forms of discrimination based on sexual preference or sex identity. Reconstructionist and Reform Jewish groups, and in the most recent decade also Conservative Jewish governing bodies, have all come out with statements in support of certain or all civil and/or religious rights of gay, lesbian, transgender and queer-identified people.[7] Often in alliance with

---

[7] For an overview of such trends see Ellen M. Umansky, "Jewish Attitudes towards Homosexuality: A Review of Contemporary Sources," in Gary D. Comstock and Susan E. Henking (eds), *Que(e)rying Religion: A Critical Anthology* (London; New York: Continuum, 1997), 181–87.

these Jewish groups are Unitarians, representatives of the United Church of Christ, and Episcopalians, who are among the most readily mobilized in campaigns against sexuality-based discrimination within their immediate religious communities and beyond. Other Christian denominations, such as the Evangelical Lutheran Church of America, have made statements within the last decade to accept monogamous same-gender couples and also the ordination of gay and lesbian clergy without a requirement for celibacy.

In the contest over which alliance will have dominating influence, it is frequently jurisdiction-by-jurisdiction, case-by-case contests in what has been seen as a larger cultural war. My aim in evoking the metaphor of war and borderlands is not to portray those with strong stakes in the matter as militaristic or belligerent, and much less is it to depict ossified sides of good and evil. Although, in places where queer coalitions and anti-queer coalitions come head-to-head, there can, in fact, be markedly delineated sides, and at times positions are, in fact, deeply entrenched and fortified, as bolstered by vitriolic or bellicose spirits. Yet, I do not envision intractable boundaries between the queer identified and allies vs. the anti-queer parties. Instead, I envision a porous and irregularly constructed divide that is further complicated by additional axes of intersection, such as "race" or ethnicity. As with territorial borders, some places in the divide between queer and anti-queer coalitions are more clearly demarcated and/or fortified, other places are more ambiguous and traversable. The borders are constantly being remade.

Anti-queer religious coalitions promote compulsory heterosexuality and gender complementarity, often in tandem with efforts to mobilize public sentiments through fear-laden depictions of a social order gone bad. On the other side, queer individuals and movements are aiming to skew the power of cisgender and heteronormative regimes in order to transform their structures in radical ways. In places where substantive territorial/legal and ideological/public opinion gains have been made by gay and queer-identified coalitions, these gains are somewhat precarious, subject to the vagaries of public opinion, and frequently obstructed by the timidity of judiciaries fully to enter into the fray on behalf of gay and queer-identified persons. Adding to the uncertainty is an array of often contradictory socio-scientific studies related to the biological and neuropsychological bases for sexual attraction and sex identity.

Feminist and queer hermeneutic struggles for identity and (r)evolution occur in Jewish, Christian and Muslim congregational settings and within the academy. In the latter half of the twentieth century, feminist critiques of religious texts and traditions facilitated and inspired a broader dismantling of such notions as gender complementarity and compulsory heterosexuality. Considerable numbers of Jewish, Christian and Muslim scholars employed historical and philological methods to highlight gender biases and formulate alternative interpretations. Although un-reading religious proscriptions on female-female eroticism was an immediate objective of such scholarship, the results were further reaching, taking aim at the very forces that stood to determine which sexualities and sex identities were included in a particular definition of religious polity.

With regard to the recognition and non-persecution of alternate sexualities and genders within Christian and Jewish contexts, Judith Plaskow, Bernadette Brooten and Charlotte Elisheva Fonrobert, are among the most well-known scholars advancing this philological and historically oriented approach. Julia Watts Belser and Teresa J. Hornsby are also distinguished in their efforts to reconfigure religiously grounded sexual ethics from a vantage point that aims to be non-hegemonic, non-heterosexist, non-patriarchal and grounded in human dignity, spiritual well-being and community cohesion. Often the overarching thesis of works in this genre is that biblically based views on sexuality are not relevant to the mores of modern society.

This is captured particularly well by Catholic feminist Mary Hunt, who in her 2005 essay, "Eradicating the Sin of Heterosexism," elaborates how lesbians within religious communities face the *kyriarchal* bind—to evoke the neologism coined by Catholic feminist scholar Elisabeth Schüssler Fiorenza—of being both female in a sexist church and lesbian in a heterosexist one. As Hunt details, this doubly marginalized position leads to the desire for "substantive changes" and not simply incorporation into preexisting structures.[8] Taking this insight into the geographical metaphor of contested borderlands and contestation in yet another way, the place of intersection of two prominent features, e.g., "woman" and "lesbian," can frequently create a key lookout from which strategically to advance. Critical insights often derive from the vantage point created by a nexus of marginalized identities: womanhood, queerness, dis/ability, etc. Not only does the nexus itself allow for critical insights into regimes of power and privilege, the experience of marginality can itself form the impetus for crafting visions for broader social transformation.

This is precisely the point at which disparate studies of same sex attraction, or intersex, or bi-sexuality join to create a field of inquiry that is vested in not just investigating marginal sexualities, but is in fact seeking to critique the very forces that determine which sexualities and sex identities are perceived and regulated as legitimate. Scholars of such ambition,

---

[8] Mary E. Hunt, "Eradicating the Sin of Heterosexism," in Gary D. Comstock and Susan E. Henking (eds), *Heterosexism in Contemporary World Religion: Problem and Prospect* (Cleveland: Pilgrim, 2007), 155-76.

including Christian ethicist Marvin J. Ellison, speak of moving beyond mere acceptance or mere incorporation, to developing radically responsive and affirming strategies based on "big love," the concept put forth by one of the most influential black feminists, Patricia Hill Collins.[9] Big love is centered on the ideal of social and economic justice for all persons, and Ellison advances the concept by including "erotic empowerment" within the frame of economic and social empowerment.

In her 2011 monograph, *Controversies in Queer Theology*, Christian theologian Susannah Cornwall elaborates the ways in which queer theology "serve[s] a vitally liberative function in the lives of queer Christians and others who have found themselves and their modes of life and love written out of signification."[10] Particularly salient here is the conceptual link between queer theology and liberation theology, with its roots in the struggle of politically and economically oppressed persons, often within regimes of terror, violent autocracies and brute military dictatorships, where the official church appeared to be complacent or complicit in the crime and oppression. Within such theoretical interventions as queer and liberation theology, the underlying principle is that oppressive regimes of knowledge and power are also detrimental to those wielding the authority and, as such, liberative frameworks serve to benefit a widely inclusive spectrum of the populace.

Both feminist and queer fields, while they take sex identity, sexuality and gender as a starting point, are not only aimed at benefitting "women" and "queers" respectively, but are interrogating a broad spectrum of identity configurations and the underlying power dynamics. Both avenues of inquiry are concerned with "que(e)rying"[11] what behavior and identity conformations counts as normative, which are privileged, which are discriminated against, and why discrimination is undesirable or unmerited. With regard to sexual desire and gender identities, feminist and queer theorists provide a vast range of strategies for contending with anti-gays and queer opponents, who typically disavow non-literalist readings of Scripture, or who express concerns for going down a so called "slippery slope" of morality, or who take anatomy to be the determining indicator of gender and sexual desire, or who see alternative sexualities as threats to traditional gender roles and hence social stability, or who fear that changing gender dynamics will lead to familial dysfunction, etc. Feminist and queer theologians

---

[9] Marvin M. Ellison, *Same-Sex Marriage? A Christian Ethical Analysis* (Cleveland: The Pilgrim Press, 2004), 167.

[10] Susannah Cornwall, *Controversies in Queer Theology*, Controversies in Contextual Theology Series (London: SCM, 2011), 7f.

[11] See the title of the 1997 edited volume by Comstock and Henking, op. cit. (note 7).

continue to demonstrate that for as many advances launched in defense of heteronormative sexuality and binary gender, there are counter-advances and targeted interventions. Hence, (r)evolution occurs from the peripheries to the center, from marginalization and persecution to acceptance and social transformation.[12]

Fostering (r)evolution on issues related to sexual identity, queerness and their intersections with religious identities, is not only happening at the peripheral borderlands, but also at the epicenters of central institutions of social and cultural life. This is to recognize that the center and the periphery are not static. It is often a basic underlying aim of those at the margins to imagine, articulate, justify and enact a political and social order that transfigures the concept of margin and center. There is a risk of reifying stereotypes of the queer individual as a rebel, potentially anarchist, non-conforming agitator, and other such stereotypes. There is a certain appeal, glamour and mobilizing potential inherent in a claim to be (r)evolutionary, particularly in youth culture, but this rebellious spirit can also entrench and exacerbate divides between socially conservative and socially liberal Muslims.

Lest it need to be rearticulated, sexuality and the regulation thereof, is in fact a political, public issue, not simply a private one. Hence, to speak of liberation with regard to sexuality, as many feminist and queer theorists are exploring, often entails one to stake out a position that explicitly aims to infiltrate, or circumvent, dominant institutions of religion, culture, or state. The world visions and principles that queerness represents, and the aims that queer movements struggle to realize, still remain marginalized, and struggles over the control of resources, authority, legitimacy, etc., are ongoing with no signs of ceasing. My thoughts on potential resolutions of the tensions within Muslim communities are preliminary, but in short, there may be ways to integrate queer identities into the fold of communities while still standing by core Islamic frameworks and ethical values regarding intimate relations. This includes, for instance, the general value on moderation and the prohibition on anal penetration, a prohibition that pertains to cisgender relationships as well. Much more work needs to be done on this topic, but the legal maximum that actions are licit unless explicitly forbidden may be a fruitful avenue to achieve balance between

---

[12] In this extended geographic metaphor I am inspired by the approach of Rachel Havrelock as well as to colleagues in the Massachusetts Institute of Technology Women and Gender Studies Program. It is from the latter that my adaptation of the term (r)evolution is indebted. I am also indebted to Bernadette Brooten and to Michael Singer for their provocative teaching and engagement with the ideas presented in this section.

the priority of integrating rather than isolating persons of non-cisgender identity and the salient importance of upholding core values and religious law. The balance of spousal rights and responsibilities in modern contexts is a related topic where much intellectual output and activism is occurring, much of it under the leadership of *Musawah,* the global movement for equality and justice in Muslim families. Increasingly, mixed-ethnic, inter-religious, and transnational family configurations are the norm; theology and religious law must keep pace with these realities.

IDENTITY AND RENEWAL

There are multiple competing interests and visions for what being "renewed" looks like. Much like the renovation of an historic home, what is essential to preserve in its original form? What can be replaced but still look and feel authentic? What elements of the house have, sadly, been irrecoverably lost to time? What part must be demolished on account of a weak foundation? What furnishings can be put in the basement for sorting through at a future date? And perhaps most importantly in this extended analogy: who is hired to manage and implement this delicate process of renewal? Or, phrased another way, if the house has many rooms, than how can we collaborate to each design our own comfortable spaces under one roof?

I began this paper thinking about the various ways in which identity, and religious identity in particular, can be considered from within academic paradigms and critical theories. I then looked at the conception of Muslims at large as belonging to a nation or community that was comprised of members of many different identity conglomerations and that spanned nation-state borders and stood in for them at times and places of crisis and political disintegration. I provided snapshots of different contemporary junctures of identity and identified further questions that were raised at these junctures. Finally, I explored queer identity as one cite wherein many of the dynamics surrounding religious identity and renewal are brought to the fore.

Who are We and What Constitutes Our Identity

Suneel Bhanu Busi

> Identity is an unfathomable as it is all-pervasive. It deals with a process that is located both in the core of the individual and in the core of the communal culture.
> Erik Erikson

Introduction

"Identity" is an integral part of every human being. However, understanding and identifying a person's identity is a complex process and depends on various factors. It is a life-long search and struggle. Identity is multiple, changeable and can be overcome. One can change one's national identity through immigration and naturalization; one can also change one's gender identity from male to female and female to male and to transgender; and one can change one's religious and political identities. I sometimes wonder at these unending possibilities that offer some of us the freedom to develop alternate identity/ identities. But when it comes to "caste," especially in our Indian context, one is born into it and hence dies with the same caste-identity. When I reflect on my self-identity I am reminded of the saying of Prophet Jeremiah, "Can Ethiopians change their skin or leopards their spots? (Jer 13:23a).

Identity and the creation narrative

I was born into and brought up in a well-educated, Christian family. My father was a well-placed government official and my mother was a school teacher.

We lived in a town, about twelve kilometers from my father's ancestral village. Once a month, on the weekend, my father would visit his parents who lived in the village. He would ride his bicycle and I used to accompany him as a pillion rider. To my surprise, my father would always get down from his bicycle upon reaching the entrance of his village and would walk only on either of the extreme sides of the village path and all the way to his parents' house, a kilometer-long stretch of dirt road. To my dismay, he would also ask me to get down from the bicycle and walk, knowing well that as a small boy it was difficult for me to cover that distance. Whenever I insisted to remain seated on the bicycle, he would convince me to get down and to walk. Even after I reached the age when I could ride my own bicycle, I was made to get down from it at the entrance to the village and to walk to my grandparents' house. Whenever I protested and demanded an answer for this practice, my father always had two responses: one, that it was the custom of the village that no one should ride on a bicycle or use any other transport vehicle on the road of the village (but I did notice others of the village riding); and second, "it is our *karma*." Only later, I came to know that we were strictly forbidden to enjoy our rights and privileges of the facilities available in the village, because we belong to the communities of the "untouchables"–the Dalits.

In Indian society, certain categories of people who were not included in the *catur-varna* (the four-fold caste) system are known historically as the untouchables. Today, these people call themselves Dalits. One is not sure about the exact period in which the evil of caste was became part of the Indian social fabric, but it was the *Itihāsa* (Epics) and *Dhramasāstra* (Manuals of Law) period that consolidated and codified the rules and regulations, rights and responsibilities, related to caste and many other social, religious, political and economic factors. There are different theories and views about the origin of the caste system in India, the most popular being, the arrival of the fair complexioned *Āryans* on the Indo-Gangetic plains, which marked the beginning of the practice of *varnā* or caste. The Āryan settlers not only devised and implemented the four main divisions of peoples–the *Brāhmin, Kshatriya (Rājanya), Vaisya* and *Sūdra*, but also gave the system strong religious moorings with the introduction of a "creation story" in the *Rigved*

> When they divided the *Purusa*, into how many parts did they arrange him? What was his mouth? What were his two arms? What were his thighs and feet called? The *brāhmin* was his mouth, his two arms were made the *rājanya* (Warrior), his two thighs the *vaisya* (trader and agriculturist), from his feet the *sūdra* (servile class was born).[1]

---

[1] Shriram Sharma Acharya (ed.), *Rigveda* (Bareilly: Sanskrit Sansthan, 1985), X. 90:11–12.

Added to this, *Manusmriti* offered a systematic articulation and interpretation of caste:

> But the Sudra, whether bought or unbought, he may compel to do servile work; for he was created by the self-existent (*svayambhu*) to be the slave of a Brahmin. A Sudra, though emancipated by his master, is not released from servitude; since that is innate in him, who can set him free from it?[2]

These inunctions were further reinforced by the Puranic myths and the renditions of the great epics, *Rāmāyana* and *Mahābhārata*.

Accordantly, Brahmins, the pure Āryans, declared themselves as *Bhūdevās* (gods on earth) and placed themselves at the helm of affairs, both social and spiritual, with access to learning and knowledge as their birth right; and further, to impart the acquired knowledge to deserving pupils was their duty. They had the right to command and demand respect, as well as to enjoy unquestioning loyalty, support and service from anyone and everyone. Even the Kings were to rule and could only rule by obeying and accepting the guidance of the Brahmin priests. Thus the Brahmins elevated themselves to the top status of both as temporal and spiritual leaders.

Next on the ladder is *Kshatriya (Rājanya)*, or the warriors group who rule; their duty is to protect the land and its people from external and internal threats and enemies. They were expected to rule, keeping in view the advice given by the Brahmin ministers and teachers who were considered to be well versed in *Dharmasāstrās*. Third in the hierarchy was the *Vaisya*, the trading community, whose duty is to provide for the needs of society. This business community was to carry on their tradecraft within the parameters of the rules and regulations provided in the *Dharmasāstrās*. These three upper castes are also known as *dvija* (the twice born—physical as well as spiritual birth) and enjoyed the privilege of being adorned with the sacred thread, a religious sign of superior birth and a qualification to learn the sacred Vedas. The last in the caste hierarchy was the *Sūdra*, the servile caste, whose only duty is to serve the above-mentioned three upper castes.

ASSIGNED IDENTITY VS. CHOSEN IDENTITY

While all these four castes fall within the framework of caste in the majority Hindu religious tradition, there is also a large percentage of people who

---

[2] Arthur Coke Burnell (transl.), *The Ordinances of Manu* (Delhi: Motilal Banarsidas, 1971), VIII. 413-14.

are differentiated from the other four castes. The *Arthasastra* of Kautilya,[3] written sometime between the fourth and fifth centuries BCE, mentions separate wells for the exclusive use of these people known as *candāla* and restrictions from entering the village proper during the night. Thus their segregation and ritual pollution gradually resulted in their untouchability. Further, Manu, the Brahmin Law-giver, in one stroke fashioned and consolidated the outcaste and untouchable status of the *candāla* forever in the following passage:

> [T]he dwelling of *candālas* and svapākās shall be outside the village, they must be made *apapātrās*, their wealth (shall be) dogs and donkeys. Their dress shall be the garments of the dead, they shall eat their food from broken dishes, black iron (shall be) their ornaments and they must always wander from place to place. A man who fulfils a religious duty shall not seek intercourse with them; their transactions (shall be) among themselves and their marriages with their equals. Their food shall be given to them by others (other than Aryan giver) in a broken dish; at night they shall not walk about in villages and towns. By the day (they) may go about for the purpose of their work [...] that is a settled rule.[4]

Today, these *candālas,* popularly known as untouchables, constitute about 16.6 percent of the total Indian population. These people are identified as the "untouchables." According to the latest 2011 enumeration, of a total population of 1.21 billion, they constitute about 167 million. There is not much agreement with regard to the actual population of the untouchables as public and private estimates vary between 175 and 225 million. For the present purpose, it might be useful to consider a conservative estimate of 180 million. The figures would be substantially higher if the Dalits who embraced non-Hindu religions were taken into account. The Indian government considers only those Dalits within the Hindu fold, and all those who have converted to Christianity, Buddhism, Sikhism and Islam are not considered as a part of this social category since these religions claim to be casteless.[5] Although estimates vary, of the 2.34 percent of the total Indian population who are Christian, between fifty and seventy percent

---

[3] T. Ganapati Sastri (ed.), *The Arthasastra of Kautilya*, 3 vols. (Trivandrum: N.p., 1952), 114.

[4] Wendy Doniger and Brian K. Smith (transl.), *Manusmriti* (New Delhi: Penguin Books, 1992), X.31, 92–94.

[5] See *Census of India*, vol. 11 (New Delhi: Ashish Publishing House, 1982), 15, Appendix I, figure 1. And Census of India, Table A-series, 2011; Cf. T. K. Oommen, "Sources of Derivation and Styles of Protest: The Case of the Dalits in India," in *Contributions to Indian Sociology*, vol. 18, no. 1 (1984).

are of Dalit background. Of the 0.76 percent of the total population who are Buddhists, about 0.65 percent are of Dalit origin.[6]

These untouchables are a proud group of people, who zealously guarded and maintained their separate identity and freedom as long as possible from the domination of the Āryan invaders.[7] Several derogatory and degrading terms were and are being used and employed by the upper castes to describe and deface them—*amānusya* (no-people), *antyaja* (last caste/exterior castes), *asprisya/achūta* (untouchable), *asura/rākshasa* (demon), *avarna* (casteless), *chandāla* (uncivilized), *dāsa/dāsyu* (servant), *mleccha* (locals/natives), *Nisāda* (primitive hunting/food-gathering people), *panchama* (fifth caste), *svapāka* (one who cooks the meat of dead-animal), etc., and some other identities such as scheduled castes (de-notified groups), depressed Classes and *Harijan* (children of God).

Harijan, today is a popular name for the untouchables/Dalits; the name was given by Mahatma Gandhi, the father of the nation. On 7 November 1933, while in Yeravada prison, Gandhi went on a fast as a protest against the segregation of untouchables in the electoral arrangements planned for the new constitution. For Gandhiji, the scrapping of separate electorates was the beginning of the eradication of untouchability and outcaste stigma. With his inspiration, *Harijan Sevak Sangh* (Association of the Servants of *Harijans*) and a weekly paper entitled *Harijan* were started in order to confront and combat the evils of caste. *Harijan* was Gandhiji's name for the untouchables to denote that that even the untouchables are "children of God." However, today, a majority of Dalit scholars denounce the credibility of Gandhiji and the term *Harijan*, branding it as derogatory as it also points to the '"children of anonymous paternity," or even children of a lesser god.

While the term Dalit really came to mean and reflect the existential reality and never-ending plight of those communities who suffer from caste (social and religious) oppression and the resultant (economic and political) poverty, today it has also come to be understood as the need to revolt against the double oppression of ritual degradation and socio-economic-political deprivation. The term *dalit*[8] emerged more as a concept from the writings of two great Indian reformers, Mahatma Jyotirao Govindarao Phule and

---

[6] John C. B. Webster, "From Indian Church to Indian Theology: An Attempt at Theological Construction," in Arvind P. Nirmal (ed.), *A Reader in Dalit Theology* (Madras: The Christian Literature Society, 1990), 27.

[7] For further discussion, see Prabhati Mukherjee, *Beyond the Four Varnas: The Untouchability of India* (Shimla: Indian Institute of Advanced Study, 1988).

[8] Monier Williams, *A Sanskrit–English Dictionary* (Delhi: Motilal Banarsidas, 1988) (reprint). *Dal* is the root word for Dalit in Sanskrit which means, to crack, to spilt, to be broken or torn asunder, trodden down, scattered, crushed, destroyed. Further. as a noun and adjective it can applied to all genders.

Babasaheb Bhimrao Ramji Ambedkar. For Phule, while Sudras are last in the caste structure, *ati-sūdras* are the least of the people who are outside the caste system.[9] In two of his books, *Who were the Sudras* and *The Untouchables*,[10] Ambedkar deals with the issue of the untouchables. For the Dalit Panthers, who popularized the concept, the term *dalit* became a symbol of assertive pride and resistance as well as the rejection of the unending oppression of caste. Further, it meant change and revolution, rather than remaining perpetually subjugated to caste and its bondage.[11] *Dalit,* therefore, has become the hallmark of self-respect, self-identity and self-assertion of the untouchable communities and their fighting slogan against the de-humanizing caste oppression. Highlighting the relevance and importance of the term *dalit* in the lives of the oppressed and suppressed people, Antonyraj, a Dalit leader and an academician, declares,

> Against all kinds of derogatory and humiliating names imposed and forced on Dalits which attribute hereditary impurity, the Dalits chose to call themselves as "Dalit." The term *dalit,* in fact identifies our oppressors, the non-Dalits that are the cause of our dehumanization. The word reflects the consciousness of our own un-free existence and outcaste experience, which form the basis for a new cultural unity and *dalit* ideology [...] it also, indicates certain militancy. The name *dalit* is a symbol of change, confrontation and revolution.[12]

Submissiveness and the silent acceptance of discrimination and de-humanization have been characteristic of the behavior of Dalits. This silent surrender of selfhood resulted in Dalits voluntarily sacrificing their very lives for the benefit of the upper castes on the altar of their self-respect, self-dignity and self-identity, thereby becoming a "no-people." V. Devasahayam, a Dalit theologian, opines that caste as a totalitarian system not only forced Dalits into a comprehensive syndrome of slavery—social, political and economic—but has also enforced a cultural annihilation through perpetual psychological genocide, resulting in the Dalit psyche being distorted and disfigured.[13] In other words, one can observe the internalization of a lowered self-esteem, confusion of self-identity and self-hate in the very psyche of Dalits. In spite of the ever-growing atroci-

---

[9] D. K. Khapde, *Mahatma Jyotiba Phule. Samajik Evam Sanskrutik Kranti ke Praneta Rashtrapita Jyotirao Phule Evam Savitribai Phule* (New Delhi: N.p., 1990), 119–120.
[10] Vasant Moon (ed.), *Dr. Babasaheb Ambedkar's Writings and Speeches*, vol. 7 (Bombay: The Education Department, Govt. of Maharastra, 1990).
[11] Barbara R. Joshi, "Dalit Panthers Manifesto," in *Untouchables: Voice of the Dalit Liberation Movement* (New Delhi: Select Book Service Syndicate, 1986), 141–42.
[12] Antonyraj, "The Dalit Christian Reality in Tamilnadu," in *Jeevadhara*, vol. XXII, no. 128 (March 1992), 96.
[13] V. Devasahayam (ed.), *Frontiers of Dalit Theology* (Madras: ISPCK, 1990), 13–14.

ties perpetuated against Dalits, today one can also notice the non-complaining, non-protesting nature of a majority of Dalits and acceptance of the inhuman treatment being meted out to them day in and day out, simply because of the strong religious orientation of everything as their *karma*. Therefore, the need of the hour is to regain the genuine identity that they are being robbed and deprived of by the so-called upper castes under the complex and sacrosanct garb of religious teachings, dogmas and doctrines of "ritual purity" and the avoidance of ritual "impurity" to maintain the moral cosmic order.

In such a context, the step forward for Dalits is to initiate a concerted effort to regain their self-image and identity as God's people from the status of "no-people." That is, to disown the tarnished image of ritually polluted beings and the deprivation of self-dignity through a refreshed and life-renewing alternate social identity. This means the recognition of the root-causes of the evil of caste, and boldly and firmly naming and affirming the institutions, conditions and contexts that have been put into place to dehumanize them. Today, choosing the name Dalit has indeed become an affirmative symbol for their quest for an identity and rejection of alien identities forced on them. In other words, *dalit* identity basically is an irreversible counter-cultural identity and consciously choosing the name *dalit* is nothing but an awareness of selfhood, self-respect and self-dignity. Without a doubt this rejects the morals and methods as well as the values and vagaries that romanticize caste as something socially desirable and religiously inevitable. Here James Massey's assertion is helpful.

> Dalit is [...] not a mere descriptive name or title, but an expression of hope for the recovery of their past identity. The struggle of these "outcastes" has given the term, Dalit a positive meaning. The very realisation of themselves as Dalit, the very acceptance of the state of "Dalitness" is the first step on the way towards their transformation into full and liberated human beings.[14]

A DALIT HOPE AND ASPIRATION

For the majority of Dalits, Hinduism through its multi-faceted shades and dimensions—its philosophical nuances, mythical mysteries, reflections of art and architecture and culture conundrums—conveys an irrevocable message of "accept caste or perish." Thus, the imposed conscious identity

---

[14] James Massey, *Down Trodden: The Struggle of India's Dalits for Identity, Solidarity and Liberation* (Geneva: World Council of Churches, 1997), 3; cf. Walter Fernandes (ed.), *The Emerging Dalit Identity: The Re-Assertion of the Subalterns* (New Delhi: Indian Social Institute, 1996), 42.

of the very existential reality as ritually impure people, the forced acceptance of victimization through unrelenting religious discourses, and the determination to seek a spirituality to wriggle out of such a hopeless life situation marked the beginning of a search of Dalits for an alternate religion that offers a liberative transformation that spells out humanization.

In fact, caste is invisible and cannot be equated with racism; and caste principles and practices that dehumanize people cannot be identified with apartheid. And yet, it controls the very behavior and nature of Indians through the invocation of religion. Not only for Dalits, but also for many good-willed upper caste people, caste is unique to India and the parent of all evils and constitutes an impediment to the harmony in society. While several Hindu social reformers, for example Rajaram Mohun Roy (1772–1833) and Mahatma Gandhi, endeavored to bring internal change or even eradicate caste from within the depths of Hinduism, they still upheld some of its religious and moral values. Others like Mahatma Jyotirao Phule (1826–1890) and Babasaheb Ambedkar (1891–1956) were crystal clear about the direct and discrete role being played by Hinduism in the promotion and practice of caste, and strongly advocated for the need to critique Hinduism to the extent of adopting an alternate religion for the total emancipation of Dalits.

Some people who, having experienced the oppressive role religion played in Hinduism, declared, "Caste is a curse which must be abolished; to abolish caste, religion must be abolished; to abolish religion, God must be abolished."[15] But, in reality, instead of rejecting and moving away from religion altogether, a majority of Dalits found liberating streams in other religious traditions such as Buddhism, Christianity, Islam and Sikhism. These liberating streams, with an egalitarian vision reflected in their traditions, religious teachings and practices, displayed the potential, unlike Hinduism, to break down the oppressive structures in society and root out caste distinctions and inequalities. Having inherited the identity as Christian, let me briefly examine the role and contributions of Christianity in the liberation of and offering an identity *par excellence* to Dalits.

"CREATED IN GOD'S IMAGE"

Even a century before Ambedkar advocating that Dalits should convert to a religion other than Hinduism in order to regain their lost identity and self-

---

[15] Quoted in R. L. Hardgrave, Jr., *The Dravidian Movement* (Bombay: Popular Prakashan, 1965), 48; Somen Das, "Christian Response to Some Selected Movements for Social Change in India in the 19th and 20th Centuries," in Vinay Samuel and Chris Sugden (eds), *The Gospel Among Our Hindu Neighbours* (Bangalore: Partnership in Mission-Asia, 1983), 34.

respect, India witnessed mass conversions to Christianity of untouchables in search of a new identity and liberation from the oppressive structures of caste. In fact, the history of the Dalit liberation movement is interwoven with the history of the Christian church in India. A strong tradition traces its beginnings to the first century CE with the arrival of St Thomas, one of the disciples of Jesus.[16] However, the more credible version is that the Portuguese Vasco da Gama reached India in 1498 CE and shortly afterwards, in 1500, friars of the Franciscan Order came to India to teach the Christian faith and Christian morality.[17] However, much credit for laying strong foundations of Christianity on the Indian soil can be attributed to the work and witness of Francis Xavier, who arrived at Goa on 6 May 1542.

With reference to caste discrimination and the resulting conversion of Dalits, one of the missionaries to remember is Robert de Nobili, a young, aristocratic, Italian priest, who arrived in Tamilnadu in south India in 1605 and came to Madurai in 1606. He found out that Christianity, being the religion of the *Parangis* (a derogatory term for the Portuguese, meaning meat-eating, wine-drinking, loose-living and arrogant persons), failed to make any in-roads to reach the upper caste Hindus who considered it the religion of a foreign people who embodied a lifestyle that was considered incompatible with Indian social and cultural norms.[18] De Nobili concluded that the best way to penetrate the Hindu bastion with the gospel of Christ was to adapt the view and way of life of the majority in the society, that is, to uphold the values of caste with the Brāhmins at its apex. Holding on to this view as a strategy to win the upper castes for Christ Jesus, de Nobili,

> [...] believed and taught explicitly that, when a man becomes a Christian, he need not leave his caste or station in life; for he was persuaded that caste was a social custom parallel to distinction of class and rank in Europe, and an inevitable feature of the Indian way of life [...].[19]

As a result, the Madura Mission of de Nobili allowed the caste distinctions and differences to enter into and continue in the church. It also divided the priests as *sanyāsis* to minister to the upper castes, and *pandaraswāmis* to

---

[16] C. B. Firth, *An Introduction to Indian Church History,* published for the Senate of Serampore College (Madras: The Christian Literature Society, 1961), 4; Mathias Mundadan, *History of Christianity in India,* vol. 1, From the Beginning up to the Middle of the Sixteenth Century (up to 1542), published for Church History Association of India (Bangalore: Theological Publications in India, 1984), 21.

[17] Firth, ibid., 51.

[18] Ibid., 109.

[19] Ibid., 111.

sustain and nurture the faith of the lower and outcastes. In other words, the Roman Catholic Church of seventeenth-century India fostered a policy of adaptation, in which caste was considered to be a social system, rather than an adversary of the gospel.[20]

Compared with the early beginnings of the Roman Catholic Church, the Protestant missions began their work at the beginning of the eighteenth century. Although the trading companies from Europe, such as the Dutch, British, Danish and French, had been in India since the early sixteenth century, they did not embark on any evangelistic enterprise. Under the initiative and patronage of King Frederick IV of Denmark, two German seminarians, Bartholomew Ziegenbalg and Henry Pluetschau, came to the southern part of India on 9 July 1706, and in 1793, William Carey, Joshua Marshman and William Ward from England, popularly known as the "Serampore Trio," arrived in Bengal. Like the Roman Catholic missionaries, the Protestants also preached the gospel, emphasizing the consequences of sin and the offer of grace of God and salvation through the death and resurrection of Jesus Christ.

In the early decades of their missionary enterprise, the Protestant missionaries considered caste and culture as inseparable elements. However, as time passed, gradually they came to the understanding of caste as a dehumanizing force of Hindu religious tradition and therefore chose to attack its evil nature.[21] Thus, during nineteenth century, the Protestant missionaries spent their energies condemning caste and minimizing its influence in the church, if not actually eliminating it completely. For example, a report of the Missionary Conference that met in Madras in February 1850 unequivocally declared,

> Caste is one of the greatest obstacles to the progress of the Gospel in India. It meets and thwarts the Missionary, not only in bearing the unsearchable riches of Christ to the unconverted Hindus, but in building up the Native Church in faith and love.

---

[20] John C. B. Webster, *Dalit Christians: A History* (New Delhi: ISPCK, 1996), 25.

[21] G. A. Oddie, "Protestant Missions, Caste and Social Change in India, 1850-1914," *Indian Economic and Social History Review*, vol. VI (September 1969), 273; Duncan B. Forrester, *Caste and Christianity: Attitudes and Policies on Caste of Anglo-Saxon Protestant Mission in India* (London and Dublin: Curzon Press Ltd., and Atlantic Highlands, NJ, USA: Humanities Press, 1980), 87ff; Sundararaj Manickam, *Studies in Missionary History: Reflections on a Culture-Contact* (Madras: The Christian Literature Society, 1988), 32-61; Hugald Grafe, *History of Christianity in India*, vol. IV, part 2: *Tamilnadu in the Nineteenth and Twentieth Centuries*, published for Church History Association of India (Bangalore: Theological Publications in India, 1990), 97-113.

This has been painfully felt in Southern India, wherever Natives at their baptism have been permitted to retain it.[22]

With such a conviction, they took an active role in highlighting the evils and disadvantages of the caste system and the disabilities suffered by the outcastes, such as being deprived of the use of public roads and wells and the banning of Dalit women from wearing clothes to cover the upper part of their bodies.

The message of Jesus' love for humankind, irrespective of the distinctions of caste and creed, and the critical attitude of missionaries to caste, ignited mass conversion movements among Dalits who were deprived of their religious aspirations by the prohibition to enter temples to worship God. Beginning in the 1840s, the mass conversion of Dalits continued into the 1920s. Though these mass conversion movements did not occur at the pan-Indian level, these remarkable conversions took place among untouchables known as the *Mādigās* and *Mālās* of Andhra Pradesh, *Chuhrās*, *Bhangis* and *Chamars* in Punjab, and *Parayārs* and *Pulayās* in Tamilnadu. And further, the proportion of the converted Dalits varied from group to group and region to region.

In 1900, the South India Missionary Conference listed five motivational factors for the Dalit mass conversions: (i) the conviction that Christianity is the true religion; (ii) the desire for protection from oppressors; (iii) the aspiration to educate their children; (iv) the acknowledgement that those who have become Christians improved both in character and social stature; and (v) the influence of Christian relatives. The missionaries noted that the injustice perpetrated by caste tyranny was one of the strongest factors that motivated Dalits to embrace Christianity.[23] On the one hand, Christianity offered Dalits a new and better social and religious identity that was not dependent on the approval and acceptance of the upper caste Hindus and, on the other, the Christian message of God's sacrificial love, "even for the untouchable," appealed to them greatly.[24] In short, the search for improved social status, greater self-dignity, self-respect and self-satisfying new

---

[22] Quoted in M. D. David, "Social Background of Basil Mission Christians: The Problem of Caste," *Indian Church History Review*, vol. XVIII, no. 2 (December 1984), 142.

[23] H. B. Hyde, "South Indian Missions – The Present Opportunity," in *The East and the West*, vol. VI (January 1908), 78; Henry Whitehead, "The Progress of Christianity in India and Mission Strategy," in *The East and the West*, vol. V (January 1907), 23.

[24] Sundararaj Manickam, *The Social Setting of Christian Conversion in South India: The Impact of the Wesleyan Methodist Missionaries on the Trchy-Travancore Diocese with Special Reference to the Harijan Communities of the Mass Movement Area 1920-1947* (Wiesbaden: n. p., 1977), 80–82; James P. Alter, *In the Doab and Rohilkhand: North Indian Christianity, 1815–1915* (Delhi: ISPCK, 1986), 140.

identity, liberation from the oppressive and dehumanizing caste system, and a hope of fulfilling of religious and spiritual needs inspired Dalits to embrace Christianity. However, the most important gospel message for Dalits is that first and foremost they are "created in the image of God" and hence not "ritually impure" and that "divine nature" is an integral part of their very being. Secondly, being created by God almighty they are equal to other human beings, whether upper, lower or outcastes or adherents of other religious faiths and ideologies, with self-dignity and self-identity. A new vision and openness of a new *ekklesia* and *koinonia* without differences and boundaries or hierarchical statuses have become a reality for Dalits who have determined to "imitate Christ."

TRANSFORMING IDENTITY—THE GIFT OF CHRIST

As we have seen, caste, a perennial symbol of Indian traditional social stratification, is non-egalitarian and exploitative, leading to India's characterization as a caste society *par excellence*. Robert Stern is right in saying, "Caste is of the warp and woof of Indian civilization and the Indian civilization is of the warp and woof of caste."[25] In such a system of legalized inequality, the allocation of roles and statuses to people is governed by a non-rational principle.[26] The interpretation of Hinduism, the majority religion of India, by a privileged few is the creator and perpetuator of this illogical and unethical principle.

Speaking about the role Hinduism has played in the discrimination of Dalits, Kothapalli Wilson points out that in spite of the numerous powerful *avatārs* (incarnations) of God and the emergence of spiritual gurus and religious reformers, the inhuman social system, powered by religious justification from Hinduism, remains entrenched in Indian society.[27] For Dalits, Hinduism has become a religion of oppression with its powerful and popular creation myth, the doctrines of *karma* and *samsāra* and sacred Scriptures that are being used to justify and legitimize their outcaste status and untouchability. Even today, Dalits feel that in India the religious establishment is one with the oppressive political forces on all crucial issues. They operate hand in hand.

---

[25] Robert W. Stern, *Changing India* (Massachusetts: Cambridge University Press, 1993), 50. Cf. E. Senart, *Caste in India* (Bombay: Oxford University Press, 1963). 50.

[26] S. P. Nagendra, "The Traditional Theory of Caste" in D. H. Nathan (ed.), *Towards a Sociology of Culture in India* (Bombay: Prentice Hall (India) Ltd., 1965), 262.

[27] K. Wilson, *The Twice Alienated* (Hyderabad: Booklinks Corporation, 1982), 13.

Religion is a vibrant force and for the average Indian religion is everything—the very basis of social and cultural traditions, the life-regulating spring of ethical values and the provider and sustainer of life-enriching spirituality. With such an understanding, Dalits in India, who have been denied a life-fulfilling religion, have been actively searching for a metaphysical force that could provide inspirational dynamism, spiritual potential and moral strength, a force that could empower them effectively to fight caste infused oppression and the resultant discrimination as well as achieving a holistic liberation and a new identity. And this they found in Christianity.

Since caste was a major factor in the conversion of Dalits to Christianity, Christian missionaries of that period struggled with difficult issues such as whether Christianity would provide what the Dalits are seeking and fulfill their aspirations; whether it would ameliorate their social status and conditions; and whether the condemnation of caste would adversely affect their diverse ministries among the majority upper caste Hindus.[28]

While on the one hand Dalits found an egalitarian message in the gospel, the missionaries on the other hand felt caste becoming a major and insurmountable problem in the conversion of upper castes. In a survey of the American Arcot Mission, undertaken for the period between 1907 and 1948, Andrew Wingate reports that, "Caste remains the biggest obstacle to conversion amongst the high caste; the final test which causes so many to turn away sorrowful is this demand to give up one's social superiority."[29] Although the missionaries came with a strong zeal to convert, they were also social activists and immersed themselves in attempts to improve the conditions of the oppressed and suppressed people, the Dalits. On their part, Dalits, after conversion to Christianity, remained in their villages, continued in their occupations and sustained their familiar social and economic relationships in spite of continued discrimination. For example, missionary John Clough observes,

> The village washermen were told not to work for the Madigas (a sub-caste of the Dalit converts); the potter was told not to sell pots to them; their cattle were driven from the common grazing ground; the Sudras combined in a refusal to give them the usual work of sewing sandals and harness; at harvest time they were not allowed to help and lost their portion of grain.[30]

---

[28] Webster, op. cit. (note 6).

[29] Andrew Wingate, *The Church and Conversion: A Study of Recent Conversion to and from Christianity in the Tamil Area of South India* (Delhi: ISPCK, 1997), 58.

[30] John E. Clough, *Social Christianity in the Orient: The Story of a Man, A Mission and Movement* (New York: Max Muller Company, 1914), 171-72.

In this way, even after the conversion to Christianity, Dalits continued to be socially, economically and politically discriminated against, and in the villages they experienced numerous social restrictions.[31]

If this was the situation about a century-and-a-half ago, today the situation has not changed much. The separation of castes in a typical village set-up is a very common feature and Dalits are made to live outside the village boundaries where there is little water and the whole area is enveloped by dirt and filth. Even the educated and successful Dalits, such as doctors, engineers and academics living in cities, face difficulties in securing a house for rent in the upper caste localities where the housing is much better, comfortable and convenient. In order to avoid renting their houses to Dalits, the upper caste landlords often put up signs saying accommodation is only for vegetarians, as vegetarianism is synonymous with Brahmins. And if financially prosperous Dalits are able to build their own houses in the residential areas of the upper caste people, they are culturally and socially isolated.[32] In the rural areas, the services of barbers and washermen are curtailed and access to grocery shops is rendered limited, if not prohibited. In some villages, certain arterial streets are off limits to the Dalits and if they are allowed to use them then they are forbidden to use their footwear. One also comes across numerous customs and traditions that govern food and food habits. In a majority of villages, the upper castes still believe it ritually polluting to eat or drink with the Dalits or to accept and taste food cooked by them. One example of such an attitude is very much prevalent and evident in the rural areas, where Dalits are prevented from entering restaurants and coffee shops, and if they are entertained, separate tumblers are provided for their beverage. In addition, Dalits are deprived of their right to be involved in the decision-making process of the village *panchayat* (administrative council) and the upper castes invariably exercise a dominant role by dictating terms to the Dalits in the governance of the village.[33]

For about three millennia, education was controlled by the upper castes in India. The enterprise of learning was their exclusive domain and centered around temples where the Brahmin priests imparted the knowledge only to the "twice-born," that is, the *Brāhmins*, *Kshatriyas* and *Vaishyās*. While the *Sūdras* were allowed to possess some skill training, Dalits were left out and remained completely illiterate.[34] Reflecting on this monopoly over

---

[31] David Haslam, *Caste Out!: The Liberation Struggles of the Dalits in India* (London: CTBI, 1999), 31–40.

[32] Kancha Ilaiah, *Why I am not a Hindu: A Sudra Critique of Hindutva Philosophy, Culture and Political Economy* (Calcutta: Samya, 1996), 68.

[33] Ibid., 47–48.

[34] Haslam, op. cit. (note 31), 38.

education and the attitude of the upper castes in educating Dalits, Kancha Ilaiah observes,

> Many of them (teachers in the educational institutions) considered most of us as "undeserving" and felt that our coming to higher educational institutions would only lead to the deterioration of standards. In the opinion of some Hindu teachers we did not deserve a place in the university [...] .They felt that instead of pulling down the standards of higher education by pushing us into the educational institutions, we should be provided with improved living conditions within our own setting.[35]

If this is the situation in the Centers of Higher Learning, the naked truth in the rural areas, especially at the primary education level, is even more appalling and discriminatory. The caste centered culture that is very much visible in the villages deprives the children of Dalit background of a competitive and conducive atmosphere for pursuing their studies. In these schools, the practice of untouchability is on public display as Dalit pupils are made to sit as a separate group at the back of the classroom; upper caste teachers treat Dalit children with indifference and contempt and instructors regularly state and emphasize Dalit students as good for nothing.[36]

However, in spite of these accepted and ingrained forms of discrimination that constitute n active impediment to the growth of a person, once converted to Christianity, Dalits never renounce their new faith, because it firmly remains as a liberating channel to achieve self-dignity and self-esteem by offering various avenues to fight against caste invoked humiliation. Conversion to Christianity has indeed become a tool for Dalits to fulfill their long neglected and deliberately denied rights, hope and aspirations. Christianity helps them in their struggle to liberate themselves from the inherited disadvantages of a socially ingrained inferiority complex, economic backwardness, political powerlessness and life-negating religious stigma of ritual pollution. In the gospel message that overwhelmingly reflects Jesus' love, healing and compassionate ministries, his caring and concern for the poor, oppressed and outcastes of society, as well as his sacrificial death for the people "outside the camp," Dalits identified themselves as the subjects and objects of this liberating, life-renewing and identity offering message. Along with opening avenues to learn religious truths and to nurture their faith, Christianity has become a force offering holistic liberation to the untouchables through the opening and establishing of educational and other allied institutions, technical training programs, health-care centers

---

[35] Ilaiah, op. cit. (note 32), 55–56.
[36] Godwin Shiri, *The Plight of Christian Dalits—A South Indian Caste Study* (Bangalore: CISRS, 1997), 130.

and social projects in and around Dalit localities. The gospel message helps and encourages Dalits to raise their voices in protest and to fight against the injustice being perpetrated by the caste system.

In his study of the conversion of Dalits to Christianity, Duncan Forrester rightly observes,

> The search for material improvement or enhancement of status is seldom if ever the sole or even the dominant motive [...]. Dignity, self-respect, patrons who will treat one as an equal, and the ability to choose one's own identity, all these are powerful incentives to conversion.[37]

Until today, embracing Christianity has focused the Dalits' desire for socio-cultural, politico-economic and religious liberation and the rejection of the discriminatory caste hierarchy that kept them at the bottom of society and stigmatized their lives as non-human beings. Without Christianity, Dalits could never dream of coming out of their extreme degradation.[38]

Without a doubt, for some groups of Dalits in India Christianity offers the possibility to change to a new way of life endowed with freedom, self-respect, human dignity and a life-renewing new identity. That is to say that faith in Christ Jesus has also been reflected in a new identity of coming out of the feeling of a ritually polluted personality and the humiliating experience of being the lowest as untouchables in the socio-religious hierarchy. These are now being eroded with the powerful gospel message of egalitarianism that advocates and emphasizes that every person is equal and created in the image of God, and thereby an integral part of the Divine, precious in the sight of God. From its arrival in India, with exception of the first few decades, Christianity has offered a space for Dalits to become aware of their human rights and to initiate movements to fight for and to protect these rights. Overall, Christianity was and is a powerful catalyst in the transformation of Dalits and their identity as human beings. It is evident that both in the urban and rural areas, Dalit Christians are winning the grudging respect and admiration of the upper castes for their transformed and transforming view and way of life that is being continuously refined by their adherence to the message of the gospel of Christ. The non-Christian upper castes often wonder at Dalit Christian neighborhoods progressively

---

[37] Forrester, op. cit. (note 21), 75.

[38] G.A. Oddie, *Hindu and Christian in South-East India* (London: Curzon, 1991), p. 159; the census data of 1991 reported the total number of Christians as 19,640,284 and of this there is a consensus that while at least half of them are from Dalit background, one fourth are from the ādivāsi communities and the rest from the upper castes.

becoming cleaner, their behavior and habits gradually becoming more acceptable, and their industriousness and honesty becoming more noticeable and admirable. This new and transformed view and way of life is a result of their understanding of the existential reality of their life as untouchables and the recognition of the liberating presence of God in Jesus Christ

Christianity has become a powerful channel and catalyst in the emancipation of Dalits. Because of their unwavering faith in Jesus Christ, in spite of life-threatening challenges, Dalits today cling to life in the middle of life-negating forces and they continue to move forward to achieve their freedom and realize their just rights. Against a tsunami of adverse conditions and contexts they slowly and steadily inch forward to demolish the inhuman caste structures. Christ as their anchor and the gospel message as their firm foundation, they have begun to rewrite their own history and to enjoy and take pride in a transformed and transforming identity as children of God. Christianity has offered me this new and unique identity. I am no more a ritually-polluted untouchable whose touch and even shadow would pollute others, but a human being created in the image of God and, hence, ritually pure.

Christ Jesus beckons the discriminated against to take center stage in forging alliances to stake their claim to human dignity and identity, whether they are Dalits in India or other oppressed masses elsewhere in the world. In other words, the liberating God irrupts into the lives of people who are forced to sit in darkness for thousands of centuries. Religion, in this case, offers an invitation to summon the courage to join God and God's people in this historical and challenging task of humanizing the universe—where the needs of the suffering take priority over the luxuries of the rich; where their freedom takes priority over the liberty of the powerful; and where their wholesome participation in society takes priority over the preservation of an order that excludes them.[39]

Conclusion

For some groups of Dalits religions such as Buddhism, Sikhism, Islam and Christianity have become an impeccable foundation for a new and creative individual self-identity as well as a collective/communal identity. These religions offered a new consciousness, a clear-cut path to de-sacralize caste complexes and a means of social protest and social transformation. At the personal level, religion is becoming a *dharma* to deal with adversity;

---

[39] David Hollenbach, *Claims in Conflict: Retrieving and Renewing the Catholic Human Rights Tradition*, (New York: Paulist Press, 1979), 204.

a rich source of personal dignity, confidence, creativity and empowerment; an enriching resource for personal self-redefinition, healing of the
"wounded psyche"[40] and the strong urge for inner spiritual transformation
that drives off the branding of "non-human" to human being with equal
dignity; and the quest to experience and explore the compassionate love of
the Divine, which is the ground of hope and an ever-flowing fountainhead
for a meaningful life in a harsh and uncaring world. These are available
aplenty in Christianity.

Like many others, I enjoy multiple identities. In terms of family relationships, I am the son of my parents, husband of my wife, father of my
children; by nationality, I am an Indian, and linguistically a Telugu; pro-
fessionally, an ordained minister of the largest Lutheran church in India,
and a theological educator at a reputed ecumenical theological seminary;
ethnically, I am a member of an outcaste/untouchable community and in
terms of religion, a Christian and denominationally, a Lutheran. In other
words, I am a product of and conditioned by many relationships and influences. When I reflect on these identities, what saddens me even today is
that in spite of all my accomplishments, when I visit my father's ancestral
village, the caste communities irrespective of their faith affiliations, still
consider me as an untouchable. However, what refreshes and renews me
is my religio-confessional identity—thank God, I am a practicing Christian
and a Lutheran. What does that mean for me?

UNWRAPPING RELIGIOUS IDENTITY: A CHRISTIAN OPENNESS

For the average Indian, religion is never only one of the several functions
of life. In fact, it is an integral whole of one's view and way of life. In general, this is especially true of religious traditions in Asia in general and in
India in particular. Thus, religion not only provides meaning and purpose
to human and cosmic life in relation to the transcendent Ultimate, but also
relates to the struggles of people everywhere to share common human
concerns in their desire to live with dignity and an honorable identity in
a peaceful and harmonious manner in relation to their neighbors.

With an "identity" as Christian, somehow I continue to cherish and
live in the misunderstanding and distortion of more than twenty centuries
of the gospel witness. Wading through the deep and disturbed waters of
history, my wish is to explore an authentic religious identity. According
to the New Testament, as we are all aware of, the "disciples" in Antioch
were called "Christians" (Acts 11:26) because they accepted Jesus of Naza-

---

[40] For a detailed discussion on this term, see Masilamani Azariah, *A Pastor's Search
for Dalit Theology* (Madras: DLET/ISPCK, 2000).

reth as the fulfillment of the Jewish expectation of the Anointed One, the Messiah. But in the context of continued interaction with our Jewish and Muslim neighbors, we reread the Bible and realize that the title, Christ is one of a few confessional identities attributed to Jesus. Others we are familiar with include Lord and Saviour. We also need to acknowledge Jesus' life had many facets of identity, such as rabbi which the Jews accept unquestioningly and prophet which the Muslim communities all over the world accept with reverence. However, most of my Christian colleagues and fellow believers hasten to point out the other identities of Jesus such as the only *avatār* (incarnation/God taking the human form) of the Eternal Word or Son of God and one of the persons of the Trinity. In such a context, I believe it to be vital that in order for me to enrich my religious identity I need to reeducate and reoriente myself about the contextually ever evolving perceptions about Jesus Christ without losing my identity as a practicing Christian. That is, the need to unwrap the teachings and doctrines that I have inherited, which is possible through the reclamation of the common roots that will hopefully propel me towards a common mission. Here my confessional identity as a Lutheran comes into play with the powerful phrase, *ecclesia reformata and semper reformanda secundum verbum Dei* (The church reformed and always being reformed according to the Word of God).

RECLAIMING COMMON ROOTS: TOWARDS A COMMON MISSION

I have to confess that in spite of my Christianized articulations and promotion of a contextual theology, known as Dalit theology, which is firmly rooted in the experience and quest of "a wandering Aramean" (Dt 26:5-9) and the pathos of the suffering masses, I have a feeling that I am slowly and steadily disassociating myself from this Hebrew experience of liberation from slavery, the exodus event, covenant and the prophetic challenges to restore peace, justice and human dignity as well as explosive and vibrant visions of a new day of freedom with equality and fraternity. Without taking this experience seriously, I may have begun to relegate my Christian identity to a dubious framework of promise and fulfillment. That means, the doctrines, liturgies, teachings, etc., that I cherish may be perpetuating a false notion that I can live in Christ without ever referring to my common roots that relate me to my neighbors. The fact is that I share with Jews and Muslims a common experiential identity though there are certain significant areas of differences. I realize that when Jesus encountered people of other faiths and philosophies at the borders and was challenged by them to extend the original covenant, he moved to the Gentile territories and at the very moment of establishing the Eucharist he threw the doors wide open by declaring, "for this is my blood of the covenant, which is poured out for many" (Mt 26:28, Mk 14:24). I praise God in Jesus Christ that I am being included in that many. The question that I grapple with and which is enmeshed in the multiplicity of my identities is, Does my Christian identity obscure my vision to understand and respect the religious identities of others in an effort to reclaim the common roots and the quest to discover possible new horizons?

As a practicing Christian I am called to be faithful to God and participate in God's mission in the context where I am placed. When Jesus condemned proselytization (Mt 23:15), he called on a particular group of people for discipleship. He sent his disciples to be witnesses to his life, ministry and mission. But the reign of God was greater than what Jesus' disciples could accomplish. Jesus recognized those outsiders who cast out demons, etc., and declared the truth that "whoever is not against us is for us" (Mk 9:40). Undeniably, goodwill and a spirit of continued reforming visions prevail among people of other faiths—Jews, Muslims, Hindus, Buddhists and those who subscribe to diverse ideologies. We are invited to join hands with them to engage in a common mission for the social and spiritual well-being of all people. This moving toward a common vision and mission constitutes a unique identity as people of God to Christians in India in light of the challenging, rapidly growing proselytizing activities of both the Hindus and Muslims. In the context of the existence of "Christians" who identify themselves as belonging to the Jesus' movement, the possibility of collaborating with like-minded people from other faiths, who are committed to challenge the evils, change society and to bring smiles to people, is a reflection of the God-given unique identity.

As we are aware, every individual carries multiple identities. Religious identity, with unwavering commitment and faithfulness to God faithfulness, is to be assessed and reassessed, reformed and re-reformed time and again in the light of the life-giving Word of God so that we can go to the roots and to the depths of our faith, whatever the socio-religious and politico-economic contexts in which we live may be. The Judeo-Christian roots lie in the liberating experience of the exodus event of the suffering and bonded labor in Egypt. Muslims acknowledge these roots although they have different versions and views on it. In a context of plurality of faiths, each religious community needs to search for their own respective roots as well as common roots in relation to the neighbors. This would further shape one's own individual and communal identity.

For me as a Christian, the Christian missionary model identity that endeavors to liberate people from de-humanization is most important. As it is evident in the sermons and teachings as well as in the work and witness of Stephen and Paul, their missionary message begin in God's liberation of the Hebrew slaves and the covenant, which bound God and God's people by a bond of faithfulness. First, Jesus' mission was focused on the "lost sheep of Israel" but, later, new dimensions were added in the suffering, death and resurrection of Jesus Christ. Many a time, one's identity may be obscured by the others' self-understanding of their religio-cultural traditions and interpretations of the sacred Scriptures. In such a context, the need of the hour is to encourage the rereading and reinterpreting Scriptures by those who possess and cherish them on their own terms so as to find a common thread for the whole of humanity. It is important to constitute and enjoy our larger communal identity along with our individual identity, which is also interfaith in nature. This calls for all concerned to spare no effort and to leave no stone unturned in building and strengthening a continued harmonious interfaith relations at the grassroots level, to engage in continued interfaith conversations of cooperation and interaction, to search for transforming scriptural insights to enrich and strengthen the bonds of community as children of God and to inspire the communities to move forward on a pilgrimage of forging friendship and fellowship toward an *oikumene* wherein the well-being of every community becomes the responsibility of the other, culminating in a one holistic community of "God's people" for the sake of the future of humankind.

LIST OF CONTRIBUTORS

Borelli, John, Dr, Special Assistant for Interreligious Initiatives to President John J. DeGioia of Georgetown University, USA, and coordinator for dialogue for the Jesuit Conference of the Canada and the United States

Busi, Suneel Bhanu, Rev., Prof. Dr, teaches at Gurukul Lutheran Theological College and Research Institute at Chennai and heads the Department of Research and Doctoral Studies as its Dean, Madras, India

Ibrahim-Lizzio, Celene, Islamic Studies Scholar-in-Residence at Hebrew College and Andover Newton Theological School and co-director of the Center for Interreligious and Communal Leadership Education

Junge, Martin, Rev., Dr, General Secretary, The Lutheran World Federation, Geneva, Switzerland

Lander, Shira L., Rabbi, Dr, Professor of Practice and Director of Jewish Studies, Southern Methodist University, Dallas, USA

Laytner, Anson Hugh, Rabbi, Interreligious Initiative Program Manager at Seattle University's School of Theology & Ministry, Seattle, USA

Moyo, Herbert, Rev., Dr, lecturer in Practical Theology at the School of Religion, Philosophy and Classics at the University of KwaZulu-Natal, South Africa

Pakpahan, Binsar Jonathan, Rev., Dr, Associate Professor and Dean of Student Affairs of Jakarta Theological (Sekolah Tinggi Teologi Jakarta), Jakarta, Indonesia

Punsalan-Manlimos, Catherine, Dr, Director of the Institute for Catholic Thought and Culture and Associate Professor in the Theology and Religious Studies department at Seattle University, USA

Sandmel, David Fox, Rabbi, Dr., Director of Interfaith Affairs for the Anti-Defamation League, New York City, USA

Sinn, Simone, Rev., Dr, Study Secretary for Public Theology and Interreligious Relations, The Lutheran World Federation, Switzerland

Strasko, Paul Moses, Rabbi, Congregation Kol Shalom on Bainbridge Island, Washington, USA

Trice, Michael Reid, Dr, Assistant Professor of Constructive Theology and Theological Ethics and Assistant Dean for Ecumenical and Interreligious Dialogue at the Seattle University School of Theology and Ministry, Seattle, USA

van Doorn-Harder, Nelly, Dr, Professor of Islamic Studies, Department for the Study of Religion, Wake Forest University, Winston-Salem, North Carolina, USA

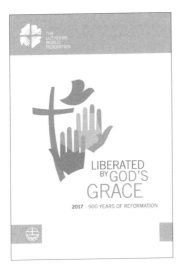

Anne Burghardt (Ed.)
Liberated by God's Grace
2017 – 500 Years of Reformation

332 pages | paperback | 15,5 x 23 cm
4 booklets in a box
ISBN 978-3-374-04160-2
EUR 19,90 [D]

In these four booklets, theologians from all parts of the world reflect on the main theme and three sub-themes (Liberated by God's Grace: Salvation–Not for Sale; Human Beings–Not for Sale; Creation–Not for Sale) of the Lutheran World Federation's commemoration of the 500th Anniversary of the Reformation.

This collection of essays provides profound insights into the crucial issues and challenges daily faced by the members of the worldwide Lutheran communion in very diverse contexts. The theological concept of justification by God's grace and its consequences for different dimensions of life serve as the main guiding principles for the essays, each one of which is accompanied by three questions that invite to further contextual reflection on the subject.

EVANGELISCHE VERLAGSANSTALT
Leipzig   www.eva-leipzig.de

Tel +49 (0) 341/ 7 11 41 -16   vertrieb@eva-leipzig.de

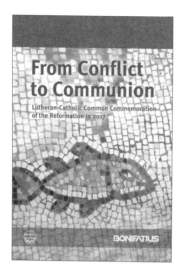

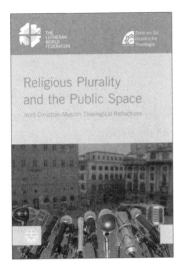